Canadian Cataloguing in Publication Data

Main entry under title:

International Film Festival Guide -1998-

1st ed.
Text in English
Includes index.

ISBN 1-896909-02-7 (bound)

1. Listing of international film festivals

FESTIVAL PRODUCTS
713 Euclid Avenue
Suite 002
Toronto, Ontario
M6G 2V1
416-410-0867
festival@interlog.com
www.festivalproducts.com

Acknowledgments

160101

In now our second year, the International Film Festival Guide has grown with two new sections and many more festival entries. Its acceptence and popularity at film festivals by the industry and festival goers as well as bookstores (though distribution by A.P.G. in the Unitied States and Hushian House in Canada) and universities has made this new edition possible. I would especially like to thank the Oldenburg International Film Festival, Aspen Filmfest, Hot Docs! Documentary Film Festival, Hong Kong International Film Festival, San Luis Obispo International Film Festival and the Melbourne International Film Festival for their support, words of encouragement and genuine interest in this guide

I also would like to give a special thanks to Steven Olivieri, Roy Frumkes, Scott Felixson, Michael Rechtshaffen, Petra Hobel and Josef Wutz of Filmfest Hamburg, Tor Fosse of the Tromso International Film Festival, Michael Lumpkin of the San Francisco Gay & Lesbian Film Festival, Jeff Rechtshaffen, Mary Colbert, Debbie Tiffin, and James Cooper for their wonderful contributions to this guide.

Since last year's guide was a success, I saw no need in breaking up the team which helped me put this second guide "in the can." For the second year this team includes Allan Lowson and Tom Haw. Their contributions were invaluable to the completion of this guide.

Finally, I would like to thank all my friends and family whose support and enthusiasm were crucial to repeating the success of the first guide. This last year has been extremely exciting, but frought with the loss of some people close to me who can never be replaced. Most importantly, I would like to thank my parents, one in memory and the other in belief.

INTERNATIONAL FILM FESTIVAL GUIDE

- 1998 -

EDITED BY

SHAEL STOLBERG

Contents at a Glance

Introduction

This guide was created to make it easier to find information about an international film festival circuit that includes hundreds of events through out the world showcasing and promoting all types of films. The guide presents the "where, when, why and how" about hundreds of film festivals as well as their awards, with interesting but brief description of festival focus. The reference section includes listings of Canadian and international producers and distributors, Canadian private and public funding agencies and a listing of training programs. Even though many post-secondary institutions have media and/or fine arts programs, we have a listing of certain schools which have a good reputation or specialize in the study of film and TV.

General information can be very useful on its own but when it is applied to an individual's specific situation it becomes powerful. Many of the descriptions and festival comments that appear in this edition, aside from being interesting, assist filmmakers in deciding which festivals would be best for their film. For example, certain festivals encourage a wider distribution of their award-winning films by granting part of the prize money to the distribution company that picks up and releases these films. Knowing which festivals offer these incentives can benefit filmmaker and distributor alike.

Whether you are involved in the film industry or not, anyone interested in films will find this guide fascinating. The original articles were created to go past the functional requirements of filmmakers, to extend and elaborate on what they already know or may have heard of in passing. One example: In *A Festival Experience* by Roy Frumkes he enlightens us on the pros and cons on attending a festival and Steven Olivieri in *Degrees of Separation* explains the various types of independent film (including where *Smoke, Laws of Gravity* and *The English Patient* fit in).The festival descriptions go beyond a dry recital of facts like "permitted" film categories to include the details that make each festival unique. To get to the Midnight Sun Film Festival in Finland, festival goers take a train that has been converted into a rolling cinema and the all-night screening of 5 films then breakfast overlooking the water at the La Rochelle International Film Festival in France.

The new section, Festivals Firsthand, include a Festival Spotlight and Festival Comment's, which give the reader a personal view point by people who have attended and/or participated in festivals around the world. In the former, the reader finds out what the festival has to offer as well as what it was like "being there" to experience the festival first hand. In the latter, various filmmakers talk about there experiences at certain festivals.

So even though this guide is an invaluable and convenient source of current information about festivals for the industry insider as well as helpful to newcomers, it will also be enjoyed by the fan of film who wants to get beyond the limits of the conventional.

Part 1

Opening Articles

Festivapalooza

by Michael Rechtshaffen

Home offices aside, the film festival currently ranks as one of the world's leading growth industries. Once the exclusive domain of Cannes, then embraced by the likes of Venice, Berlin, Chicago, New York, Toronto and Montreal, each adding a little individual cosmo-spolitan flair, the film festival has, in recent years, become as prevalent as the web site. Virtually any hole-in-the-wall town with a multiplex or even a community center with an old Bell & Howell pull-up screen and extra fold-up chairs can hop aboard the filmfest bandwagon, where glamor and glitter stand alongside incorrect aspect ratios, blown projector bulbs and sound qualities that make announcements on certain subway systems sound digitally state-of-the-art by comparison.

Of course, before the advent of the film festivals and the realization that a little glitz can go a long way in the tourism department, most major cities got by with film societies---those gatherings of film dweebs who would pack stuffy screening rooms for a retrospective of the films of Georges Franju or Carl Theodor Dreyer.The product was there, but good luck attracting any paparazzi. Going back farther still, some recently discovered archaelogical finds actually trace an early prototype of today's film festival back almost 80,000 years, when members of neighboring clans gathered in caves to perform an assortment of shadow pictures against a designated cave wall in the flickering fire-light, using only their hands and other extremities.The rest of the clan members would sit crosslegged on the cold dirt floors, grunting or smashing rocks on the ground appreciatively.

While technology has certainly come a long way from that time (although some may argue that audiences haven't), the current film festival explosion is unfortunately bound to give way to considerable fallout. As any experienced filmfest organizer will tell you, cramming dozens of movies into a week-long slot and flying in a handful of stars and directors does not necessarily a successful event make. Programming is everything, and as more and more towns and cities, villages and burgs vie for a piece of the filmfest circuit, finding an identifying hook becomes increasingly crucial for survival.

As a public service, following are a selection of easily adaptable models which are still available (as of press time) and can be yours for the asking (plus a minimal charge).

The Guam International Phil Festival

Dedicated to honoring our rich and varied Phil heritage, this year's edition shines the spotlight on the late, great Phil Silvers with a feature film retrospective that proves his comic genius went far beyond TV's Sgt. Bilko. Included in the program will be multiple screenings of "Follow That Camel" (1967), "The Boatniks" (1970) and "The Chicken Chronicles" (1977), not to mention a special gala presentation of "Forty Pounds of Trouble" (1963) which also happens to be Norman Jewison's directorial debut, to be introduced by funnyman Phil Hartman. The Festival will also pay tribute to Phil Harris, (perhaps best known as the voice of Baloo the Bear in "The Jungle Book") with a special, restored screening of his little-seen 1932 romantic musical comedy "Melody Cruise," featuring the hit song, "He's Not the Marrying Kind." Plus Phil Donahue will moderate the discussion"Phil(ip) Marlow on Screen," with panelists including musical greats Phil Collins and Phil Everly as well as sports legend Phil Esposito.

The [insert struggling Communist country name here] Festival of Meaningful Reflection

Contending that motion pictures should exist strictly for the better-ment of the mother country and that any notion of entertainment value can only lead to deviant behavior, The Festival of Meaningful Reflection will this year screen films from several newly renamed republics, including "Water in My Eardrums," "Little Sparrows Become Warriors Too," "For the Good of the People, Part III," "Hartmut, My Sweet" and the sweeping, "A Great Melancholy in the Loins." No film is under three hours and there will be no intermissions in between screenings. While not a competitive festival, per se, the film deemed the most worthy by the Festival's secret judging committee will honor it with its most prestigious award, The Golden Ferret.

The Kuala Lumpur Cinedisco Festival

A festival devoted to the power of movies, music and movement, this year's edition kicks off with a double blast from the past--a twin bill screening of those 1979 gems, "Roller Boogie"and "Skatetown, U.S.A." (which, incidentally marked Patrick Swayze's feature debut). Both will be presented with digitally remastered Dolby Surround sound. Casts from both movies will be in attendance, with confirmations to date from Linda Blair, Beverly Garland, Scott Baio, Ruth Buzzi and Billy Barty. Also on this edition's roster: "'Thank God, It's Friday" (1978), which introduced Donna Summer's Oscar-winning "Last Dance" "Can't Stop the Music" (1980), the only motion picture in the history of the medium to feature both The VillagePeople and Bruce Jenner; and the long unavailable "Lambada" (1990), shot in Super 35. There will also be a special gala presentation of the electrifying "Sanjay's Disco Dreams" (1977), often referred to as an East Indian "Saturday Night Fever."

The Can Film Festival

Not to be confused with that venerable festival along the Croissette, or the Canine International Film Festival (see below) this bi-annual festival in Frobisher Bay presents the bathroom as celluloid shrine, pointing to such notable films as "Psycho," "The Shining"and, the more recent "Trainspotting," as just a few examples of what the French call "Cinemade la Toilette." This year's installment sets the tone with a special screening of Peter Wier's "The Plumber" (1980), a black comedy originally made for Australian TV about an obnoxious plumber who terrorizes tenants; to be preceded by a world premiere screening of the short, "She Came in Through the Bathroom Window," a dramatization of the old Beatles song that packs a surprise wallop.

The Canine International Film Festival

The only film festival that guarantees "Dogs, Only Dogs," makes good its claim with new and classic pooch pictures. Figuratively, the Duluth, Minnesota festival runs the gamut from the Bunuel-Dali surrealist masterpiece, "Un Chien Andalou" to the Jayne Mansfield clunker, "Dog Eat Dog" to Lumet's "Dog Day Afternoon" and the screen adaptation of Frederick Forsythe's "The Dogs of War" to the Australian punk picture, "Dogs in Space" right through to ultraviolent Belgian entry "Man Bites Dog" and likewise Tarantino's "Reservoir Dogs." Literally, selections include "Baxter," "Beethoven" "Benji the Hunted," "Big Red," "Bingo," "Chips, The War Dog," "Cujo," "Digby, the Biggest Dog in the World," "Dusty," Elmer," "Fabulous Joe," "Fluke," "Frankenweenie," "George!," "Greyfriars Bobby," "Hambone & Hillie," "K-9," "K-9000," "Kavik the Wolf Dog," "Lassie," "Milo and Otis," "Mongrel," "Monster Dog," "My Dog Shep," "Nikki, the Wild Dog of the North," "Old Yeller," "Poco," "Pound Puppies and the Legend of Big Paw," "Rin Tin Tin," "Rover Dangerfield," "Savage Sam," "Scruffy," "Shep Comes Home," "Sherlock: Undercover Dog," "Shiloh," "Top Dog," "The Ugly Dachshund," "Wolfheart's Revenge" and, last but certainly not least, "Zoltan...Hound of Dracula." New titles, meanwhile, vie for the Festival's solo prize--The Silver Flea Collar.

The It Plays in Peoria Film Festival

Long considered a trusty barometer for major studios, the just-your-average movie going town of Peoria, Illinois makes its long-awaited film festival debut with a line-up of titles that have yet to play other festivals. Based on their reaction here, filmmakers and distributors may then work out their festival game plans, accordingly, rather than spend needless amounts of money on prints, subtitles, entry fees and travel.

Good luck.

A 20-year film festival veteran, Hollywood Reporter film critic Michael Rechtshaffen has covered the festival circuit for numerous print and broadcast outlets in the United States and Canada. His "Film Festival Primer" was an extremely popular part of last year's International Film Festival Guide.

Degrees of Separation:
Feature film production expansion and diversification in current U.S. Independent Cinema
by Steven Olivieri

Degrees

It used to be that there were about 40 independent feature films in production per year and twenty or so film schools and film festivals to check into around the U.S. in the seventies and early eighties. Today, there are over 1,000 film projects in the works in the U.S. alone, hundreds of film programs to check into around the country and, as evidenced by this book, over 300 film festivals humming around the world to investigate. Not exactly a lack of interest and growth in feature film production these days.

With the advent of the amazing improvements in the (super) 16mm to 35 mm liquid-gate blow-up process for film prints becoming commonplace now, a well shot, 16mm low-budget feature film can convince buyers at the film markets into thinking that the film is worth a vast amount more than its actual cost of production (I'm speaking of course, of productions that were not shot with light bulbs or dads' "excellent" flood lights alone!). So, the independent feature filmmaking world has come a long way from a few maverick outsiders vs. the studios, to formidable Oscar-takers from those same studios.

But what about this brave, new (relatively speaking) "independent" world? With feature film budgets ranging from $7,000.00 in pocket change to over $20,000,000.00 in corporately backed bucks, is there a singular definition left for the term "independent" feature film? I hardly think so. This is not necessarily a bad thing, but, with the hip, pinpoint mega marketing of a few ultra-low budget independent feature films in the past few years, you wonder if everyone and literally their grandmother are diving head first into production because they feel that they can achieve that .1% phenomenon or will they wait until all of the quality pieces of the project are in place? And even if they wait and create a great film, can they compete with the 10-15 million independent motion picture that already has a formidable publicity unit in place long before they get their first print back from the lab? The scope of independent feature filmmaking in New York ranges from using school-borrowed 16mm Bolex wind up cameras to 35mm Panaflex cameras and lenses, step stools to Chapman cranes and pizza to sushi. There is a critical difference between $50,000.00 and $201,000.00 budgets, $499,000.00 and $1,999,000.00 budgets.

Fortunately, SAG (Screen Actors Guild) has developed different contract agreements to meet the needs of various budgets constraints in the low-budget world. Talented, union actors want to work, and SAG wants them to get exposure. But again, will they get enough exposure if the "awesome" ultra low-budget film cannot afford the (relatively) huge publicity campaign that the high-budget independent feature film can? (By the way, looking for other avenues of exposure is where this book becomes indispensable). Indeed, there is a distinct hierarchy in the independent film world now. The ultra-low budget, independent filmmakers now look at the ultra-high budget independent filmmakers almost as mini studios, to be as much admired as feared or even disliked (really only disliked when the high-budget script is a total sellout - this is what the studios were supposed to be famous for over the years). Film festivals are actually a great place to rub shoulders with the good, the bad, the rich, the poor and the ugly as well as the funny. If you go to enjoy your films' reception (if you came with one) as well as other films, you can basically demystify alot of current hype and cliches for yourself along the way that always pervade the film world (no, Sharon Stone is not currently "attached" to 167 projects and no, *"SHINE"* was not made for just 100,000 U.S. $). You can actually talk straight with filmmakers who have been around the block and learn alot. Film festivals are essentially an enjoyable celebration and recognition of outstanding films. It is not as though there are no promotional politics percolating around every print, but if you go to a film selling market, be prepared to do alot of business with little romance left over.

But, back to the United States. As far as the many degrees of separation between the relentlessly creative production budgets throughout the independent feature film arena in the U.S., the "hierarchy" might roughly break down (from the ground up) something like this:

1.) The $7,000.00 rarity - Add at least $100,000.00 in post-production renovation and a super slick half-million dollar advertising campaign and you just might have a household name. Robert Rodriguez', *"EL MARIACHI"* and very few other films make it into this "miracle" category. 2.) The $25,000.00 - $75,000.00 guerrilla shoot - Resourcing is paramount here. Free locations, vehicles, equipment, etc. will help fill the gaps where hard costs must be met. (Nick Gomez' *"LAWS OF GRAVITY"* and Ed Burns' *"THE BROTHERS McMULLEN"* recently made this category famous again.) The film can proceed under the SAG Limited Exhibition Agreement with a few competent (possibly even name) union actors. Many producers here may choose not to go through with the time and risk factors associated with the rigorous "first time" complications of incorporating a company and adhering to the intimidating SAG guidelines. They opt to use non-SAG actors they know well or have auditioned which may produce incredible results or a total amateur flop. Generally begging for post-production completion funds after the film is "in the can". Shooting in 16mm unless the producers' uncle owns a 35mm camera package. 3.) The $75,000.00 - $199,000.00 hustle shoot. The film may have good deferred post-production deals in place, so that the money can still be prioritized for better equipment, all fresh film stock, some deferred salaries, etc. Can still proceed under the SAG Limited Exhibition Agreement and probably will. Might shoot in super 16mm, possibly 35mm. I should note that the previous three categories of film production occur much more frequently in New York than in Los Angeles. Gretchen Somerfeld, an independent filmmaker residing in Los Angeles, recalls shooting her directorial debut, *"Interruptions"* throughout the streets of L.A. recently. She felt that if you were attempting to shoot your feature film with a budget described in any of the three previously mentioned categories, that "most people in the business would look askance at you for working in 16mm in an overwhelmingly 35mm town." SAG, permits and deal cutting are all much more of an obstacle to overcome in L.A. than in New York. I have produced feature films myself in both New York and L.A. and notice the film savvy nature of even average L.A. residents who have learned that they should coerce you into using huge, expensive rental generators for tiny lighting set-ups (as opposed to tying in directly to their fuse box) to avoid a remotely possible power failure. Never mind how this drains a low-budget films' "already feeble" bank acct. 4.) The $200,000.00 - $499,000.00 relatively civil shoot. Smart producers should be able to make this look good. SAG Modified Low-Budget Agreement in place. Publicity and legal fees actually attended to. Generally shooting in 35mm. Food starts getting noticeably better. Transportation between locations may become less frantic. 5.) The $500,000.00 - $1,999,000.00 shoot. Name actors (or their agents) more responsive here. Honey wagons (trailers) begin to appear. The director hopefully still has complete artistic control. Distribution strategy (negative pick-up deals, music licensing deals, etc.) begins to underscore the project. 6.)The $5,000,000.00 - $15,000,000.00 shoot. *"SMOKE"* would fit into the lower end of this category. Takes on a very low-budget studio feel. More complex produsorial and promotional politics emerge. Actors get paid at least scale. Name actors get above-scale chunks. Hopefully manageable without too many "suits" mucking up the works. Of course it's shot in 35mm and the food is great! (Exotic locations don't hurt either). 7.)The 20 million and over shoot. The Cadillac (so to speak) productions of the independent film world. Corporate dollars and board of directors generally in control. Final cut for the director possibly in question. Basically competing with studios for more exhibition slots. Hopefully, the story may still be the original focal point amidst the overriding objective of attaining very large box office returns. *"THE ENGLISH PATIENT"* has, in fact, ascended to these lofty production heights.

With the overwhelming success of independent feature films at the Oscars this past year, it is encouraging to see the independents give the studios a run for the money (even if in fact the promotional costs for some of those independent films all but killed their profit margin for the moment). If independent films can keep their focus on the story, a great script, then the maverick movement will always be worthwhile. Maybe American Cinema can eventually take on a more European sensibility and variance (gasp) in its choices of future megaplex bookings around the country and reevaluate the rampant production of blockbuster flicks that can only ever hope to entertain audiences in a sociologically shallow way. It will take more multi-theatre art houses like the Angelika in New York to float more independent fare or huge multiplexes with a broader commitment to independent films to increase their visibility across the country.

America still has the potential to produce a majority of quality motion pictures for the world market. If it takes the most touching and profound independent films to lead the way to better and better cinema in this country and abroad, then so be it.

Steven Olivieri is an independent screenwriter/director/producer based in New York City. He has produced the award winning feature film, "DESOLATION ANGELS" which won for best first film in both the '95 Telluride and Toronto film festivals. He has just secured distribution for his own directorial debut, "THE IRREVERSIBLE YEAR" and is working on his latest screenplay, "FURNACE".

The Geopolitics of the Film Industry

by James Cooper

Hollywood no longer just depicts the world - it is now a major player in it.

Geopolitics have moved from the bipolar nuclear nightmare diplomacy of the Cold War and emerged into a new world order where international trade is the new battlecry. The film industry has quickly followed suit.

Where over the years, films coming out of the major studios dealt with themes of global import - *The Hunt for Red October, Reds, Red Dawn, Russia House* all come to mind - the motion picture industry itself has increasingly become the subject of international relations. Indeed, Hollywood has long recognized the value of global relations. As U.S. films dominate the screens across the globe, the foreign box office receipts for American-produced films have added handsomely to the bottom line.

Where the U.S. used to approach the power brokers in Moscow on issues of global security, the agenda has changed. Jack Valenti, the U.S. film industry's leading lobbyist and spokesman, attended the 20th Moscow International Film Festival in July 1997 and paid a diplomatic call to the Kremlin. The aging President of the Motion Picture Association of America, and former Johnson Administration bureaucrat, managed to secure promises from Russian Prime Minister Viktor Chernomyrdin that the Russian government would increase efforts to combat video piracy.

It is estimated that video piracy - the illegal copying and distribution for sale of copyrighted works - costs Hollywood hundreds of millions of dollars annually in lost licensing and royalty fees. It also costs the Russian government money that it could obtain through taxation - an estimated $250 million to $300 million a year. As Mr. Valenti visited Moscow, bootlegged video copies of *Batman & Robin* were for sale within blocks of the meeting, even before the film was making its cinematic debut in the beleaguered capital.

And while video piracy is only part of the billions of dollar piracy industry that exists in Russia - name brand watches, fashion items, compact disks, and video games are but a few of the illegally manufactured products for sale without the proper licenses - it is the film industry that has made a significant commitment to international cooperation.

It is not surprising. It was a controversy over the reduction of trade barriers concerning the film industry which nearly brought about the collapse of the world's trading regime. During the Uruguay Round of negotiations for the General Agreement of Tariffs and Trade, started in 1986, the French government vehemently opposed American film penetration of French cinema screens. The Elysée Palace saw it simply as American cultural imperialism and refused to withdraw regulations which limited American access to French film distribution. The issue was finally concluded in December 1993, thanks to last-minute compromises by U.S. and French diplomats.

Such French intransigence should have been no surprise to the world's trading partners. Fiercely nationalistic in its cultural policies, France has put itself in the vanguard of the efforts by the European Union to block further saturation of the Continent's movie and television screens by Hollywood. Not surprisingly, the Cannes festival, which is getting nearly three-quarters of the 1997 budget (totaling $5.9-million) from the government and the local municipality, is an element in that policy. French Culture Minister Philippe Douste-Blazy, merely a month away from losing his job, proudly expounded on the value of the Cannes Film Festival: "This is an occasion to show that French cinema is second in the world."

Despite such protestations of "We're number two!", the festival is United States-friendly. The fiftieth anniversary celebrations saw the opening of the Cannes location for Planet Hollywood. It was not by accident that the festival opened with the Luc Besson film *The Fifth Element* and that the film's star Bruce Willis is a shareholder in the glamorous hamburger franchise. Nor was it coincidental that Hollywood had managed to lure the celebrated French director into the production of a summer blockbuster.

In short, despite episodic French protestations, the film industry is global. Or rather, the international film industry is fast becoming American. It is not just by accident that the fiftieth anniversary of the Cannes Film Festival occurred around the same time as the fiftieth anniversary of the Marshall Plan, the economic aid package the Unitied States provided to war-torn Europe. Such American hegemony in what used to be sacrosanct cultural industries like film is not necessarily a bad thing.

The American dream is about merit and hard work winning in the end. If this means good films will get made and championed by critics and bad films scrapped or lambasted by the press, so be it. It is quite telling that only one of the films nominated for Best Motion Picture in the 1997 Academy Awards came from a big Hollywood studio. As American audiences open their hearts to smaller and foreign films and film-makers, American studio chequebooks too will open.

So too will Hollywood mindsets. The U.S. film industry has already taken note of the changes affecting the globe and acted accordingly. Bridget Bardot has made a second career as an animal rights activist. Richard Gere has rallied pubicly for the people of Tibet. Tim Robbins and Susan Sarandon have gone global with their respective campaigns. At the 1995 Academic Awards, when presenting the Award for Best Foreign Motion Picture, Jeremy Irons referred to *Before the Rain* as a film from "The Former Yugoslav Republic of Macedonia", keeping in tune with the nomenclature of the time and the political sensitivities of the film and the situation in the Balkans. Hollywood had stood up and taken notice.

But then again the U.S. film industry has been at the height of international intrigue for years. In the late 1940s and 1950s, the film industry was the main target for attack by the U.S. Senate Committee on Un-American Activities and its ringleader Senator Joseph McCarthy. Many fine actors, producers, and directors were blacklisted by

Hollywood and ostracized by the spheres of power at the time. With the globalization of culture, Hollywood will continue to take an international perspective. It will not be just for plots and actors, but for marketshare and liberal trading partners.

At the end of the day, however, the film industry has a leg up on the evolving arena of world politics. Hollywood is long seasoned in the politics of posing and the propaganda of the deed. Ronald Reagan already showed us that.

James Cooper teaches international law at the University of Toronto. He has also written and produced independent films.

The Festivals

● Flickerfest International Outdoor Short Film Festival

Flickerfest showcases quality short films from around the world. It takes place annually ,in Sydney, at Bondi Beach during the month of January. The films are all screened outside to take advantage of the beautiful surroundings. In March, the films go on tour thoughtout Australia.

FESTIVAL DATES
January, 1998
SUBMISSION DATES
October, 1997
ADDRESS
31 Hickson Rd., Level 1
Millers Point NSW 2000
Australia

TEL:	61 2 926 67242
FAX:	61 2 926 24774
E-MAIL:	flickerf@tmx.com.au
CONTACT:	**Craig Kirkwood**

FILM TYPE
Short
COMPETITIVE
Yes
LANGUAGE
Any
COUNTRY
Any
ENTRY FEES
$25

AWARDS
Awards to Best Film, Best Animated Film and Best Student Film.

● Palm Springs International Film Festival

Historically, this festival has premiered the Academy Award nominations prior to the announcements. It also places emphasis on student entries. Over 130 films from over 40 countries will be showcased in six venues in Palm Springs. This festival screens World Premieres, U.S. Premieres and films submitted for an Oscar . International directors, celebrities and film critics will be in attendance or representing their latest films.

FESTIVAL DATES
January 8-25, 1998
SUBMISSION DATES
November 1, 1997
ADDRESS
PO Box 2230
Palm Springs, CA 92263
USA

TEL:	760-322 2930
FAX:	760-322 4087
E-MAIL:	filmfest@ix.netcom.com
WEB SITE:	
http://www.psfilmfest.org/eighth.htm	
ENTRIES:	400
ATTENDEES:	50,000
CONTACT:	**Craig Prater**

FILM TYPE
All
COMPETITIVE
No
LANGUAGE
Any
COUNTRY
Any
ENTRY FEES
$25 short/$60 feature

AWARDS
Each year Palm Springs honours individuals with acheivement awards that include; the Charles A. Crain Desert Palm Acheivement Award; International Filmmaker Award; Director's Lifetime Acheivement; Frederick Loewe Acheivement Award and the Outstanding Acheivement in Craft Award.

● Cine Latino

January

Cine Latino focuses on feature and short films from Latin America. It also screens films from Germany as well as international premieres.

FESTIVAL DATES
Mid-January to Mid-February, 1998
ADDRESS
Postfach 1549 (PO Box)
D-72005 Tubingen
Germany

TEL: 49-7071-32828
FAX: 49-7071-31006
ENTRIES: 20
ATTENDEES: 3,000
CONTACT: **Dieter Betz**

FILM TYPE
Feature, Short
COMPETITIVE
No
COUNTRY
Latin American
ENTRY FEES
None

● International Film Festival of India (New Delhi)

This festival's goal is to provide a forum for films from around the world, contribute to an understanding of different cultures as well as to promote friendship and cooperation among various cultures. Their programs include a competition for female Asian directors, Cinema of the World, Retrospectives, Tributes, Mainstream Indian Cinema and a Market section held during the festival.

FESTIVAL DATES
Middle of January, 1998
ADDRESS
Directorate of Film Festivals, Ministry of
Information and Broadcasting
4th Floor, Lok Nayak Bhavan, Khan Market
New Delhi 110 003
India

TEL: 91-11 461 5953/469 7167
FAX: 91-11 462 3430
ENTRIES: 70-80
ATTENDEES: 2,500
CONTACT: **Malti Sahai**

FILM TYPE
Feature
COMPETITIVE
Yes
LANGUAGE
Any (English subtitles)
COUNTRY
Any
ENTRY FEES
None

AWARDS
This festival awards the Golden Peacock for best film by an Asian woman director (Rs. 500,000), Silver Peacock for most promising female Asian director (Rs. 250,000) and the Special Jury Award for an individual's artistic contribution (Rs. 250,000).

● Sundance Film Festival

Sundance was created by Robert Redford to enhance the artistic vitality and diversity of American filmmaking. Sundance is internationally recognized as the single most important showcase of American independent cinema. Its programs include American Spectrum, World Cinema and Shorts. The competition selects the best independent dramatic and documentary film.

FESTIVAL DATES
  January 15-25, 1998
SUBMISSION DATES
  October, 1997
ADDRESS
  Sundance Institute, PO Box 16450
  Salt Lake City, UT 84116
  USA

TEL: 801-328 3456
FAX: 801-575 5175
E-MAIL: sundance@xmission.com
WEB SITE: http://www.sundance.org/
ENTRIES: 100+
ATTENDEES: 9,000
CONTACT: **Nicole Guillemet**

AllFILM TYPE
  All
COMPETITIVE
  Yes
LANGUAGE
  Must be an American film
COUNTRY
  Any (US for competition only)
ENTRY FEES
  $20-$50

AWARDS
  The awards include a Grand Prize, Cinematography Award, Audience Award and Filmmaker's Trophy.

● KidFilm Festival

KidFilm is sponsored by the USA Film Festival and is the largest children's media arts event in the US. Programs include best contemporary and classic films from around the world as well as a guest filmmaker. A goal of KidFilm is to use a familiar, accessible medium to communicate important ideas, and to provide children with an early introduction to the media arts.

FESTIVAL DATES
  January 15-18, 1998
SUBMISSION DATES
  December, 1997
ADDRESS
  2917 Swiss Ave.
  Dallas, TX 75204
  USA

TEL: 214-821 6300
FAX: 214-821 6364
WEB SITE: http://www.usafilmfestival.com/
ENTRIES: 300
ATTENDEES: 15,000
CONTACT: **Alonso Durlade**

FILM TYPE
  All
COMPETITIVE
  Yes/No
LANGUAGE
  Any
COUNTRY
  Any
ENTRY FEES
  None

AWARDS
  The competition is called "Kids in the Directors Chair" and admittance is free to this event.

● Slamdance International Film Festival

Slamdance is going on to its 4th year and has expanded into a support system for the new filmmaker. It features films of all genres primarily devoted to first-time directors and films which do not have domestic distribution or wealthy budgets. The screenwriting competition selects six finalists which include three grand prize winners from over 1,000 entries. By showcasing new talent, Slamdance is continuing to create opportunities for new writers and directors while helping them to grow.

FESTIVAL DATES
  January 16-23, 1998

SUBMISSION DATES
  October 15, 1997 (early); November 12, 1997 (final)

ADDRESS
  6381 Hollywood Boulevard , No. 520
  Los Angeles, CA 90028
  USA

TEL:	213 466 1786/310 204 7977
FAX:	213 466 1784
E-MAIL:	slamdance@earthlink.net
WEB SITE:	http://www.slamdance.com/
ENTRIES:	1,000+ submitted
CONTACT:	**Jeremy Taylor**

FILM TYPE
  All

COMPETITIVE
  Yes

LANGUAGE
  Any (English subtitles)

COUNTRY
  Any

ENTRY FEES
  $25 under 40 mins. $40 over 40 mins. (early; $10 more at final deadline)

AWARDS
  Grand Jury Prizes for Best Short and Best Feature Audience Awards for Best Short and Best Feature. In the screenplay competition 1st , 2nd and 3rd place receive $2,000, $750 and $250 dollars, respectively as well as a submission to a Major Literary Agency , Major Studio & "MovieBuff" Film Credits/Contacts Software.

● Solothurn Film Festival

Solothurn gives a representative survey of all forms of creative film and video-making in Switzerland of the preceding year. It presents a selection of films and videos by Swiss authors and foreign authors resident in Switzerand as well as co-productions between Switzerland and foreign countries.

FESTIVAL DATES
  January 20-25, 1998

ADDRESS
  Unt. Steingrubenstrasse 19, PO Box 1030
  CH-4502 Solothurn
  Switzerland

TEL:	41-32-625 8080
FAX:	41-32-623 6410
E-MAIL:	felmtage@cuenet.ch
WEB SITE:	http://www.cuenet.ch/felmtage/
ENTRIES:	180
ATTENDEES:	30,000
CONTACT:	**Ivo Kummer**

FILM TYPE
  All

COMPETITIVE
  Yes

LANGUAGE
  Any

COUNTRY
  Switzerland and coproductions with Switzerland

ENTRY FEES
  None

● Max Ophuls Preis Film Festival

Max Ophuls is Europe's most important German-language film festival, especially for young directors. It intends to give a yearly synopsis of German-language film production. Many films from Austria and Switzerland are therefore presented in competition. Other programs include Saarbrucker Premieres, a Retrospective, and films from another European country.

FESTIVAL DATES
January 20-25, 1998 (tbc)

ADDRESS
Filmburo Sarrbruken, Max Ophuls Preis
Mainzer Str 8
66111 Saarbruken
Germany

TEL:	49-681-39452
FAX:	49-681-905 1943
E-MAIL:	erbach@coli.uni-sb.de
WEB SITE:	http://www.coli.uni-sb.de/~erbach//mop95.html
ENTRIES:	250
ATTENDEES:	20,000
CONTACT:	**Christel Drawer**

FILM TYPE
Feature, Short

COMPETITIVE
Yes

LANGUAGE
German

COUNTRY
German language country

ENTRY FEES
None

● Brussels Film Festival

Brussels screens various types of films throughtout its 11-days. Sections include Kaleidoscope of the World Cinema, open to all feature films over 60 mins shot in 35 mm; Night of the Short Film, for shorts under 20 mins, shot in 35mm or 16mm and Belgian Focus, competitive for Belgian features and shorts. Belgian docs are shown, but are not part of a competition. Special sections showcased at this festival include tributes and retrospectives.

FESTIVAL DATES
January 21-31, 1998

SUBMISSION DATES
October 30, 1997

ADDRESS
30 Chaussee de Louvain
B-1020 Brussels
Belgium

TEL:	32-2-227 3980
FAX:	32-2-218 1860
E-MAIL:	infoffb@netcity.be
WEB SITE:	http://www.ffb.cinebel.com/
ENTRIES:	180-200 screened
ATTENDEES:	47,000
CONTACT:	**Christian Thomas**

FILM TYPE
All

COMPETITIVE
Yes

LANGUAGE
Any

COUNTRY
Any

ENTRY FEES
No

AWARDS
In the European Competition, features and shorts compete for the Crystal Star Awards (that offer support for European promotion and distribution worth over $100,000).

● Tromso Film Festival

Tromso is the northernmost film festival and presents international films. The chosen films are mostly art house and documentary. Young filmmakers, new talents and unknown directors are an important part of this festival's programs as well as Asian and European films.

FESTIVAL DATES
January 21-25, 1998

SUBMISSION DATES
January, 1998

ADDRESS
Georgernes Verft 3
5011 Bergen
Norway

TEL: 47-55 32 25 90
FAX: 47-55 32 37 40
E-MAIL: tiff@bgnett.no
WEB SITE: http://www.bgnett.no/tiff
ENTRIES: 40-50
ATTENDEES: 4,000
CONTACT: **Tor Fosse**

FILM TYPE
Feature, Documentary

COMPETITIVE
Yes

LANGUAGE
Any

COUNTRY
Any

ENTRY FEES
Small fee

AWARDS
The Audience Award is presented every year.

● Clermont-Ferrand Short Film Festival

Clermont-Ferrand is one of the most popular and largest short film festivals in the world. It focuses on international short films with prizes awarded to both national and international entries. Its programs include retrospectives, debates and a market for shorts.

FESTIVAL DATES
January 23-31, 1998

ADDRESS
26 rue des Jacobins
F-63000 Clermont-Ferrand
France

TEL: 33-4-73 91 65 73
FAX: 33-4-73 92 11 93
WEB SITE: http://fcmwww.in2p3.fr/
ENTRIES: 200+
ATTENDEES: 100,000+
CONTACT: **Christian Guinot**

FILM TYPE
Short

COMPETITIVE
Yes

LANGUAGE
Any

COUNTRY
Any

ENTRY FEES
None

AWARDS
This festival awards the Grand Prix, Prix special du jury, and Prix du public to both national and international films.

● Tokyo Video Festival

Tokyo Video accepts all types of video compositions, and the competition results are announced in the beginning of the following year. It endeavours to entertain and improve video-making efforts and support video productions. It has played a significant role in promoting "global communications through video images" and in creating a new video-imaging culture.

FESTIVAL DATES
January 24, 1998

SUBMISSION DATES
October 5, 1997

ADDRESS
c/o Victor Building, 1-7-1 Shinbashi, Minato-ku
Tokyo 105
Japan

TEL: 81-3-3289 2811
FAX: 81-3-3289 2819
ENTRIES: 1,750+
CONTACT: **Minoru Sato**

FILM TYPE
All types of video composition

COMPETITIVE
Yes

LANGUAGE
Any

COUNTRY
Any

ENTRY FEES
None

AWARDS
The awards include, the Video and JVC Grand Prize (US$5,000, 10-day round trip to Japan, trophy and citation), Gold (5), Silver (10) and Bronze (15) Awards worth $2,500 and $2,500 in video equipment, $1,500 and $1,500,respectively.

● Internationales Filmwochenende

This festival focuses on recent European and International productions (competitive) plus a non-competitive section that includes tributes to directors as well as panoramas.

FESTIVAL DATES
January-February, 1998

SUBMISSION DATES
November, 1997

ADDRESS
Gorbersteige 2
D-97082 Wurzburg
Germany

TEL: 49-931-414098
FAX: 49-931-416279/408561
CONTACT: **Berhold Kremmler**

FILM TYPE
Feature, Short

COMPETITIVE
Yes

LANGUAGE
Any

COUNTRY
Any

ENTRY FEES
None

AWARDS
Audience Award for Best Feature Film (5,000DM).

● Gerardmer Fantastic' Arts International Fantasy Film Festival

Fantastic Arts is dedicated to screening films that are part of the fantasy genre. Films showcased can be science-fiction, horror, supernatural or any other "fantastic" film from any part of the world. Other events take place during the festival that fit into the "fantasy" motif.

FESTIVAL DATES
January 28-Feb. 1, 1998
SUBMISSION DATES
January 8, 1998
ADDRESS
c/o Le Publis Systeme
36 rue Pierret
F-92200 Neuilly-sur-Seine
France

TEL: 33-1-46 40 55 55
FAX: 33-1-46 40 55 39
ENTRIES: 100 (15 screened)
ATTENDEES: 35,000
CONTACT: **Laurent Geissmann**

FILM TYPE
All, but documentary (french shorts)
COMPETITIVE
Yes
LANGUAGE
Any (French subtitles)
COUNTRY
Any
ENTRY FEES
None

AWARDS
The Grand Prix Gerardmer Fantastic' Arts is awarded each year at this festival.

● Rotterdam International Film Festival

Rotterdam is one of the largest and most popular film festivals in the world. The main program includes the Tiger Awards Competition, international and European premieres and a "slice" from certain recent festivals. Its sidebars include retrospectives on different genres and directors as well as on new Dutch films. Other highlights are connections with major independent distributors (which in 1996 helped release over 30 new films), Cinemart (a meeting place for all industry professionals showcasing certain film projects) and the Hubert Bals Fund (which awards $50,000US to 20 film-projects).

FESTIVAL DATES
January 28-February 8, 1998
SUBMISSION DATES
November 1, 1997
ADDRESS
PO Box 21696
NL-3001 AR Rotterdam
The Netherlands

TEL: 31-10-411 8080
FAX: 31-10-413 5132
E-MAIL: iffr@luna.nl
WEB SITE: http://www.iffrotterdam.nl/
ENTRIES: 210 screened
ATTENDEES: 100,000+
CONTACT: **Simon Field**

FILM TYPE
All
COMPETITIVE
Yes
LANGUAGE
Any
COUNTRY
Any
ENTRY FEES
None

AWARDS
Rotterdam has the Tiger Awards competition which focuses on the promotion of new talent. An international jury chooses three films which receive $10,000US. Other awards are the Citroen Audience Award (for favorite feature film) and the Fipresci and KNF Prizes awarded by film journalists.

● Cinequest, San Jose Film Festival

Cinequest focuses on those films considered part of Maverick Cinema, films which successfully stretch to and achieve something new and different. Special sections are devoted to Latino, Asian, After Hours and High-Tech cinema as well as tributes held each year to showcase certain filmmakers.

FESTIVAL DATES
January 29-February 4, 1998
SUBMISSION DATES
October 11, 1997
ADDRESS
PO Box 720040
San Jose, CA 95172-0040
USA

TEL:	408-995 6305
FAX:	408-277 3862
E-MAIL:	sjfilmfest@aol.com
WEB SITE:	http://www.webcom.com/~sjfilm/
ENTRIES:	100
ATTENDEES:	35,000-40,000
CONTACT:	**Mike Rabehl**

FILM TYPE
All
COMPETITIVE
Yes
LANGUAGE
Any
COUNTRY
Any
ENTRY FEES
$25

AWARDS
Awards include Best Drama and Comedy Feature, Best Documentary and Best Short Film.

● Goteborg Film Festival

Goteborg is the largest and official Swedish film festival. It has grown to be one of Scandinavia's most important. The aim of the festival is to expose films considered important to buyers, to an interested audience. Over the years, more then 220 films have received distribution in Scandinavia, as a result of screenings at this festival.

FESTIVAL DATES
January 30-Feb. 8, 1998 (tbc)
SUBMISSION DATES
November, 1997
ADDRESS
Box 7079
S-402 32 Goteborg
Sweden

TEL:	46-31-410 546
FAX:	46-31-410 063
E-MAIL:	goteborgfilmfestival@mailbox.swip-net.se
WEB SITE:	http://www.goteborg.se/kultur/film/festival/
ENTRIES:	300+
ATTENDEES:	15,500
CONTACT:	**Gunnar Bergdahl**

FILM TYPE
All
COMPETITIVE
No
LANGUAGE
Any (English or Swedish subtitles)
COUNTRY
Any
ENTRY FEES
None

AWARDS
The awards include the Goteborg-Postens Nordiska Filmpris, Film of the Year and the Goteborg Stora Filmpris.

● Miami Film Festival

Miami presents premieres of the best films from the US, Europe, Asia and Latin America. During the festival there are seminars, as well as Q&A sessions after many films. It has also become known as the gateway for Spanish language films into the US.

FESTIVAL DATES
  January 30-February 8, 1998
SUBMISSION DATES
  November 1, 1997
ADDRESS
  444 Brickell Avenue, Suite 229
  Miami, FL 33131
  USA

TEL: 305-377 3456
FAX: 305-577 9768
E-MAIL: info@filmsocietyofmiami.com
WEB SITE:
http://www.miamifilmfestival.com/
ENTRIES: 25-28
ATTENDEES: 37,000
CONTACT: **Stephanie Martino**

FILM TYPE
  All (35mm only)
COMPETITIVE
  No
LANGUAGE
  Any
COUNTRY
  Any
ENTRY FEES
  No

Brief Entries

● MIDEM

ADDRESS
Reed Midem Organization
11 rue de Colonel Ave.
17726 Paris Cedex
France

FESTIVAL DATES
January 18-22, 1998
TEL: 33-1-41 90 44 00
FAX: 33-1-41 90 44 09
CONTACT: **Xavier Roy**

● FIPA (International de Programmes Audiovisuels)

ADDRESS
215 rue du Faubourg Saint-Honore
75008 Paris
France

TEL: 33-1-45 61 01 66
FAX: 33-1-40 74 07 96
CONTACT: **Michel Mitrani**

● New York Festivals

ADDRESS
780 King Street
Chappaqua, NY 10514
USA

TEL: 914-238 4481
FAX: 914-238 5040
CONTACT: **Joan McLoughlin**

● NATPE (National Association of TV Programming Executives)

ADDRESS
2425 Olympic Boulevard, Suite 550E
Santa Monica, CA 90404
USA

TEL: 310-453 4440
FAX: 310-453 5258
CONTACT: **Bruce Johanden**

● Travelling-Rennes Film Festival

ADDRESS
Clair Obscur 6
avenue Gaston Berger
F-35043 Rennes Cedex
France

TEL: 33-2-99 14 10 00
FAX: 33-2-99 33 50 05
CONTACT: **Jocelyne Regnier**

● Cineasia (Singapore)

ADDRESS
244 West 49th Street, Suite 200
New York, NY 10019
USA

TEL: 212-246 6460
FAX: 212-265 6428
CONTACT: **Jimmy Sunshine**

● Fajr Film Festival

Fajr is a competitive event which primarily showcases Iranian films. Even though its focus is on these films, it also endeavors to screen a sampling of international fare. This helps to accomplish one of its goals, which is to establish a bridge between Eastern and Western Cinema.

FESTIVAL DATES
February, 1998
SUBMISSION DATES
December, 1997
ADDRESS
Farhang Cineman
Dr Shariati Avenue
Gholhak, Tehran 19139
Iran

TEL: 98-21265 086/200 2088/89/90
FAX: 98-21-237 082
E-MAIL:
WEB SITE:
http://www.gpg.com/film/simargh.html
ENTRIES: 100-150
ATTENDEES: 400,000
CONTACT: **E. Zarghami**

FILM TYPE
All
COMPETITIVE
Yes
LANGUAGE
Persian, English and French
COUNTRY
Any country, but Israel
ENTRY FEES
None

AWARDS
Awards are given out in all the major categories including Best Film, Director, Screenplay, Cinematography, Actor, Actress, Music as well as Best First Film.

● Cairo International Film Festival for Children

This Middle-Eastern festival focuses strictly on films for children. It takes place approximately two months after its cousin, the Cairo International Film Festival ,which has a more general focus and accepts all types of international feature films.

FESTIVAL DATES
February, 1998
ADDRESS
17 Kasr el Nil Street
Cairo
Egypt

TEL: 202-392 3562
FAX: 202-393 8979
ENTRIES: 200
CONTACT: **Saad Eldin Wahba**

FILM TYPE
All
COMPETITIVE
Yes
LANGUAGE
Any
COUNTRY
Any
ENTRY FEES
None

● San Diego Film Festival

San Diego's mandate is to show the "best" in contemporary cinema from around the world. Since "best" is so subjective, selections are based solely upon the aethetic sensibilities of the selection committee. In general; the committee is looking for well-crafted films of all kinds and subject matter reflecting a unique personal vision on the part of the filmmaker(s). San Diego, prides itself on the merit of its selections and has included films rejected by other, larger festivals, and also rejected submissions accepted at those festivals. The festival exists as a 4- month program starting at the beginning of February and ending in late May each year.

FESTIVAL DATES
  February to May, 1998
SUBMISSION DATES
  November 30, 1997
ADDRESS
  University of California-San Diego Dept. 0078
  Rm. 3.332, 3rd Floor , Price Center
  Meyers Drive
  La Jolla, CA 92093
  USA

TEL:	619 534-0497
FAX:	619 534-7665
E-MAIL:	rbaily@ucsd.edu
WEB SITE:	http://www.ueo.ucsd.edu/
ENTRIES:	500 (42 screened)
ATTENDEES:	18,900+
CONTACT:	**Ruth Baily**

FILM TYPE
  All
COMPETITIVE
  Yes
LANGUAGE
  Any (English subtitles)
COUNTRY
  Any
ENTRY FEES
  $25US short and animated films only

AWARDS
  The awards include Festival Award for Best Film; Patrons Award for Best Film, Festival Award for Best Short Film; Festival Award for Best Animation and 2 special achievment awards.

● Tropfest (Tropicana Short Film Festival)

Tropfest showcases short films that are less than seven minutes in length. Their is a competitve component to this festival in which all the films take part and can win prizes. A common theme, decided by the festival, must be incorporated into all the entries. In 1997 the theme was a pickle.

FESTIVAL DATES
  February, 1998
SUBMISSION DATES
  January, 1998
ADDRESS
  24/2A Bayswatch Rd.
  Kings Cross NSW 2011
  Australia

TEL:	612 9368 0434
FAX:	61 2 9356 4531
E-MAIL:	tropfest@infolearn.com.au
WEB SITE:	
	http://www.infolearn.com.au/tropfest/
CONTACT:	**Gina Hall**

FILM TYPE
  Short
COMPETITIVE
  Yes
LANGUAGE
  Any
COUNTRY
  Any
ENTRY FEES
  $10

● Mardi Gras Film Festival

The Mardi Gras Film Festival focuses on films about, of interest to, and/or made by gays and lesbians. It takes place every year as part of the month-long Sydney Gay & Lesbian Mardi Gras Arts Festival. This event is the largest of its kind in the world. Aside from films, Mardi Gras also features a screening/discussion program, parties, and the "Festival Cafe", a place to meet and talk with the filmmakers.

FESTIVAL DATES
February 11-25, 1998 (tbc)
SUBMISSION DATES
December 12, 1997
ADDRESS
PO Box 1081
Darlinghurst, NSW 2010
Australia

TEL: 61-2-9332 4938
FAX: 61-2-9331 2988
E-MAIL: info@queerscreen.com.au
WEB SITE:
http://www.queerscreen.com.au/filmfest/index.html
ENTRIES: 90
ATTENDEES: 18,000
CONTACT: **Tony Grierson**

FILM TYPE
All
COMPETITIVE
No
LANGUAGE
Any (English subtitles)
COUNTRY
Any
ENTRY FEES
None

● Berlin International Film Festival

Berlin is one of the most prestigious festivals in Europe and the world. Apart from the international competition, its program has many others sections, including an International Forum of New Cinema, an International Panorama, New German Films, a Children's Film Fest and a Retrospective. During the festival, there is also an European film market showcasing films in various stages of production.

FESTIVAL DATES
February 11-22, 1998
ADDRESS
Budapester Strasse 50
D-10787 Berlin
Germany

TEL: 49-30-25 48 90
FAX: 49-30-25 48 92 49
E-MAIL: info@filmfest-berlin.de
WEB SITE: http://www.filmfest-berlin.de/
ENTRIES: 200+
ATTENDEES: 50,000+
CONTACT: **Moritz De Hadeln**

FILM TYPE
All
COMPETITIVE
Yes
LANGUAGE
Any (German subtitles)
COUNTRY
Any
ENTRY FEES
Contact Festival

AWARDS
The awards include the Golden Berlin Bear (best feature), Silver Berlin Bear for best director, actor (female & male) and outstanding achievement, Alfred Bauer Prize and the Blue Angel to a European film.

● Portland International Film Festival

Portland is an annual 18 day survey of contemporary world cinema. It screens aprroximately 100 feature and short films from around the world. Special programs include A Pacific Rim Showcase, Children's Series, New Directors, Archival Treasures, Visiting Artists and New French Cinema.

FESTIVAL DATES
February 12-March 1, 1998
SUBMISSION DATES
December 1, 1997
ADDRESS
Northwest Film Centre
1219 S.W. Park Avenue
Portland, OR 97205
USA

TEL: 503-221 1156
FAX: 503-226 4842
E-MAIL: theboss@nwfc.org
WEB SITE:
http://www.nwfc.org/~library/piff.html
ENTRIES: 400 (93 screened)
ATTENDEES: 30,000+
CONTACT: **Bill Foster**

FILM TYPE
All, but animation
COMPETITIVE
Yes
LANGUAGE
Any (English subtitles)
COUNTRY
Any
ENTRY FEES
None ($15 to return tape)

AWARDS
The awards presented at this festival include Best Film, Blockbuster Audience Award, New Director Award and Best Short Award.

● East Village Armchair Film Festival

The East Village Armchair Film Festival is an alternofest for film lovers. It screens narrative shorts in a cosy, warm, living roomish setting. It takes place each year during the middle of February.

FESTIVAL DATES
February 12, 1998 (tbc)
ADDRESS
Orange Roughy Production Arts
c/o Constance Van Flandern
101 St Mark's Pl #28
New York, NY 10009
USA

TEL: 212 982-3818
E-MAIL: CONNIEVF@aol.com
WEB SITE:
http://www.interactive.net/~chris/Armchair-Film-Festival/
ATTENDEES: 150+
CONTACT: **Constance Van Flandern**

FILM TYPE
Short in live action, animation or documentary
COMPETITIVE
Yes
ENTRY FEES
$10 (VHS copy note format)

AWARDS
Different prizes are awarded each year at this festival. Previous prizes were $500 in film stock from Kodak and the "comfy award" which is in the shape of an armchair.

● International Forum of New Cinema (Berlin)

This festival aims to inform participates about new formal and thematic developments in film in different countries of the world. By staging discussions with the filmmakers following the screenings and by supplying informative background material, this festival provides an appropriate forum for the films.

FESTIVAL DATES
February 13-23, 1998

SUBMISSION DATES
November 30, 1997

ADDRESS
Budapester Strasse 50
D-10787 Berlin
Germany

TEL:	49-30 2548 9229
FAX:	49-30-25 48 92 49
ENTRIES:	600
ATTENDEES:	87,700
CONTACT:	**Karen Moeller**

FILM TYPE
All, but short

COMPETITIVE
Yes

LANGUAGE
Any (German subtitles)

COUNTRY
Any

ENTRY FEES
None

AWARDS
The prizes include the Wolfgang Staudte Award (20,000DM), Mionetto Film Award, Caligari Film Prize (5,000DM), and the Berliner Zeitung Reader's Jury Prize (5,000DM).

● United States Super 8mm Film/Video Festival

This festival encourages entries from all genres of film as long as they originated on Super 8mm film or video. Its mandate is the promotion of 8mm films. To this end, the Rutgers Film Co-op/NJMAC has sponsored four touring programs selected from Super 8 festival prizes winners from past years. "Selections of the U.S. Super 8 Film/Video Festival Touring Program" has been screened at media arts centres, festivals, and universities worldwide.

FESTIVAL DATES
February 13-15, 1998

ADDRESS
Rutgers Film Co-op/NJMAC, Program in Cinema Studies
108 Ruth Adams Bldg-Douglass Campus, Rutgers University
New Brunswick, NJ 08903
USA

TEL:	(908) 932 8482
FAX:	(908) 932 1935
E-MAIL:	NJMAC@aol.com
WEB SITE:	http://www.rci.rutgers.edu/ ~nigrin/super8.html
ENTRIES:	180
ATTENDEES:	800-1000
CONTACT:	**Albert G. Nigrin**

FILM TYPE
All (NTSC only)

COMPETITIVE
Yes

LANGUAGE
Any (English subtitles)

COUNTRY
Any

ENTRY FEES
None

AWARDS
A panel of judges award $1200US dollars' worth of prizes each year. They include a Grand Prize, Honorable Mentions and the Audience Choice Prize.

● Brussels Cartoon and Animated Film Festival

Brussels is a non-competitive animation film festival, screening international films from the world, retrospectives, exhibitions, and workshops. Its aim is the promotion of quality animation. It is one of the top festivals on the international cartoon and computer-generated images circuit.

FESTIVAL DATES
February 17-March 1, 1998

SUBMISSION DATES
November 1, 1997

ADDRESS
Folioscope
19 rue de la Rhetorique
1060 Brussels
Belgium

FILM TYPE
Animation

COMPETITIVE
No

LANGUAGE
Any

COUNTRY
Any

ENTRY FEES
None

TEL: 32 2 534 41 25
FAX: 32 2 534 22 79
E-MAIL: folioscope@skynet.be
WEB SITE:
http://www.awn.com/folioscope/festival/index.html
ENTRIES: 100-150
ATTENDEES: 35,000
CONTACT: **Doris Cleven**

● World Animation Celebration

As the title indicates, this festival is an annual "celebration" of animation from all over the world. In its first year, 1997, it was frequented by filmmakers, screenwriters, artists, executives, "tech-heads" and animation film lovers. Aside from the regular screenings future projects from Warner Bros., Fox Animation, MTV, Nickelodeon and Klasky Csupo were shown. The festival also has an International Business Conference for Television Animation, a New Animation Technology Expo, and an ASIFA-Hollywood Opportunities Expo.

FESTIVAL DATES
February 17-22, 1998

SUBMISSION DATES
October 15, 1997

ADDRESS
5889 Kanan Road, Suite 317
Agoura, CA 91301
USA

TEL: 818-991 2884
FAX: 818-991 3773
ENTRIES: 1,200 (250 screened)
ATTENDEES: 25,000
CONTACT: **Marisa Materna**

FILM TYPE
Animation

COMPETITIVE
Yes

LANGUAGE
Any

COUNTRY
Any

ENTRY FEES
$35-$75

AWARDS
There are 40 categories of prizes which include (all, but the Grand Prize award 1st and 2nd place): Best Film of the Festival (Grand Prize), Best Theatrical Feature Film, the Jim Henson Award, Best Stop Motion produced by an Independent, Best Computer-Assisted Animation Produced by an Independent, Best Stop Motion Produced by a Professional, Best Work Produced by a Student, Best First Work produced by an Independent, and many more.

● Victoria Independent Film & Video festival

Victoria is "committed to fostering the culture of independent cinema and aims to provide a forum for non-commercial, independently produced film & video in any format". The festival will also include seminars, workshops and a three-day trade forum conducted by visiting industry professionals from across the US and Canada.

FESTIVAL DATES
February 17-25, 1998
SUBMISSION DATES
October 30, 1997
ADDRESS
Society of Independent Filmmakers
#203-732 Princess Ave.
Victoria, British Columbia V8T 1K6
Canada

TEL: 250 389 1590
FAX: 250 389 1590
E-MAIL: randomrd@islandnet.com
WEB SITE: http://www.islandnet.com/~ran-
domrd/filmfest/festival.html
CONTACT: **Kathy Kay**

FILM TYPE
All
COMPETITIVE
Yes
LANGUAGE
Any (English subtitles)
COUNTRY
Any
ENTRY FEES
$10 (Canada); $20 (International)

● Les Rendez-Vous du Cinema Québecois

This festival is a retrospective of all Québec film and video of the previous year.

FESTIVAL DATES
February 19-28, 1998
SUBMISSION DATES
October 31, 1997
ADDRESS
4545 avenue Pierre-de-Coubertin
C.P. 1000, Succursale M
Montréal, Québec H1V 3R2
Canada

TEL: 514-252 3021
FAX: 514-251 8038
E-MAIL: rendez-vous@coproductions.com
WEB SITE:
http://www.coproductions.com/rendez-vous/
ENTRIES: 100
ATTENDEES: 5,000
CONTACT: **Michel Coulombe**

FILM TYPE
All
COMPETITIVE
No
LANGUAGE
French or English with French subtitles
COUNTRY
Quebec or made by Quebec director
ENTRY FEES
None

● Fantasporto (Oporto International Film Festival)

The aim of this festival is to promote new forms and methods of filmmaking. Fantasporto will also include lectures, meetings, exhibits, or any other manifestation of creativity compatible with the promotion of Cinema as Art and Entertainment.

FESTIVAL DATES
February 20-28, 1998

SUBMISSION DATES
November 30, 1997

ADDRESS
Rua Da Constitucao 311
P-4200 Oporto
Portugal

TEL:	351-2-550 8991/1/2
FAX:	351-2-550 8210
ENTRIES:	150
CONTACT:	**Mario Dorminsky**

FILM TYPE
Feature, Short

COMPETITIVE
Yes

LANGUAGE
Portuguese,Spanish,French or English subtitles

COUNTRY
Any

ENTRY FEES
None

AWARDS
This festival sponsors a competitive Fantasy section as well as a New Directors Week that offers awards to first and second time directors.

● PanAfrican Film and TV Festival of Ouagadougou (Fespaco)

FESPACO showcases films made by African filmmakers and people of the African Diaspora. Films made by others are accepted but do not participate in the competition. This festival is held biennially.

FESTIVAL DATES
February/March, 1999

ADDRESS
Secretariat General Permanent du Fespaco
2505 Ouadougou O1
Burkina Faso

TEL:	226-30 7538
FAX:	226-31 2509
ENTRIES:	272
ATTENDEES:	400,000
CONTACT:	**Filippe Sawadogo**

FILM TYPE
All

COMPETITIVE
Yes

LANGUAGE
Any (English or French subtitles)

COUNTRY
Any

ENTRY FEES
120 FF/entry

● Bombay International Film Festival for Documentary, Short and Animation Films- Mumbai

This is a biennial film festival focusing on short, documentary, and animated films.

FESTIVAL DATES
February, 1998

SUBMISSION DATES
October 31, 1997

ADDRESS
Film Division, Ministry of Information and Broadcasting, Government of India
24-Dr G Deshmukh Marg
Bombay 400 026
India

TEL:	91-22-386 1461
FAX:	91-22-386 0308
ENTRIES:	700
ATTENDEES:	10,000+
CONTACT:	**D. Gautaman**

FILM TYPE
Short, Documentary and Animation

COMPETITIVE
Yes

LANGUAGE
Any (English subtitles)

COUNTRY
Any

ENTRY FEES
None

AWARDS
First and second prizes are awarded for: non-fiction films over 40 minutes long; non-fiction under 40 minutes; fiction under 60 minutes; animated films; video-vista film. All of these prizes include a monetary award as well as the Golden or Silver Conch. Also awarded are the International Jury Award, Critics Award, and Lifetime Achievement Award.

● Green Screen (London)

Green Screen is a celebration of filmmaking of all "green" issues. This international environmental film festival is also taken on tour to several UK cities and a few foreign capitols. One of its most popular features is the discussion periods following most of the screenings.These discussions engage well-known experts and celebrities in debates and Q & A sessions with audience members. Other programs include exhibitions, parties, lunches and dinners which provide the festival goers with many opportunities to meet other enthusiasts and visiting filmmakers.

FESTIVAL DATES
February/March, 1998

SUBMISSION DATES
November 30, 1997

ADDRESS
114 St. Martin's Lane
London WC2H 4AZ
UK

TEL:	44-171-379 7390
FAX:	44-171-379 7197
ENTRIES:	800 (200 screened)
ATTENDEES:	up to 700/screening
CONTACT:	**Victoria Cliff-Hodges**

FILM TYPE
All

COMPETITIVE
Yes

LANGUAGE
English

COUNTRY
Any

ENTRY FEES
No

AWARDS
The Bill Travers "Insight" Award for the best detective film.

● Comedy Film Festival

This is the UK's only film festival devoted strictly to the genre of comedy. It accepts all film types (excluding documentaries) as long as it is of a comedic nature.

FESTIVAL DATES
End of February, 1998

SUBMISSION DATES
December, 1998

ADDRESS
Harbour Lights Cinema
Ocean Village
Southampton SO14 3TL
UK

TEL:	44-1703-635 335
FAX:	44-1703-234 444
ENTRIES:	20-30
ATTENDEES:	2,500
CONTACT:	**Rod Varley**

FILM TYPE
All, but documentary

COMPETITIVE
No

LANGUAGE
English (contact for exceptions)

COUNTRY
Any

ENTRY FEES
None

February

IVCA Film & Video Communications Festival Program & Production Awards (London)

ADDRESS
IVCA, Bolsover House
5-6 Clipstone Street
London W1 8LD
UK

TEL: 44-171-580 0962
FAX: 44-171 436 2606
CONTACT: **Ginny Williams**

Monte Carlo Television Festival

ADDRESS
Centre de Congress Auditorium
Boulevard Louis 11
98000 Monte Carlo
Monaco

TEL: 33-93 30 49 44
FAX: 33-93 50 70 14
CONTACT: **Wilfred Groote**

MILIA (Cannes)

ADDRESS
Reed Midem Organisation
179 avenue Victor Hugo
F-75116 Paris
France

TEL: 33-1-44 34 44 47
FAX: 33-1-44 24 44 00
E-MAIL: 100321.1310@compuserve.com
CONTACT: **Laurine Garaude**

American Film Market (AFM)

ADDRESS
10850 Wilshire Boulevard, 9th Floor
Los Angeles, CA 90232
USA

TEL: 310-446 1000
FAX: 310-446 1600
WEB SITE: http://www.afma.com/
CONTACT: **Brady Craine**

Oslo Filmdager (Oslo Film Event)

ADDRESS
c/o Oslo Kinematografer
PO Box 1584 Vika
N-0118 Oslo
Norway

TEL: 47-22 42 71 54
FAX: 47-22 33 39 45
CONTACT: **Guttorm Petterson**

● Jewish and Israeli Film Festival (Montpellier)

The goals of the festival are to promote the Jewish and Israeli culture through "World Cinema". The films are chosen according to specific themes which represent and enhance the different aspects of Judaism and the Israeli people.

FESTIVAL DATES
Beginning of March, 1998
SUBMISSION DATES
December, 1997
ADDRESS
500 Boulevard d'Antigone
3400 Montpellier
France

TEL:	33-4-67 15 08 76/67 72 32 63
FAX:	33-4-67 15 08 72/67 72 32 62
ATTENDEES:	10,000
CONTACT:	**Corine Rouffi**

FILM TYPE
All
COMPETITIVE
Yes
LANGUAGE
Any
COUNTRY
Any
ENTRY FEES
None

● Fribourg Film Festival

Fribourg's aim is to institute and nourish a dialogue between the North and the South by means of the cinema. It is the only European festival that offering a simultaneous platform for all types of film from Africa, Asia and Latin America.

FESTIVAL DATES
March 1-8, 1998
SUBMISSION DATES
December 31, 1997
ADDRESS
Rue de Locarno 8
1700 Fribourg
Switzerland

TEL:	41-26-322-2232
FAX:	41-26-227 950
ENTRIES:	80
ATTENDEES:	15,000
CONTACT:	**Martial Knaebel**

FILM TYPE
All
COMPETITIVE
Yes
LANGUAGE
Any (English or French subtitles)
COUNTRY
Africa, Asia or Latin America
ENTRY FEES
None

AWARDS
The director who wins the Grand Prix (for best feature film) receives 15,000 Swiss Francs and its distributor gets 10,000. The director who's film is considered second best receives 3,000 Swiss Francs and the director who receives the Technical Award is given the equivelent of 5,000 Swiss Francs worth of film stock.

● Tampere Short Film Festival

Tampere is a competitive festival for animated, documentary, and fiction films up to 30 minutes in length (35 or 16mm). It also offers a national competition for new Finnish productions. It is regarded as one of the top short film festivals in the world. The jury prefers films that take risks and offer a more "innovative intellectual social analysis", especially for documentaries. Programs include "Cinema Mexico", "Short Films & Art", and a retrospective.

FESTIVAL DATES
March 4-8, 1998
SUBMISSION DATES
January 5, 1998
ADDRESS
PO Box 305
SF-33101 Tampere
Finland

TEL: 358-3-213 0034/219 6149
FAX: 358-3-223 0121
E-MAIL: film.festival@tt.tampere.fi
WEB SITE:
http://www.tampere.fi/festival/film/
ENTRIES: 2,500-3,000
ATTENDEES: 38,000
CONTACT: **Mikko Rahikka**

FILM TYPE
Short
COMPETITIVE
Yes
LANGUAGE
Any
COUNTRY
Any
ENTRY FEES
None

AWARDS
Awards include the Grand Prix ("Kiss" statuette and 25,000FIM) , the Special Prize of the Jury (small statuette "Kiss" and 4000FIM) and Diplomas of Merit. Winners in the animation, documentary and fiction categories receive a small "Kiss" statuette and 4000FIM.

● Santa Barbara Film Festival (SBIFF)

SBIFF is a 11-day annual event which has taken place in Santa Barbara since its inception in 1986. Throught out those years it has grown in size and stature and has received worldwide recognition for its diverse programming. A focus of the festival is the discovery of new independent films, documentaries, shorts and videos.

FESTIVAL DATES
March 5-15, 1998
SUBMISSION DATES
December 1, 1997
ADDRESS
1216 State Street, Suite 710
Santa Barbara, CA 93101-2623
USA

TEL: 805-963 0023
FAX: 805-962 2524
E-MAIL: sbiff@west.net
WEB SITE: http://west.net/~sbiff/
ENTRIES: 125 screened
ATTENDEES: 32,000
CONTACT: **Diane M Durst**

FILM TYPE
All
COMPETITIVE
Yes
LANGUAGE
Any (English Subtitles)
COUNTRY
Any
ENTRY FEES
$40US; $45 international

AWARDS
A jury of motion picture professionals selects winners in 9 categories including Best US Feature, Best Foreign Feature, Best Director, Best Documentary Feature and Short, Best Live Action Short, Award for Artistic Excellence, Best Santa Barbara Filmmaker and an Audience Choise Award.

● Bradford Film Festival

Bradford focuses on wide-screen cinemascope, IMAX, cinerama, and world cinema. This is one of three films festivals that take place in Bradford throught out the year.

FESTIVAL DATES
  March 6-21, 1998
SUBMISSION DATES
  December 31, 1997
ADDRESS
  National Museum of Photography, Film and Television
  Pictureville, Bradford BD1 1NQ
  UK

FILM TYPE
  Feature, Short
COMPETITIVE
  No
LANGUAGE
  Any
COUNTRY
  Any

TEL: 44-1274-727 488
FAX: 44-1274 723 155
ATTENDEES: 15,000
CONTACT: **Bill Lawrence**

● Cartagena Film Festival

Cartagena Film Festival is over 35 years old and competitive for Ibero-Latin-American films. The festivals programs include international films, premieres, special tributes, a short film competition, meetings, forums and workshops. During the festival, regional television channels broadcast news about the films as well as interviews with directors, actors, actresses etc.

FESTIVAL DATES
  March 6-14, 1998 (tbc)
SUBMISSION DATES
  February, 1998
ADDRESS
  Calle San Juan de Dios,
  Baluarte San Francisco Javier A.A.
  1834 Cartagena
  Colombia

FILM TYPE
  All
COMPETITIVE
  Yes
LANGUAGE
  Any
COUNTRY
  Any

TEL: 57-5-660 0966/664 2345
FAX: 57-5-660 0970/660 1037
WEB SITE: http://www.escape.com/~spy-der/CART.HTML
ENTRIES: 60+
ATTENDEES: 85,000
CONTACT: **Victor Nieto**

● Cinema du Reel (International film festival of anthropology)

Cinema du Reel screens a wide selection of film to reach its ethnographical goal; the promotion of documentary cinema. The films submitted to this festival must be full or short length sociological or ethnographical documentaries in 35mm, 16mm or video format. These entries must also have been completed by the end of the previous year.

FESTIVAL DATES
  March 6-16, 1998 (tbc)
SUBMISSION DATES
  November 1, 1998 (tbc)
ADDRESS
  Cinema du Reel, Bibiliotheque Publique d'Information
  19 Rue Beauborg
  75197 Paris 04
  France

TEL:	33-1-44 78 45 16/44 78 44 23
FAX:	33-1-44 78 12 24
ENTRIES:	20 (competition)
CONTACT:	**Suzette Glenadel**

FILM TYPE
  Must be documentary format
COMPETITIVE
  Yes
LANGUAGE
  Any
COUNTRY
  Any
ENTRY FEES
  None

AWARDS
  The awards include the Prix du Cinema Reel, Prix du Court Metrage (15,000), Prix Jaris Ivens (15,000), Prix des Bibliotheques (30,000), Prix du Patrimoine (15,000), Prix de la SCAM (30,000) and the Prix Louis Marcorelles. All prize money is awarded in Francs.

● San Francisco Asian-American Film Festival

The San Francisco Asian-American Film Festival is the largest showcase and launching pad, in North America, of films & videos by/about the Asian & Asian American Diasporas. Every year the festival includes exhibits and premieres over 100 feature length, short, documentary, experimental and animated films.

FESTIVAL DATES
  March, 1998
SUBMISSION DATES
  Mid-October, 1997
ADDRESS
  346 Ninth Street, 2nd Floor
  San Francisco, CA 94103
  USA

TEL:	415-863 0814
FAX:	415-863 7428
E-MAIL:	naata@sirius.com
ENTRIES:	125
ATTENDEES:	15,000+
CONTACT:	**Corey Yi/Paul Tong**

FILM TYPE
  All
COMPETITIVE
  No
LANGUAGE
  Any (English subtitles)
COUNTRY
  Any (must be Asian themes)
ENTRY FEES
  $10 US (or NAATA member)

● Bergamo Film Meeting

The first aim of Bergamo is to present of that could be acquired for theatrical or cultural distribution in Italy. Bergamo also publishes catalogues feature film directors and works ignored or neglected by commercial distributors.

FESTIVAL DATES
Mid-March, 1998

SUBMISSION DATES
February, 1998

ADDRESS
Via Pacou 3
I-24121 Bergamo
Italy

TEL: 39-35 234011
FAX: 39-35 233129
ATTENDEES: 20,000
CONTACT: **Angelo Signorelli**

FILM TYPE
Feature

COMPETITIVE
Yes

ENTRY FEES
None

AWARDS
The Gold, Silver and Bronze "Rosa Camuna" are awarded each year at this festival.

● Dublin Film Festival

One of Dublin's key objectives is "To make a significant and lasting contribution to the film culture of Ireland in general, and Dublin in particular". Aside from regular screenings, Dublin also features live musical concerts, discussions, seminars and workshops. A unique event presented by Dublin is "The Music for the Movies Competition". This competition comprises muscial scores written to accompany old silent Irish films. The scores are performed live with the accompaning film at one of the many theatres used.

FESTIVAL DATES
March 3-12, 1998

ADDRESS
1 Suffolk Street
Dublin
Ireland

TEL: 353-1-679 2937
FAX: 353-1-679 2939
E-MAIL: dff@iol.ie
WEB SITE: http://www.iol.ie/dff/
ENTRIES: 240 screened
ATTENDEES: 34,000
CONTACT: **Oine O' Halloran**

FILM TYPE
All

COMPETITIVE
No

LANGUAGE
Any

COUNTRY
Any

ENTRY FEES
Contact festival

● Local Heroes International Screen Festival

Local Heroes focuses on distinctive independent films from Canada and around the world. It screens Canadian shorts and international features. Guests include up-and-coming Canadian filmmakers, international writers, directors, producers, and industry experts. Many of them will take part in the morning industry seminars and panel discussions.

FESTIVAL DATES
March 8-14, 1998
SUBMISSION DATES
December 1, 1997
ADDRESS
National Screen Institute
10022-103rd Street, 3rd Floor
Edmonton, Alberta T5J 0X2
Canada

TEL:	403-421 4084
FAX:	403-425 8098
E-MAIL:	filmhero@nsi-canada.ca
WEB SITE:	http://www.nsi-canada.ca/
ENTRIES:	25 screened
ATTENDEES:	3,000
CONTACT:	**Debbie Yee**

FILM TYPE
Feature, Short
COMPETITIVE
No
LANGUAGE
Any (English subtitles)
COUNTRY
Only short films must be Canadian
ENTRY FEES
$25 (for Canadian short entries)

● International Festival of Films on Art

This festival encompasses all the arts, of any period or style, in the following disciplines: painting, sculpture, architecture, design, crafts, fashion, decorative arts, museology, restoration, photography, cinema (portraits of directors and actors, film shoots, special effects), literature, dance, music, and theatre.

FESTIVAL DATES
March 10-15, 1998
SUBMISSION DATES
October 10, 1997
ADDRESS
640 St.Paul Street West, Suite 406
Montréal, Québec H3C 1L9
Canada

TEL:	514-874 1637
FAX:	514-874 9929
E-MAIL:	fifa@maniacom.com
WEB SITE:	http://www.maniacom.com-
fifa.html	
ENTRIES:	500
ATTENDEES:	50,000
CONTACT:	**Rene Rozon**

FILM TYPE
Documentary, Animation
COMPETITIVE
Yes
LANGUAGE
Any (English or French subtitles)
COUNTRY
Any
ENTRY FEES
$35 US

AWARDS
The awards include a Grand and Jury Prize, a Creativity, Best Portrait, Best Essay, Best Film for Television, Best Media Work, and Best Educational Film Award.

● The Festival of Italian Film, Cinema Itaiano Oggi "SM"

This festival annually brings a contribution of Italian art and culture to South Florida through its fine selection of Italian produced films.

FESTIVAL DATES
March 11-17, 1998

SUBMISSION DATES
December, 1997

ADDRESS
Cultura Italiana Inc.
2600 SW 3rd Avenue, Suite 770
Miami, FL 33129
USA

TEL: 305-532 4986
FAX: 305-532 8696
ENTRIES: 15 screened
ATTENDEES: 10,000
CONTACT: **Giulio Santero**

FILM TYPE
Feature

COMPETITIVE
Yes

LANGUAGE
Italian (English subtitles)

COUNTRY
Italy

ENTRY FEES
None

AWARDS
Prizes for Best Film, director, actor and actress

● Femme Totale Women's Film Festival (Dortmund)

Femme Totale highlights films that come into being largely as the result of women's efforts. It has become a meeting place for women filmmakers and film buffs. The "Frauenfilmfestival" is a showcase for films focusing on a central theme. "Uncanny Pleasures" is the theme for the 1997 festival. The genres featured will be thrillers, women detectives, avant-garde, and the vortex of horror.

FESTIVAL DATES
March 11-15, 1998 (tbc)

SUBMISSION DATES
November 23, 1997

ADDRESS
c/o Kultuburo der Stadt Dortmund
Kleppinstr. 21-23
44122 Dortmund
Germany

TEL: 49-231 5 02 51 62
FAX: 49-231 5 02 24 97
E-MAIL: femmetotale@compuserve.com
WEB SITE: http://www.inter-net-work.de/
ENTRIES: 100 screened
ATTENDEES: 7,000
CONTACT: **Anne Schallenberg**

FILM TYPE
All

COMPETITIVE
No

LANGUAGE
Any

COUNTRY
Any

ENTRY FEES
None

● London Lesbian and Gay Film Festival

This two week event showcases films dealing with the Lesbian and Gay identity and experience.

FESTIVAL DATES
March 12-26, 1998

SUBMISSION DATES
December, 1997

ADDRESS
National Film Theatre, South Bank
London SE1 8XT
UK

TEL: 44-171-815 1323/815 1324
FAX: 44-171-633 0786
E-MAIL: jane.ivey@bfi.org.uk
ATTENDEES: 16,400+
CONTACT: **Jane Ivey**

FILM TYPE
All

COMPETITIVE
No

LANGUAGE
Any

COUNTRY
Any

ENTRY FEES
None

● Newport Beach International Film Festival (NBIFF)

The NBIFF is a competitive film festival composed of approximately 100 films from all categories. Festival screening are held at several theatres which range in capacity from 250-1,250 seats. One theatre used, the Balboa, was restored to its "1930's glory" in the fall of 1996. During the festival's run there are seminars, book signings, special tributes, charitable events, various parties and Q&A sessions at the end of many screenings. Campus screenings and a pub party for student filmmakers at the University of California, Irvine was a part of the 1997 festival

FESTIVAL DATES
March 12-22, 1998

SUBMISSION DATES
January, 1998 (tbc)

ADDRESS
4400 MacArthur Blvd., 5th Floor
Newport Beach, CA 92660
USA

TEL: 714 851 6555
FAX: 714 851 6556
WEB SITE: http://www.nbiff.org/
ENTRIES: 100 screened (550 submitted)
ATTENDEES: 17,000
CONTACT: **Jeff Conner**

FILM TYPE
Any

COMPETITIVE
Yes

LANGUAGE
Any (English subtitles)

COUNTRY
Any

ENTRY FEES
$35 feature; $25 short

AWARDS
The awards given out at this festival include The Jury Award presented by the NBIFF Jury, The Producers Guild Award given to the best produced feature film, The Audience Award selected by audience participation and balloting, The Maverick Award is awarded to either the best use of film on a budget, noteworthy filmmaker of the future, or industry innovator,The BLOCKBUSTER Student Film Award Regional Competition, national award winner to play on the Sundance Channel and The Short Film Award honouring the top short film of the Festival.

● Brussels International Festival of Fantasy, Thriller & Science Fiction Films

This festival has organized next to its film programming a series of animation films centred on fantasy including expositions, a make-up competition, a body painting contest, a fantasy fashion show, a creative workshop, and the "Bal Des Vampires" which is annually attended by 1000 people in costume.

FESTIVAL DATES
March 13-28, 1998
SUBMISSION DATES
January 15, 1998
ADDRESS
144 Avenue de la Reine
Koninginnelaan
B-1030 Brussels
Belgium

TEL:	32-2-201 1713
FAX:	32-2-201 1469
ATTENDEES:	49,000+
CONTACT:	**Guy Delmote**

FILM TYPE
Feature, Short
COMPETITIVE
Yes
LANGUAGE
Any
COUNTRY
Any
ENTRY FEES
None

AWARDS
The awards include the Raven (Grand Prix), Special Prizes of the Jury, and the Pegasus (prize of the audience).

● Minimalen Short Film Festival

Minimalen focuses on low-budget/no budget short films. The films chosen will be presented in the "New International Short Films" section.

FESTIVAL DATES
March 13-15, 1998
SUBMISSION DATES
December 15, 1997
ADDRESS
c/o Filmhuset Rosendal, PO Box 1083
N-7002 Trondheim
Norway

TEL:	47-73 52 27 57
FAX:	47-73 53 57 40
ENTRIES:	150
ATTENDEES:	2,000
CONTACT:	**Karine Kristiansen**

FILM TYPE
Short
COMPETITIVE
No
LANGUAGE
Any (English subtitles)
COUNTRY
Any
ENTRY FEES
None

● South by Southwest Film Festival and Conference (SXSW)

SXSW Film is an independent film festival and conference showing over 100 films in nine days. SXSW Film has proven to be a unique place to listen to and learn from from the best voices in all phases of independent filmmaking. SXSW Film has become a national showcase for independent films and videos. The Conference will continue to provide a meeting space for film and videomakers and will offer hands-on practical information on the art and craft of independent filmmaking. Increased one-on-one interaction with industry representatives through mentor sessions, roundtables and mini-meetings.

FESTIVAL DATES
March 13-22, 1998

SUBMISSION DATES
December 12, 1997

ADDRESS
PO Box 4999
Austin, TX 78765
USA

TEL: 512 467 7979
FAX: 512 451 0754
E-MAIL: film@sxsw.com
WEB SITE: http://www.sxsw.com/
ENTRIES: 700 submitted (100 screened)
ATTENDEES: 15,000+
CONTACT: **Nancy Schafer**

FILM TYPE
All (including music videos; NTSC only)

COMPETITIVE
Yes

LANGUAGE
Any

COUNTRY
Any

ENTRY FEES
$30US

AWARDS
In all categories that include full length features, shorts, documentary features, and music videos a Silver Armadillo Award is presented.

● Ann Arbor 16mm Film Festival

Ann Arbor was founded as a showplace for independent and experimental filmmakers from all over the world. Many of the films shown at the festival have been originators of popular styles and trends that have been manifested in rock videos and alternative feature films.

FESTIVAL DATES
March 17-22, 1998

SUBMISSION DATES
February 15, 1998

ADDRESS
207 East Ann Street
Ann Arbor, MI 48104
USA

TEL: 313-995 5356
FAX: 313-995 5396
E-MAIL: vicki@honeyman.org
WEB SITE:
http://www.citi.umich.edu/u/honey/aaff/
ENTRIES: 350
ATTENDEES: 5,000
CONTACT: **Vicki Honeyman**

FILM TYPE
All (16mm)

COMPETITIVE
Yes

LANGUAGE
Any (English subtitles)

COUNTRY
Any

ENTRY FEES
$32 US/ $37 foreign

AWARDS
The awards include Best of the Festival ($1,500), the Tom Berman Award for most promising filmmaker ($1,250), Marvin Felhiem Award for best experimental film ($500), the Lawrence Kasden Award for best narrative ($500), and the Michael Moore Award for best documentary ($500).

● Hot Docs! Documentary Film Festival

Hot Docs! is a 5 day festival and conference for documentary filmmakers. The films screened are international in scope and represent every part of the world. They are screened at different venues in Toronto and provide a generous cross-section of all types of documentary film. Aside from the many films screened, there are also discussions, parties and a closing night gala awards banquet where all the awards are presented.

FESTIVAL DATES
March 17-22, 1998

SUBMISSION DATES
December 31, 1997

ADDRESS
344 Dupont St., Suite 206
Toronto, Ontario M5R 1V9
Canada

TEL:	416 975 3977
FAX:	416 968 9092
E-MAIL:	debbie_nightingale@tvo.org
WEB SITE:	http://www1.sympatico.ca/hot-docs/
ENTRIES:	350 (100 screened)
ATTENDEES:	2,000
CONTACT:	**Kelly Lamorie**

FILM TYPE
Documentary

COMPETITIVE
Yes

LANGUAGE
Any

COUNTRY
Any

ENTRY FEES
$100

AWARDS
Their are 25 prizes awarded at this festival. They include the Vision Award and Best of the Festival; Best Political, Cultural, Arts and Social Issue Documentary; Best Cinematographer, Music, Writing, Sound , Editor and Director; Best Feature, Short, Experimental Short, Children's Biography/History and Arts/Culture/Biography Documentary.

● Laon International Film Festival for Young People

Laon aims to introduce to children and young adults to the best films of international production. It also attempts to contribute to the development of mutual exchange between professionals and to help in the distribution of these films.

FESTIVAL DATES
March 30-April 9, 1998

SUBMISSION DATES
February 10, 1998

ADDRESS
Festival du Cinema, BP 526
F-02001 Laon, Cedex
France

TEL:	33-3-23 20 38 61
FAX:	33-3-23 20 28 99
ENTRIES:	10 (competitive), 50(non)
ATTENDEES:	20,000
CONTACT:	**Marie Therese Chambon**

FILM TYPE
Feature

COMPETITIVE
Yes

LANGUAGE
Any

COUNTRY
Any

ENTRY FEES
None

AWARDS
The awards include the Grand Prix (70,000 FF), Prix Special Du Jury, Mention Speciale, Prix Du Jury International Jeune Public and Prix De La Ville De Laon.

● New York Underground Film Festival

New York Underground is an "annual forum for independent, uncompromising filmmakers with unique personal visions-filmmakers who choose to exist outside the mainstream". The focus is on innovative, cutting-edge work which can be controversial in nature. Other festival events include live bands at nightly parties, retrospectives and hands-on seminars. The organizers of the festival, FilmCore, continue screenings throught out the year and sponsor a post-production fund for filmmakers.

FESTIVAL DATES
March 18-22, 1998
SUBMISSION DATES
January 5, 1998 (final February 2)
ADDRESS
225 Lafayette St. , Ste. 401
New York, NY 10012
USA

TEL: 212 925 3440
FAX: 212 925 3430
E-MAIL: festival@nyuff.com
WEB SITE: http://www.nyuff.com/
ENTRIES: 800 (75 screened)
ATTENDEES: 10,000
CONTACT: **Ed Halter**

FILM TYPE
All
COMPETITIVE
Yes
LANGUAGE
Any (English subtitles)
COUNTRY
Any
ENTRY FEES
$30US; $35US (by February 2)

AWARDS
Awards include Best Feature, Short, Documentary, Animation, Experimental and the Festival Choise Award.

● Cleveland International Film Festival

Cleveland has many special sections including documentaries, American Independent features, family films, new films from Eastern Europe, PanAfrican features, Gay & Lesbian films, and the main World Tour section. Purchasing of tickets in advance is advisable at this festival, because many screenings sell out.

FESTIVAL DATES
March 19-29, 1998
SUBMISSION DATES
November 30, 1997
ADDRESS
The Cleveland Film Society
1621 Euclid Avenue, Number 428
Cleveland, OH 44115-2107
USA

TEL: 216-623 0400
FAX: 216-623 0103
E-MAIL: filmfest@cyberdrive.net
WEB SITE: http://www.clevefilmfest.org/
ENTRIES: 5000
ATTENDEES: 28,000
CONTACT: **David W Wittkowsky**

FILM TYPE
All
COMPETITIVE
Yes
LANGUAGE
Any
COUNTRY
Any
ENTRY FEES
$25 shorts/$50 features

AWARDS
The awards include the Roxanne T. Mueller Award (people's choice award), Best Ohio short, Documentary short, Student short, and Best Women's short.

● Days of Independent Film (Augsburg)

Days' is an international forum for independently produced documentary and feature films. The festival's sections include "Perspektives" (features new productions, premieres and first films), Regional Focus (personal views and insights into film work of one nation or region) and Retrospectives (showcases a famous independent filmmaker's work). Another component of the festival is a Student's Conference. Here students present their works, in the Special Programmes section, and then discuss them with an assortment of filmmakers, producers etc. Days is considered a festival with a "workshop character", because of all its seminars, workshops and discussions.

FESTIVAL DATES
March 22-29, 1998
SUBMISSION DATES
December 1, 1997
ADDRESS
Filmburo Augsburg
Schroeckstr. 8
D-86152 Augsburg
Germany

FILM TYPE
Feature and Documentary
COMPETITIVE
No
LANGUAGE
Any
COUNTRY
Any
ENTRY FEES
None

TEL:	49-821-15 30 77
FAX:	49-821-3 49 52 18
ENTRIES:	600 (70 screened)
ATTENDEES:	20,000
CONTACT:	**Sabine Tamm**

● Montevideo Film Festival

Montevideo is devoted to short, feature length, documentary, fiction, experimental, Latin American and international films. Its purpose is to promote film quality (in all genres) and human conceptional values. Another part of this festival is its meetings and discussions based on regional projects.

FESTIVAL DATES
March, 1998
SUBMISSION DATES
January 30, 1998
ADDRESS
Cinemateca Uruguaya
Lorenzo Carnelli 1311
Montevideo 11.200
Uruguay

FILM TYPE
All
COMPETITIVE
Yes
LANGUAGE
Any
COUNTRY
Any
ENTRY FEES
None

TEL:	598-2-48 24 60/49 57 95
FAX:	598-2-49 45 72
ENTRIES:	106
ATTENDEES:	35,000
CONTACT:	**Manuel Martinez Carril**

● Istanbul International Film Festival

Istanbul focuses on features dealing with arts (literature, music, cinema, dance etc.) and other thematic sections including Tributes, selections from World Festivals, " A Country - A Cinema", and a panorama of Turkish Cinema.

FESTIVAL DATES
  March/April, 1998
SUBMISSION DATES
  December, 1997
ADDRESS
  Istiklal Caddesi, No. 146
  80070 Beyoglu Istanbul
  Turkey

TEL:	298 31 33 34 35
FAX:	249 77 71
ENTRIES:	130-150
ATTENDEES:	100,000
CONTACT:	**Mrs. Hulya Ucansu**

FILM TYPE
  Feature, Documentary
COMPETITIVE
  Yes
LANGUAGE
  Any
COUNTRY
  Any
ENTRY FEES
  None

AWARDS
  The Golden Tulip is awarded. Qualifying films must deal with the arts.

● International Thriller Film Festival of Cognac

Cognac was created in 1982 to showcase any film from the mystery/thriller genre. These can include films that deal with crime, police drama, investigations, "film noir", etc. This is a 4-day event which promises a lot of "whodunnit's". Activities that fit within the genre are also part of this festival.

FESTIVAL DATES
  End of March; beginning of April, 1998
SUBMISSION DATES
  Mid-March, 1998
ADDRESS
  36 Rue Pierret
  92200 Neuilly-sur-Seine
  France

TEL:	33-1-46 40 55 55
FAX:	33-1-46 40 55 39
ENTRIES:	150 (15 screened)
ATTENDEES:	10,000
CONTACT:	**Daniel Benzakein**

FILM TYPE
  All, but documentary (French shorts only)
COMPETITIVE
  Yes
LANGUAGE
  Any (French subtitles)
COUNTRY
  Any
ENTRY FEES
  None

AWARDS
  Grand Prix "Cognac 98" will be awarded at the festival.

Brief Entries

● Annual Television Festival USA

ADDRESS
25 West 52nd Street
New York, NY 10019
USA

TEL: 212-621 6600
FAX: 212-621 6765
CONTACT: **Donna Levy**

● Cine Showcase and Awards

ADDRESS
1001 Connecticut Avenue NW, Suite 638
Washington, DC 20036
USA

TEL: 202-785 1136
FAX: 202-785 4114
CONTACT: **Joy Parisi**

● International Celtic Film and Television Festival (Bangor)

ADDRESS
c/o Cenad Quadrant
14 Stryd y Porth Mawr
Wales ll55 1AG
UK

TEL: 44-1286-675 221
FAX: 44-1286-677 449
CONTACT: **Iwan Llwyd**

● NATO / Showest (Las Vegas)

ADDRESS
116 N Robertson Boulevard, Suite 708
Los Angeles, CA 90048
USA

FESTIVAL DATES
March 2-5, 1998
TEL: 310-657 7724
FAX: 310-657 4758
CONTACT: **Herb Burston**

● Nordic Film Festival

ADDRESS
22 rue de la Champmesie
76000 Rouen
France

TEL: 33-2-35 98 28 46
FAX: 33-2-35 70 92 08
CONTACT: **Jean Michel Mongredien**

● The Television Show (London)

ADDRESS
Institute of International Research
2nd Floor, Market Towers, 1 Nine Elms Lane
London SW8 5GQ
UK

TEL: 44-171-344 3811
FAX: 44-171-344 3829
CONTACT: **Caryl Williams**

● Travelling Film Festival

ADDRESS
405 Glebe Point Rd.
Glebe NSW 2037
Australia

FESTIVAL DATES
March-May and Sept.-Oct, 1998
TEL: 61 2 966 03844
FAX: 61 2 969 28793
E-MAIL: sydfilm@ozonline.com.au
CONTACT: **Jenny Neighbour**

● Aspen Shortfest

Aspen Shortfest focuses on short dramas, comedies, documentaries and animation which awards cash prizes.

FESTIVAL DATES
April 1-5, 1998 (tbc)
SUBMISSION DATES
January 31, 1998
ADDRESS
110 E Halam, Suite 102
Aspen, CO 81611
USA

TEL: 970-925 6882
FAX: 970-925 1967
E-MAIL: geldred@aspenfilm.org
WEB SITE: http://www.aspen.com/filmfest/
ENTRIES: 700
ATTENDEES: 20,000
CONTACT: **George Eldred**

FILM TYPE
Short
COMPETITIVE
Yes
LANGUAGE
Any
COUNTRY
Any
ENTRY FEES
$30-$40

AWARDS
The Awards include the Grand Prize, Special Jury, Horizon, Animated Eye, Best Student and Short Film, and Special Recognition.

● British Academy of Film and Television Arts - The BAFTA awards

Awards are given out to the best film and television programs. The winner are arrived at by voting by BAFTA members and juries.

FESTIVAL DATES
April, 1998
SUBMISSION DATES
December 31, 1997
ADDRESS
195 Piccadilly
London W1V 9LG
UK

TEL: 44-171-734 0022
FAX: 44-171-734 1792
ATTENDEES: 2,000
CONTACT: **Harry Manley**

FILM TYPE
All
COMPETITIVE
Yes
COUNTRY
Any (film, TV only UK)
ENTRY FEES
None

● Carolina Film and Video Festival

April

Carolina screens any and all of the best available film and video produced by students and independents. This is a forum which showcases works that rarely get a chance to be seen.

FESTIVAL DATES
April 1-4, 1998
SUBMISSION DATES
March 10, 1998
ADDRESS
Broadcasting/ Cinema Program
100 Carmichael Building UNC- Greensboro
Greensboro, NC 27412-5001
USA

TEL:	910-334-5360
FAX:	910-334-5039
E-MAIL:	akheilsb@hamlet.uncg.edu
WEB SITE:	

http://www.uncg.edu/cbt/CFVF.html
ENTRIES:	300 (45 screened)
ATTENDEES:	600+
CONTACT:	**Killian Heilsberg**

FILM TYPE
All
COMPETITIVE
Yes
LANGUAGE
Any (English subtitles)
COUNTRY
Any
ENTRY FEES
$30US (independents); $20US (students)

AWARDS
At least $2500 in cash and film stock is presented every year. The categories and specific amounts awarded each work are the responsibility of the festival's jury.

● Eat My Schlock: Home Grown Trash Film Festival

Eat My Schlock screens short video productions of up to 15 minutes in length. Its goal is to screen the most "tacky and entertaining" entries they receive.

FESTIVAL DATES
April, 1998
ADDRESS
709 Ann Street
Fortitude Valley Old 4051
Brisbane Queensland
Australia

TEL:	61 7 3252 2650
CONTACT:	**Andrew Leavold**

FILM TYPE
Short
COMPETITIVE
Yes
LANGUAGE
Any
COUNTRY
Any
ENTRY FEES
Contact festival

AWARDS
Awards are given for 1st, 2nd, and 3rd with a prize also going to the film voted the worst of the festival.

● New Directors/New Films

New Directors/New Films "provides a forum for newcomers as well as veteran filmmakers who have been overlooked or are unable to present their achievements to the American public." For the last 24 years, this festival has brought attention to the works of up-and -coming film artists including Steven Spielberg, John Sayles, Spike Lee, Richard Linklater, Atom Egoyan, Gregg Araki and Tom Dicillo.

FESTIVAL DATES
  March/April, 1998
SUBMISSION DATES
  January, 1998
ADDRESS
  The Film Society of Lincoln Centre
  70 Lincoln Centre Plaza
  New York, NY 10023
  USA

TEL: 212-875 5610
FAX: 212-875 5636
WEB SITE:
http://www.film.com/filmfests/new.directors.1995.html
ENTRIES: 300 entries (21 screened)
CONTACT: **Richard Pena**

FILM TYPE
  All
COMPETITIVE
  Yes
LANGUAGE
  Any
COUNTRY
  Any
ENTRY FEES
  None

● Singapore International Film Festival

Singapore showcases about 150 features, shorts and videos. There is a competitive section for Asian cinema as well as a specialized competitive festival by the Federation of Film producers Association. Every year the the including tributes and retrospectives.

FESTIVAL DATES
  April, 1998
SUBMISSION DATES
  November, 1997
ADDRESS
  400 Orchard Rd.
  #24-09 Orchard Towers
  Singapore 238875
  Malaysia

TEL: 65-738 7567
FAX: 65-738 7578
ENTRIES: 150
ATTENDEES: 50,000
CONTACT: **Teo Swee Leng**

FILM TYPE
  All
COMPETITIVE
  Yes
LANGUAGE
  Any
COUNTRY
  Any
ENTRY FEES
  None

AWARDS
  The Silver Screen Awards for Asian films only.

● St. Kilda Short Film Festival

St. Kilda showcases national and international short films under 60 minutes in length. All formats will be accepted (including 16mm, Super 8 and video). In addition to the screenings the festival also has a competition for Australian short films with up to $10,000 given out in prizes. Once the festival is completed, a selection of films are chosen to go on tour to different parts of Australia.

FESTIVAL DATES
April, 1998
SUBMISSION DATES
February, 1998
ADDRESS
Private Bag No. 3
St. Kilda Victoria 9182
Australia

TEL: 61 3 9209 6699
FAX: 61 3 9209 6790
E-MAIL:
stkilda.filmfestival@portphillip.vic.gov.au

FILM TYPE
Short
COMPETITIVE
Yes
LANGUAGE
Any
COUNTRY
Any
ENTRY FEES
$15

AWARDS
St. Kilda offers $10,000 in prizes.

● Canyonlands Film/Video Festival

CFVF's goal is to offer audiences high quality independent film and video in a friendly "down home" atmosphere and to help film and video artists achieve their professional goals. It encourages thought provoking material regardless of viewpoints in any genre which can offer audiences "new solutions, based on positive change". Potential distributors, film/video artists as well as regional and national audiences frequent this community-based event held in local community venues.

FESTIVAL DATES
April 2-4, 1998
SUBMISSION DATES
March 1, 1998 (early)
ADDRESS
c/o Country Pumpkin Productions
435 River Sands Rd.
Moab, UT 84532
USA

TEL: 801 259-4619
E-MAIL: cfvf@moab-utah.com
WEB SITE: http://moab-utah.com/film/video/festival.html
ENTRIES: 100+

FILM TYPE
All
COMPETITIVE
Yes
LANGUAGE
Any (English subtitles)
COUNTRY
Any
ENTRY FEES
$20 (student); $25 (16mm & video); $30 (35mm)

AWARDS
A cash award may be given for the "Best of Festival" film or video. Other awards will be non-cash and offered in over 10 categories. Awards are not mandatory in all categories and judges have the right to recommend that no awards be given. Categories include best feature drama, short, outdoor adventure, student, documentary, comedy, visual art, western, improvisational, and most inspirational.

● Creteil International Festival of Women's Films

Creteil aims to promote films directed by women on subjects of their choice, and to allow for better understanding of the situation and evolution of women and their cinema in each country represented. Creteil's non-competitive programs include a tribute to the career of an actress, retrospective of the work of a major woman director, and a panorama of French women director's films.

FESTIVAL DATES
April 3-20, 1998

SUBMISSION DATES
December 15, 1997

ADDRESS
Maison des Arts
Place Salvador Allende
94000 Creteil
France

TEL:	33-1-49 80 38 98
FAX:	33-1-43 99 04 10
ENTRIES:	5,000+
ATTENDEES:	20, 000
CONTACT:	**Jackie Buet**

FILM TYPE
All

COMPETITIVE
Yes

LANGUAGE
Any (synapsis in French or English)

COUNTRY
Any

ENTRY FEES
Transportation / Insurance fees only

AWARDS
The awards are given out in three different categories; full length (Jury and Audience Prize), full length documentary (Audience and AFJ Prize), and short length fiction and documentary (Audience Prize).

● Film Fest New Haven

Film Fest New Haven is one of the two broad based, independent festivals in New England accepting works in all genres. The mandate of this festival "is to expose audiences to the work of new, innovative filmmakers and to provide to those filmmakers an opportunity to secure wider distribution for their work".

FESTIVAL DATES
April 3-5, 1998

SUBMISSION DATES
January 31, 1998

ADDRESS
c/o Wayne Buck
111 Clinton Ave.
New Haven, CT 06513
USA

TEL:	203 865-2773
FAX:	203 865-2773
E-MAIL:	73303.405@compuserve.com
WEB SITE:	

http://ourworld.compuserve.com/homepages/Film_Fest_New_Haven/

ENTRIES:	60+ screened
CONTACT:	**Wayne Buck**

FILM TYPE
All

COMPETITIVE
Yes

LANGUAGE
Any (English subtitles)

COUNTRY
Any

ENTRY FEES
$25

AWARDS
The Audience Choice awards are presented to films that are either in or out of the regular competition. Films in competition are judged by a jury of film industry professionals.

● Hong Kong International Film Festival (HKIFF)

HKIFF is a 16-day non-competitive festival that runs each year during the Easter holidays. Its goals are "to serve as a platform for international film exchange and be a window to the world for Hong Kong Cinema and present Hong Kong audiences with films of artistic merit as well as "exhibiting the history and achievements of the local film industry". The main programs are "Asian Cinema" ; "Hong Kong Cinema Retrospective" ; "Hong Kong Panorama" and "International Cinema". Special programs and tributes are also part of the festival. Six theatres with seating from 1,268 seats (the Grand Theatre) to 193 seats (Lim Por Yen Film Theatre) are used to screen the films.

FESTIVAL DATES
April 3-18, 1998 (tbc)
SUBMISSION DATES
December 1, 1997
ADDRESS
Festivals Office, Level 7 Administration Building
Hong Kong Cultural Centre, 10 Salisbury Road
Kowloon
Hong Kong

FILM TYPE
All
COMPETITIVE
No
LANGUAGE
Any
COUNTRY
Any
ENTRY FEES
None

TEL: 852-2734 2903/2900-6
FAX: 852-2366 5206
WEB SITE:
http://imsp007.netvigator.com/hkiff/
ENTRIES: 200
ATTENDEES: 80,000
CONTACT: **Angela Tong**

● International Animated Film Festival (Stuttgart)

Stuttgart is a biennial festival that showcases animated films with artistic merit. Every festival it features an international and student's competition. Its programs include an International Panorama, Best of Animation and a "Young Animation" program.

FESTIVAL DATES
April 3-8, 1998
SUBMISSION DATES
December 1, 1997
ADDRESS
Stuttgarter Trickfilmtage
Teckstrabe 56, (Kulturpark Berg)
70190 Stuttgart
Germany

FILM TYPE
Animation
COMPETITIVE
Yes
LANGUAGE
Any
COUNTRY
Any
ENTRY FEES
None

TEL: 49-711-925 4610
FAX: 49-711-925 4615/262 4980
ENTRIES: 500
ATTENDEES: 45,000

AWARDS
Several awards are given out during the festival, but their value has not been decided on for the upcoming year (1998).

● Montreal International Short Film Festival

This festival is divided into competitive and non-competitive sections. The competitive section is divided into four categories: international fiction and documentary, international animation, a Quebec University, and Quebec College competition. The non-competitive section includes special programs, tributes, retrospectives, Quebec panorama and The Long Night of the Shorts.

FESTIVAL DATES
April 6-12, 1998 (tbc)
ADDRESS
4205 St. Denis Street, Suite 326
Montréal, Québec H1V 3R2
Canada

TEL:	514-990-9676
FAX:	514-285 2886
ENTRIES:	600
ATTENDEES:	10,000
CONTACT:	**Bernard Boulad**

FILM TYPE
Short
COMPETITIVE
Yes
LANGUAGE
Any
COUNTRY
Any
ENTRY FEES
$30

AWARDS
The awards include the Grand Prize ($2,000), Best Screenplay ($500), Public Prize ($500) and the Youth Prize ($1,000).

● Deutsches Kinder-Film & Fernseh-Festival

This festival is a national competition of children's films and TV programs. It also sponsors an international forum for industry professionals.

FESTIVAL DATES
April 12-18, 1998 (tbc)
SUBMISSION DATES
January, 1998
ADDRESS
Postfach 166
D-07506 Gera
Germany

TEL:	49-365-230 63
FAX:	49-365-260 18
ENTRIES:	100
ATTENDEES:	10,000
CONTACT:	**Elke Ried**

FILM TYPE
All
COMPETITIVE
Yes
LANGUAGE
German
COUNTRY
German countries
ENTRY FEES
None

AWARDS
The "Goldener Spatz" award is given out every year.

● Los Angeles Independent Film Festival (LAIFF)

April

The LAIFF brings to Los Angeles the finest independent films from across the United States. This annual festival continues its efforts towards uniting the independent filmmaking community, bringing together a unique group of non-profit organizations to support each other and filmmakers across the country. LAIFF showcases and celebrates the diversity of American independent film, giving filmgoers a place to discover and support emerging talent.

FESTIVAL DATES
April 16-20, 1998
SUBMISSION DATES
January, 1998 (latest)
ADDRESS
5858 Wilshire Blvd., Suite 205
Los Angeles, CA 90036
USA

TEL: 213 937 9137
FAX: 213 937-7770
E-MAIL: LAIFF@aol.com
WEB SITE: http://www.laiff.com/
ENTRIES: 1300 25 features and 55-60 shorts
screened)

FILM TYPE
All
COMPETITIVE
Yes
LANGUAGE
Any (English subtitles)
COUNTRY
US
ENTRY FEES
$25-45US

AWARDS
In 1997, the LAIFF instituted the Audience Award, which is open to all films in the body of the festival (excluding opening and closing night films and any non-curated film screened during the festival). Awards are given to best Feature-length Film, Best Writer, Best Director and Best Short Film. Prize packages include cash, products and services.

● Taos Talking Pictures

The Taos Talking Picture Festival is a multicultural celebration of cinema artists, their art, and audience. This festival presents a friendly atmosphere that is inclusive rather than exclusive, allowing festival-goers easy access to filmmakers and films. The highlights include tributes, retrospectives, new independent films, a showcase of Native American film and video, the Open Street Screening and a salute to Latino cinema.

FESTIVAL DATES
April 16-19, 1998
ADDRESS
216M North Peublo Rd., #216
Taos, NM 87571
USA

TEL: 505-751 0637
FAX: 505-751 7385
E-MAIL: ttpix@taosnet.com
WEB SITE: http://www.taosnet.com/ttpix/
ENTRIES: 350+
ATTENDEES: 9,000+
CONTACT: **Kelly Clement**

FILM TYPE
All
COMPETITIVE
Yes/No
LANGUAGE
Any
COUNTRY
Any
ENTRY FEES
$15 (30 minutes or less); $25 (over 30 minutes)

AWARDS
The Innovation Award, given out at Taos Talking Pictures, is probably the most unique prize awarded by any festival. The creator(s) of the award winning feature receive 5 acres of land in Taos, New Mexico.

● USA Film Festival

April

USA Film Festival is dedicated to excellence in the film and video arts. It features eight days with filmmakers of "yesterday, today and tomorrow." These include William Wellman, Samuel Fuller, Sydney Pollack and John Waters. Throughout the festival, there are special tributes, programs and premieres.

FESTIVAL DATES
April 16-23, 1998

SUBMISSION DATES
March 4, 1998

ADDRESS
2917 Swiss Avenue
Dallas, TX 75204
USA

TEL: 214-821 6300
FAX: 214-821 6364
WEB SITE: http://www.usafilmfestival.com/
ENTRIES: 700+
ATTENDEES: 13,000
CONTACT: **Alonso Duralde**

FILM TYPE
All

COMPETITIVE
Yes

LANGUAGE
Any

COUNTRY
Any

ENTRY FEES
$40

AWARDS
The competitive part of this festival is called the National Short Film and Video competition. It awards $1,000 to films in the Drama, Non-Fiction, Animation and Experimental categories. Awards of $500 are given to the Family, Texas, and Student award winners and $250 goes to the best music video. Four Special Jury prizes are also awarded.

● Chicago Latino Film Festival

Chicago Latino presents the best of the most recent cinema from Spain, Portugal, Latin America and the United States. It also considers and presents all genres including drama, comedy, satire, animation, documentaries, musicals, epic and experimental works.

FESTIVAL DATES
April 17-27, 1998

ADDRESS
c/o Columbia College
600 South Michigan Avenue
Chicago, IL 60605
USA

TEL: 312-431 1330
FAX: 312-360 0629
ENTRIES: 100
ATTENDEES: 25,000
CONTACT: **Pepe Vargas**

FILM TYPE
All

COMPETITIVE
No

LANGUAGE
Spanish or English (English subtitles)

COUNTRY
Spain, Portugal, US and Latin America

ENTRY FEES
None

AWARDS
The Kodak Emerging Filmmaker Award and an Audience Award are given out at this festival. The winner of the Kodak award as receives receives $3,000 worth of raw film stock.

● Minneapolis / St. Paul International Film Festival

April

Minneapolis / St. Paul is the largest film event in the upper Midwest. It regularly screens about 100 films from 35-40 countries. It features a large selection of Scandinavian films , films from countries of the former Soviet Union and Canadian films. International and US directors, producers and filmmakers frequent the festival and its screenwriter's workshops. Five different venues around the Twin Cities, are used throught out this event.

FESTIVAL DATES
April 17-May 2, 1998

SUBMISSION DATES
March 1, 1998

ADDRESS
University Film Society
2331 University Ave., SE-ste 130-B
Minneapolis, MN 55414-3067
USA

TEL: 612-627 4431
FAX: 612-627 4111
E-MAIL: filmsoc@gold.tc.umn.edu
WEB SITE:
http://www.umn.edu/nlhome/g023/filmsoc/
ENTRIES: 100 screened
ATTENDEES: 25,000
CONTACT: **Bob Strong**

FILM TYPE
All

COMPETITIVE
Yes

LANGUAGE
Any

COUNTRY
Any

ENTRY FEES
$50US (feature); $35US (short)

AWARDS
The Emerging Flicker's Competition Categories include Narrative, Feature Documentary and Shorts (feature of documentary).

● Worldfest Houston

Worldfest is a festival production company which will be celebrating its 30th year in 1997. It screens a selection of its award winners at this 10 day event. It has granted Gold Awards to Randall Kleiser, Jonathan Demme, Martin Brest, The Coen Brothers, John Sayles as well as David Lynch. Worldfest began its Screenplay competition in 1988. Each year more than 600 entries are received and reviewed by a jury made up of six industry professionals. The promotion of excellence in the field of indepedent filmmaking is what Worldfest is trying to acheive.

FESTIVAL DATES
April 17-26, 1998

SUBMISSION DATES
March 1, 1998 (first week in March)

ADDRESS
PO Box 56566
Houston, TX 77246-6566
USA

TEL: 713-965 9955
FAX: 713-965 9960
E-MAIL: worldfest@aol.com
WEB SITE: www.vannevar.com/worldfest/
ENTRIES: 3,500-4,000 (screened by jury for awards)
ATTENDEES: 20,000
CONTACT: **J Hunter Todd**

FILM TYPE
All

COMPETITIVE
Yes

LANGUAGE
Any

COUNTRY
Any

ENTRY FEES
$50-$200

AWARDS
Worldfest has over 200 categories of which the nine majors ones are: theatrical feature films, television & cable productions, film and video productions, TV commercials, experimental film and video, student film and video, sceenplays, music videos and new media. There are Gold, Silver, Bronze and Certificates of Merit Awards in each category as well as Special Jury Awards given out at the sole discretion of the jury. There is also one GRAND AWARD for each of the Major Category headings and the Best overall Student winner receives a Kodak Raw Stock award equivalent to $2,500.00.

Festival International Cinema Documentaire Nyon Visions du Reel

The goal of Nyon Visions du Reel is to recognize documentary films with an international perspective and showcase them in the International Competition. Other sections of this festival include The "nonmissables" (films that must be seen), "New Perceptions" (films made by the self-taught at the beginning of their careers and students from film schools), "Insights" (a close up about one work that really matters) and Workshop where films are viewed and discussed with a filmmaker who has come to talk about his/her ideas and work methods.

FESTIVAL DATES
April 20-26, 1998

SUBMISSION DATES
January 31, 1998

ADDRESS
5 Rue du Boiron
CH-1260 Nyon 2
Switzerland

TEL: 41-22-361 6060
FAX: 41-22-361 7071
ECONTACT: **Jean Perret**

FILM TYPE
Documentary

COMPETITIVE
Yes

LANGUAGE
English, French or German

COUNTRY
Any

ENTRY FEES
None

AWARDS
An international jury, a jury of young film-makers and a public jury choose the award winners and receive the "Visions du Reel" prizes which are accompanied by monetary awards. Awards include the Grand Prix, Full Length Prize and the Short Film Prize.

Cape Town International Film Festival

Provides a cross-section of international cinema of artistic quality, with a focus on independent productions in contrast to the Hollywood mainstream, eg. documentaries of socio-political issues.

FESTIVAL DATES
April-May, 1998

SUBMISSION DATES
March 31, 1998

ADDRESS
c/o University of Cape Town, Private Bag
Rondebosch 7700
Cape Town
South Africa

TEL: 27-21 238 257/8
FAX: 27-21 242 355
E-MAIL: filmfest@Hiddingh.UCT.ac.zd
ENTRIES: 50
ATTENDEES: 12,000
CONTACT: **James A. Polley**

FILM TYPE
Feature, Documentary

COMPETITIVE
Yes

LANGUAGE
Any (English subtitles)

COUNTRY
Any

ENTRY FEES
None

● New York International Independent Film & Video Festival (NYIIFVF)

NYIIFVF is a 14-day event that features hundreds of films, artists, sculptors, painters, photographers, actors, singers and screenwriters from around the globe, all in one event. Through the sheer breadth of its program, this festival enables producers, managers, agents, art dealers, record labels, press, critics, and the general public the opportunity to view new talent in all fields of entertainment . Screenings are held at the Mark Goodson Theatre , The International Talent Network , and the Le Bar Bat. In 1996, all the screenings and many of the events were sold out.

FESTIVAL DATES
April 21-May 4, 1998 (tbc)

SUBMISSION DATES
August 1, 1997 (contact for extensions)

ADDRESS
175 5th Avenue. , Suite 2334
New York, NY 10010
USA

TEL:	212 777 2002
FAX:	212 387 0873
E-MAIL:	stu@vegasnet.net
WEB SITE:	http://www.nyfilmvideo.com/
ENTRIES:	125-150 screened
ATTENDEES:	6,000+
CONTACT:	**Stuart Alson**

FILM TYPE
All

COMPETITIVE
Yes

LANGUAGE
Any

COUNTRY
Any

ENTRY FEES
$55 Screenplays; $95 Film/Video/Artists; $150 Performance (returned if not accepted)

AWARDS
Awards are given to 1st, 2nd,3rd, and 4th place winners in each category.

● The International Electronic Cinema Festival

The objective of this Festival is "to provide a forum to promote and explore the creative synergy between cinema and television". Entries must have been completed no earlier than 14 months prior to the Festival. The festival is held in Montreux and in Japan in alternating years. The 1997 festival featured a Producers Kiosk which allowed participants to privately view a work at the festival.

FESTIVAL DATES
April 22-27, 1998 (tbc)

SUBMISSION DATES
Approx, 3 months before

ADDRESS
PO Box 1451
Rue du Theatre 5
CH-1820 Montreux
Switzerland

TEL:	41-21-963 3220
FAX:	41-21-963 8851
E-MAIL:	message@symposia.ch
WEB SITE:	http://www.montreux.ch/symposia/
CONTACT:	**Renee Crawford**

FILM TYPE
TV programme

COMPETITIVE
Yes

LANGUAGE
Any / official English

COUNTRY
Any

ENTRY FEES
200 Sfr.

AWARDS
Grand Prix Astrolabium - to best production across all categories and one Astrolabium to the best production in each category; Special Award of the City for high resolution computer imagery; Festival Citation to second place in each category; Outstanding Acheivement Awards to maximum three individuals for recognition of outstanding work; UNESCO award to productions that promote UNESCO goals.

● Golden Rose Light Entertainment

This is a TV festival that focuses on light entertainment. It takes place in Montreux, but is an international competition of TV programming from around the world.

FESTIVAL DATES
April 23-28, 1998
SUBMISSION DATES
February, 1998
ADDRESS
Television Suisse Romande
Quai E Anserment 20, PO Box 234
CH-1211 Geneva 8
Switzerland

TEL:	41-22-708 8599
FAX:	41-22-781 5249
E-MAIL:	pierre.grandjean@tsr.srg-ssr.ch
ENTRIES:	200 contest, 300 video
ATTENDEES:	500-800
CONTACT:	**Pierre Grandjean**

FILM TYPE
comedy sitcoms, variety, music, game shows & variety documentaries
COMPETITIVE
Yes
LANGUAGE
Any
COUNTRY
Any
ENTRY FEES
Contest CHF500, Video CHF150/4programs

AWARDS
Prizes include Silver Roses' for Best Sitcom, City of Montreux Prize for the Best Comedy, Variety and Music Programme, Best Game Show and Best Variety Documentary. The runner-up to each winner of the Silver Rose can be awarded Bronze Rose. Also awarded is The Golden Rose of Montreux, The Press Prize and The Unda Prize.

● Making Scenes Lesbian and Gay Film & Video Festival

Making Scenes is a lesbian, gay, bisexual and transgendered, bilingual film and video festival, held in the nation's capital, Ottawa. It began as a 5-day festival, and has been growing steadily for the past six years. The festival also offers seminars and discussions throughtout its duration.

FESTIVAL DATES
April 23-28, 1998 (tbc)
SUBMISSION DATES
September 30, 1997
ADDRESS
c/o Arts Court
2 Daly Avenue
Ottawa, Ontario K1N 6E2
Canada

TEL:	819 775 5423
FAX:	819 775 5422
E-MAIL:	scenes@fox.nstn.ca
WEB SITE:	http://Fox.nstn.ca/~scenes/
ENTRIES:	34 screened
ATTENDEES:	2,600+
CONTACT:	**Donna Quince**

FILM TYPE
All
COMPETITIVE
Yes
LANGUAGE
Any (English subtitles)
COUNTRY
Any
ENTRY FEES
Contact festival

AWARDS
Making Scenes offers awards for Best Film, Short Film/Video, Documentary, and Best Canadian Short Film/Video. There is also have an award for Best Locally-Produced Film and Video. These two prizes are each worth about $500 in equipment rentals and services.

● Munich International Documentary Film Festival

This festival's international program includes a competition and information section. A specialty of the festival is a regional showcase of new films of Bavaria, some seen for the first time. Other categories include a retrospective and special program section that changes each year.

FESTIVAL DATES
April 23-May 2, 1998 (tbc)
SUBMISSION DATES
February 20, 1998
ADDRESS
Troger Strasse 46
D-81675 Munich
Germany

TEL: 49-89-470 32327
FAX: 49-89-470 6611
ENTRIES: 500
ATTENDEES: 15,000
CONTACT: **Gudrun Geyer**

FILM TYPE
Short and Documentary
COMPETITIVE
Yes
LANGUAGE
Any
COUNTRY
Any
ENTRY FEES
None

AWARDS
The awards include Der Besondere Dokumentar film (5,000 DM) and the Der Dokumentar film preis des BR (20,000 DM).

● Oberhausen Short Film Festival

Oberhausen has been in existence for over 40 years, and is one of the most well-respected short film festivals in the world. Aside from its screening over 200 films it also has many other programs. These include parties, discussions, special film programs and a competition that awards prizes to many films in different categories.

FESTIVAL DATES
April 23-28, 1998 (tbc)
ADDRESS
Internationale Short Film Festival
Grillostrasse 34
D-46045 Oberhausen
Germany

TEL: 49-208-825 2652/2420
FAX: 49-208-852 591
E-MAIL: oberhausen@uni-duisburg.de
WEB SITE: http://www.uni-duisburg.de/HRZ/IKF/
ENTRIES: 200+
ATTENDEES: 30,000+
CONTACT: **Angela Haardt**

FILM TYPE
Short
COMPETITIVE
Yes
LANGUAGE
Any
COUNTRY
Any

AWARDS
A variety of awards are given out in different categories.

● Oslo Animation Festival

Oslo is the only festival for animated film in the Nordic countries. The festival is international , but the competition is for Baltic and Nordic films only. Its goal is to create a positive festival atmosphere and to offer unforgettable film experiences which appeal to a wide audience. This festival strives to be an important meeting place for animation professionals, students and a growing enthusiastic audience.

FESTIVAL DATES
April 23-26, 1998

SUBMISSION DATES
January 15, 1998

ADDRESS
P.B. 867 sentrum
0104 Oslo
Norway

TEL: 47 22 47 80 50
FAX: 47 22 47 80 60
E-MAIL: oaf@manelyst.filmenshus.no
ATTENDEES: 3,000
CONTACT: **Kristine Kjolleberg**

FILM TYPE
Animation

COMPETITIVE
Yes

LANGUAGE
Any

COUNTRY
Any

ENTRY FEES
Contact festival

AWARDS
The Grand Prize is awarded for best film. The prizewinner receives a total of 15 000 nkr.

● San Francisco International Film Festival

The San Francisco International Film Festival is presented each Spring by the San Francisco Film Society, a non-profit arts organization whose aim is to foster an appreciation for film and video. Its emphasis is on work that has not yet secured U.S. distribution.This festival's program is recognized as one of the most adventurous in the U.S. and draws on current international production. Retrospectives, parties, seminars and discussions are all part of the event.

FESTIVAL DATES
April 23-May 7, 1998

ADDRESS
1521 Eddy Street
San Francisco, CA 94115
USA

TEL: 415-929 5000
FAX: 415-921 5032
E-MAIL: sfiff@sfiff.org
WEB SITE: http://www.sfiff.org/
ENTRIES: 100+
ATTENDEES: 70,000
CONTACT: **Brian Gordon**

FILM TYPE
All

COMPETITIVE
Yes

LANGUAGE
Any (English subtitles)

COUNTRY
Any

ENTRY FEES
None

AWARDS
The SFIFF has two components: 1) the Golden Gate Awards competition for documentaries, television production, animation and shorter works; and 2) the invitational, non-competitive section for recent narrative features, archival presentations, retrospectives and special awards recognizing individual achievement.These works are judged in over 30 categories by juries composed of Bay Area media professionals

● The Avignon/New York Film Festival

The Avignon/New York Film Festival is part of the French-American Film Workshop. The festival "encourages innovative filmmakers to speak to audiences beyond their frontiers by establishing a unique transatlantic crossroads for contemporary, thought-provoking films." The festival offers a plethora of French and American independent films as well as seminars, interviews, prizes, retrospectives, receptions and round tables.

FESTIVAL DATES
April 23-May 3, 1998, New York; June 24-28, Avignon

SUBMISSION DATES
February, 1998 New York; May, 1998, Avignon

ADDRESS
198 Avenue of the Americas
New York, NY 10013
USA

TEL: 212-343 2675
FAX: 212-343 1849
E-MAIL: jhr2001@aol.com
WEB SITE:
http://www.francetelecom.com/twist/twist_in/AVIGNON/avi-ny97/contents.htm
ENTRIES: 30 screened in Avignon; 50 in New York
ATTENDEES: 5,000 Avignon; 10,000 New York
CONTACT: **Jerome Rudes**

FILM TYPE
All, but animation

COMPETITIVE
Yes

LANGUAGE
English/French

COUNTRY
US and France

ENTRY FEES
$25US

AWARDS
In Avignon, the "Tournage Awards" are presented by an international jury and in New York the " 21st Century Filmmaker Awards" are presented according to audience response. Four awards are give out to the best American and French feature and short film.

● Les Journées Du Cinema Africain et Creole

This festival showcases the work of African and Creole filmmakers. It will also screen a film if it revolves around an African or Creole subject or theme.

FESTIVAL DATES
End of April, 1998

SUBMISSION DATES
March 1, 1998

ADDRESS
67 Ste-Catherine Street, Suite 5
Montréal, Québec H2X 1Z7
Canada

TEL: 514-284 3322
FAX: 514-845 0631
E-MAIL: vuesda@cam.org
WEB SITE: http://www.vuesdafrique.org/
ENTRIES: 12-150
ATTENDEES: 95,000+
CONTACT: **Gerard Le Chene**

FILM TYPE
All

COMPETITIVE
Yes

LANGUAGE
Any (French subtitles)

COUNTRY
Film must be about African or Creole subject

ENTRY FEES
None

● Gyor Media Wave

Gyor Media Wave focuses on films dealing with or made by all minorities, Asians, Eastern Europeans and Native cultures. Each year the festival ends on the May day weekend.

FESTIVAL DATES
April 27-May 3, 1998
SUBMISSION DATES
January 15, 1998
ADDRESS
Mediavave Foundation
H-9028 Gyor, Soprani ut 45
Gyor
Hungary

TEL: 36-96-328 888
FAX: 36-96-415 285
E-MAIL: mediawave@arrabonet.hungary.net
ENTRIES: 900
ATTENDEES: 600+
CONTACT: **Jeno Hartyandi**

FILM TYPE
All
COMPETITIVE
Yes
LANGUAGE
Any
COUNTRY
Any
ENTRY FEES
None

AWARDS
The awards include Mediawave Prize ($1,000 US), Ministry of Culture Prize ($800 US), and prizes given by sponsor's such as Kodak and Coca-Cola.

● Washington DC Film Festival

Each year, this festival focuses on national cinema with smaller showcases from other countries. It presents premiere screenings along with international guests and special events, such as receptions, panels, and events for children as well as Filmfest DC for Kids and for Seniors.

FESTIVAL DATES
April 29-May 10, 1998
SUBMISSION DATES
January 15, 1998
ADDRESS
Box 21396
Washington, DC
USA

TEL: 202-785 0481
CONTACT: **Tony Gittens**

FILM TYPE
All
COMPETITIVE
No
LANGUAGE
Any
COUNTRY
Any
ENTRY FEES
None

● Philadelphia Festival of World Cinema

Philadelphia showcases established and emerging talent and attracts a selection of diverse films. It provides filmmakers with an opportunity to screen their films for an enthusiastic and supportive (non-industry) audience. Included in the festival is the "Set in Philadelphia" national screenwriting competition, the Cinepulse audience rating system, panel discussions, seminars/workshops and tributes.

FESTIVAL DATES
April 29-May 10, 1998

SUBMISSION DATES
January 12, 1998

ADDRESS
International House
3701 Chestnut Street
Philadelphia, PA 19104
USA

FILM TYPE
Feature and Short

COMPETITIVE
No

LANGUAGE
Any (English subtitles)

COUNTRY
Any

ENTRY FEES
Various (contact festival)

TEL:	800-969 7392
FAX:	215-895 6562
E-MAIL:	pfwc@libertynet.org
WEB SITE:	http://www.libertynet.org/~pfwc
ENTRIES:	300+
ATTENDEES:	25,000
CONTACT:	**Linda Blackaby**

● All Russian Festival Sozvezdie in Yaroslav

ADDRESS
3 Vasilievskaya Street
Moscow 123056
Russia

TEL: 7-095-254 7056
FAX: 7-095-0251 0220
CONTACT: **Ivan Mogovich**

● Buzios Cine Diners Club Festival

ADDRESS
Rua Frei Leandro,35
Rio de Janeiro 22470.21
Brazil

TEL: 55-21-246 7791
FAX: 55-21-286 1191

● Cartoon on the Bay - Amalfi

ADDRESS
66, Via Teulada 00195
Rome
Italy

TEL: 39 6 37 49 82 74
FAX: 39 6 37 01 343
E-MAIL: cartoonsbay@sacis.it
CONTACT: **Alfio Bastiancich**

● FIFREC (International Film & Student Directors Festival - Nimes)

ADDRESS
FIFREC
BP 7144, 30913
Nimes Cedex
France

TEL: 33-4-72 02 20 36
FAX: 33-4-72 02 20 36

● Grenzland Films

ADDRESS
PO Box 307
D-95632 Wunsiedel
Germany

TEL: 49-923-2 4770
FAX: 49-923-2 805 55

● Madrid International Film Festival (Imagfic)

ADDRESS
Gran Via 62, 8th Floor
28013 Madrid
Spain

TEL: 34-1-541 3721
FAX: 34-1-542 5495
CONTACT: **Rita Sonlleva**

● MIP-TV (Cannes)

ADDRESS
Reed Midem Organisation
179 avenue Victor Hugo
75116 Paris
France

TEL: 33-1-44 34 44 44
FAX: 33-1-44 34 44 00
CONTACT: **Andre Vaillant**

● National Association of Broadcasters - NAB

ADDRESS
1771 N Steet, NW
Washington, DC 20036 2891
USA

TEL: 202-429 5350
FAX: 202-429 5406
CONTACT: **Lynn McReynolds**

● Marseilles Vue Sur les Docs International Film Festival

The festival centres on accompanying the risks, explorations and escapades of the filmmakers, therefore, the selection committee considers any "classic" or creative documentary film, as well as "reality inspired" experimental films of any format.

FESTIVAL DATES
Beginning of May, 1998
SUBMISSION DATES
Jan 1- Mar 31, 1998
ADDRESS
3 square Stalingrad
13001 Marseille
France

TEL:	33-4-91 84 40 17
FAX:	33-4-91 84 38 34
ENTRIES:	200+
ATTENDEES:	20,000+
CONTACT:	**Brigitte Rubio**

FILM TYPE
Documentary
COMPETITIVE
Yes
LANGUAGE
Any
COUNTRY
Any
ENTRY FEES
No fee ($10 to return selection)

AWARDS
Variety of awards given out by an international jury. These include: "Vue sur les Docs" grand prize awarded to best director (30 000 FF), "Planete Cable" (25 000 FF) and The Public's Award (15 000 FF).

● New England Film and Video Festival

Festival celebrates excellence in film and video created by New England independents and students, at all stages of their careers, who demonstrate a strong personal vision. The award-winning films for this festival are chosen from hundreds of entries by a jury and then screened at the festival.

FESTIVAL DATES
May, 1998
SUBMISSION DATES
November 1, 1997
ADDRESS
Boston Film/Video Foundation
1126 Boyston Street
Boston, MA 2215
USA

TEL:	617 536 1540
FAX:	617 536 3576
E-MAIL:	nefvfest@aol.com
WEB SITE:	http://www.actwin.com/BFVF
ENTRIES:	Only 14 award winning films are screened
ATTENDEES:	3,000
CONTACT:	**Anne-Marie Stein**

FILM TYPE
All
COMPETITIVE
Yes
LANGUAGE
Any
COUNTRY
New England and Upstate NY Regions only
ENTRY FEES
$35 Indie, $25 Student

AWARDS
Fourteen awards given out totaling over $7000.

● Rochester International Film Festival

Rochester, sponsored by "Movies on a Shoestring", was established in 1959 and will be celebrating its 40th anniversary in 1998. After each submitted film is viewed and critiqued (a copy which will be sent to the filmmaker) a jury of three decides which films will be screened at the festival. Each film that is chosen is awarded the Shoestring Trophy. All films are screened at George Eastman House, a museum of photography and film.

FESTIVAL DATES
May, 1998 (tba)

SUBMISSION DATES
March 1, 1998

ADDRESS
Movies on a Shoestring
P. O. Box 17746
Rochester, NY 14617
USA

TEL: 716 271 2116
FAX: 716 473 4490
E-MAIL: pdoering@frontiernet.net /
moas@juno.com
WEB SITE: http://www.frontiernet.net/~pdo-
ering/5MOAS/MOASched/MOASched.html
ENTRIES:
ATTENDEES:
CONTACT: **Ellie Cherin/ Paul Doering**

FILM TYPE
Short (40 minutes and under)

COMPETITIVE
Yes

LANGUAGE
Any (English subtitles)

COUNTRY
Any

ENTRY FEES
$20US

AWARDS
The Shoestring Trophy is engraved with the title and filmmaker's name, and awarded to each film at the Festival. An Honorable Mention entry exhibits the overall excellence, but was not chosen for the Festival. The Certificate of Merit is awarded to a noteworthy work which will not be screened at the Festival.

● Women of Colour Film & Video Festival

Women of Colour Film & Video Festival has served as an important forum for women of color to meet audiences from a variety of backgrounds. Most importantly, the festival has provided an opportunity for women of color, film and videomakers to interact with a diverse audience in critical discussions about the production and circulation of their images. It features film/video screenings and conversations with independent filmmakers, videographers and visual media activists.

FESTIVAL DATES
May, 1998

SUBMISSION DATES
January 1, 1998

ADDRESS
Kresge College - UCSC Activities Office
1156 High Street
Santa Cruz, CA 95064
USA

TEL: 408 459-3349
E-MAIL: wocff@cats.ucsc.edu
WEB SITE:
http://www2.ucsc.edu/people/ktrion/fvf.html
CONTACT: **Margaret Daniel**

FILM TYPE
All

COMPETITIVE
No

LANGUAGE
Any

COUNTRY
Any

● Images Festival of Independent Film & Video

May

Images is Toronto's annual celebration of the work of independent film and video producers in Canada and throughout the world. Images incorporates new media exchange programs, student videos and film, spotlights/retrospectives, workshops, artist talks and panel discussions.

FESTIVAL DATES
 May, 1998
SUBMISSION DATES
 October, 1997
ADDRESS
 401 Richmond Street West, Suite 448
 Toronto, Ontario M5V 3A8
 Canada

TEL:	416-971 8405
FAX:	416-971 7412
E-MAIL:	images@interlog.com
WEB SITE:	
http://www.interlog.com/~images/	
ENTRIES:	300-500 (submissions)
ATTENDEES:	2,000
CONTACT:	**Deirdre Logue**

FILM TYPE
 All (including computer/website work)
COMPETITIVE
 Yes
LANGUAGE
 Any
COUNTRY
 Any
ENTRY FEES
 $10, $15 for US entries (this fee covers shipping)

AWARDS
 Telefilm Canada Prize ($5,000 CAN)

● Human Rights Watch Film Festival

The goal of this festival is to "expand public awareness of human rights issues, and encourage filmmakers around the world to address human rights subject matter in their work". Once the festival has showcased its films in New York and Los Angeles about 10 films are chosen which go on a "World Tour". Past cities that have participated are Boston, Seattle, Portland, Vienna, Venice, Prague, Sarajevo, Bogota, Rio de Janeiro, Toronto , Vancouver, Seoul, Guatemala, El Salvador and Beijing.

FESTIVAL DATES
 June 5-18, 1998 (tbc)
SUBMISSION DATES
 January 20, 1998
ADDRESS
 485 Fifth Avenue
 New York, NY 10017
 USA

TEL:	212-972 8400
FAX:	212-972 0905
E-MAIL:	hardinh@hrw.com
WEB SITE:	http://www.hrw.org/iff
ENTRIES:	17+
CONTACT:	**Heather Harding**

FILM TYPE
 All
COMPETITIVE
 Yes
LANGUAGE
 Any
COUNTRY
 Any

AWARDS
 A $5,000 prize is awarded to a filmmaker for his/her contribution to human rights filmmaking. It is given in memory of Nestor Almendros.

International Film Festival Guide   77

● National Educational Media Network

This educational media event choses works that have "subject matter, creativity, factual accuracy, technical and artistic quality as well as educational value". The winners selected by jury will have their work showcased in May. Entries are accepted from TV programming, film, video and CD-rom, anything that meets their mandate of educational media.

FESTIVAL DATES
May, 1998

SUBMISSION DATES
December 1, 1997

ADDRESS
655 13th Street
Oakland, CA 94612
USA

TEL:	510-465 6885
FAX:	510-465 2835
E-MAIL:	nemn@aol.com
CONTACT:	**Jean Paul Petraud**

FILM TYPE
All (including all types of educational media)

COMPETITIVE
Yes

LANGUAGE
English

COUNTRY
Any

ENTRY FEES
Contact festival

AWARDS
The Gold, Silver and Bronze Apple Awards are presented at this media competition.

● Cannes Film Festival

Cannes is probably the most well known film festival worldwide. Aside from its regular programs, several markets are held during the festival. A good showing at Cannes can be a tremendous help to any film and an award will almost guarantee a distribution contract, if one is needed. This festival is attended by all the major distribution houses around the world and has become an essential part of the festival circuit and a showcase for the year's new films.

FESTIVAL DATES
May 7-18, 1998

SUBMISSION DATES
Beginning of March 1998

ADDRESS
99 Boulevard Melesherbes
75008 Paris
France

TEL:	33-1-42 66 92 20/45 61 66 00
FAX:	33-1-45 61 94 94
WEB SITE:	http://cannes.zds.softway.world-net.net/cannes96/index.htm
ENTRIES:	200+
ATTENDEES:	100,000+
CONTACT:	**Gilles Jacob**

FILM TYPE
All except Documentaries

COMPETITIVE
Yes

LANGUAGE
Any

COUNTRY
Any

AWARDS
The awards include the Palme d'Or, Grand Prix, Best Actress, Actor, Director, Screenplay, Special Jury Prize, the Technical Grand Prix and the Camera d'Or.

● International Film Weekend (Augsburg)

This festival takes place during a weekend in the spring. It screens shorts of the last two years as well as documentaries, animated films, historical programs and films for children. At this festival, the audience is the jury for the yearly competition.

FESTIVAL DATES
 May 7-10, 1998
SUBMISSION DATES
 January 15, 1998
ADDRESS
 Filmburo
 Schroeckstr. 8
 D-86152 Augsburg
 Germany

TEL: 49 821 15 30 77
FAX: 49 821 3 49 52 18
ENTRIES: 80 screened
ATTENDEES: 8,000
CONTACT: **Erwin Schletterer**

FILM TYPE
 Short
COMPETITIVE
 Yes
LANGUAGE
 Any
COUNTRY
 Any
ENTRY FEES
 None

● Montreal Jewish Film Festival

Montreal Jewish screens films that deal with the jewish identity or are of interest to the jewish people. Any type of film is welcome to participate as long as it meets the above stipulations.

FESTIVAL DATES
 May 7-14, 1998
SUBMISSION DATES
 February 1, 1998
ADDRESS
 c/o 125 Brookfield Ave.
 Montreal, Quebec H3P 2A3
 Canada

TEL: 514 738 1288
ENTRIES: 18
ATTENDEES: 2,500
CONTACT: **Susan Alper**

FILM TYPE
 All
COMPETITIVE
 No
LANGUAGE
 Any (English or French subtitles)
COUNTRY
 Any
ENTRY FEES
 None

● Toronto Jewish Film Festival

The Toronto Jewish Film Festival is the second largest event of its kind in North America. It features films from all over the world that deal with subjects of interest to Jewish people. Many of the films are North American or Canadian premieres. It also features a film panel which is free to the public. In 1997, the panel dealt with an individual's Jewish identity how it shaped their work.

FESTIVAL DATES
May 7-14, 1998

SUBMISSION DATES
March 31, 1998

ADDRESS
33 Prince Arthur Ave., Second Floor
Toronto, Ontario M5R 1B2
Canada

TEL:	416-324 8226
FAX:	416-324 8668
E-MAIL:	tjff@interlog.com
WEB SITE:	http://www.web-sights.com/tjff/
ENTRIES:	100+ (22 screened)
ATTENDEES:	10,000+
CONTACT:	**Shlomo Schwartzberg**

FILM TYPE
All

COMPETITIVE
No

LANGUAGE
Any (English subtitles)

COUNTRY
Any

ENTRY FEES
None

● Seattle International Film Festival

Seattle is the largest and most highly attended festival in the US. It has been chosen as one of five North American festivals in which a film's presentation qualifies it for the Independent Spirit Awards, the independent film industry's most prestigious awards. A unique feature of this festival is its annual foreign film poster auction.

FESTIVAL DATES
May 14-June 7, 1998 (tbc)

SUBMISSION DATES
March 3, 1998

ADDRESS
801 East Pine Street
Seattle, WA 98122
USA

TEL:	206-324 9996
FAX:	206-324 9998
E-MAIL:	mail@seattlefilm.com
WEB SITE:	http://www.SeattleFilm.com/Home.html
ENTRIES:	700+
ATTENDEES:	110,000
CONTACT:	**Carl Spence**

FILM TYPE
All

COMPETITIVE
Yes

LANGUAGE
Any

COUNTRY
Any

ENTRY FEES
$25/short, $50/feature

AWARDS
The jury awards include Best New Director and Best American Independent Film whereas the audience awards include Best Film, Director, Documentary Feature, Short Film, Actor and Best Actress.

● Inside/OUT Lesbian and Gay Film and Video Festival

Inside/Out's goal is to advance cultural works, primarily film and video by and/or about lesbian, gay, bisexual and transgendered people of all races, classes, creeds and abilities in order to represent, support and develop these identities and sexualities.

FESTIVAL DATES
  May 21-31, 1998
SUBMISSION DATES
  January 15, 1998
ADDRESS
  401 Richmond St. West, Suite 216
  Toronto, Ontario M5V 1X3
  Canada

TEL: 416-977 6847
FAX: 416-977 8025
E-MAIL: inside@interlog.com
WEB SITE: http://www.insideout.on.ca/
ENTRIES: 176 screened
ATTENDEES: 15,000
CONTACT: **Ellen Flanders**

FILM TYPE
  All
COMPETITIVE
  Yes
LANGUAGE
  Any (English subtitles)
COUNTRY
  Any
ENTRY FEES
  None

AWARDS
  Inside/Out awards the Bulloch Entertainment Award worth $1,500Can. dollars every year.

● Los Angeles Asian Pacific Film and Video Festival

The Festival showcases productions by emerging and established Asian American filmmakers, as well as an international showcase of works by Asian international producers and directors. The festival is held every year during Asian Pacific Heritage month which is May.

FESTIVAL DATES
  Late May, 1998
SUBMISSION DATES
  Late January 1998
ADDRESS
  Visual Communications
  263 South Los Angeles Street, Suite 307
  Los Angeles, CA 90012
  USA

TEL: 213-680 4462
FAX: 213-687 4848
E-MAIL: ferrer@vc.apanet.org
WEB SITE: http://vc.apanet.org/viscom
ENTRIES: 200+
ATTENDEES: 5000+
CONTACT: **Abraham Ferrer**

FILM TYPE
  All
COMPETITIVE
  No
LANGUAGE
  Any
COUNTRY
  Any
ENTRY FEES
  $20 handling fee; $25 international

● Annecy International Animation Film Festival

Annecy is one of the largest and best known animation festival in the world. At this point it is a biennual with awards given to films in the categories of short fiction, full-length feature, films for TV and TV series. Commercial, educational, scientific and industrial films are also screened. Some of the festival's other programs include an international competition for student films and graduation films, retrospectives, tributes, exhibitions, debates, seminars, lectures, panel discussions, giant open-air screenings and the MIFA market that takes place during the festival. Ten theatres are used during this event.

FESTIVAL DATES
May, 1999

ADDRESS
6 Ave. des Iles Bp 399
F-74013 Annecy Cedex
France

TEL: 33 4 5067 8195
FAX: 33 4 5057 4172
E-MAIL: info@annecy-animation-festival.tm.fr
WEB SITE: http://www.annecy-animation-festival.tm.fr/
ENTRIES: 1,200+ (254 screened)
ATTENDEES: 110,000
CONTACT: **Jean-Luc Xiberras**

FILM TYPE
Animation

COMPETITIVE
Yes

LANGUAGE
Any (English or French translations)

COUNTRY
Any

ENTRY FEES
None

AWARDS
The awards for short films include the "Grand Prix" for best animated short, "Special Jury Prize" for best first film, "Special Distinction" awarded for script, backgrounds and/or quality of animation, "Special Distinction" for soundtrack quality in feature films, "Grand Prix" for best animated feature and best animated TV programme, Special Prize for best TV series (up to 12 mins), (13-26 mins) and special (up to 52 mins).

● Dreamspeakers - The First Peoples World Film Celebration

Dreamspeakers Festival showcases all types of Aboriginal films from all over the world. The three categories which a film can be entered into are: totally aboriginal, collaborative and theme (non-aboriginal work on an aboriginal theme). The film festival is a part of the Dreamspeakers Celebration. There are also sections on performing arts, arts and crafts and traditional foods.

FESTIVAL DATES
May 26-31, 1998

SUBMISSION DATES
February 28, 1998

ADDRESS
15620- 111th Avenue, Suite 201
Edmonton, Alberta T5M 4R7
Canada

TEL: 403-451-5033
FAX: 403-452-9042
E-MAIL: dream@worldhost.com
WEB SITE:
http://www.discoveredmonton.com/dreamspeakers/
ENTRIES: 130
ATTENDEES: 1,000
CONTACT: **Sharon Shirt**

FILM TYPE
All

COMPETITIVE
Yes

LANGUAGE
Any

COUNTRY
Any

ENTRY FEES
$25

AWARDS
Their are 10 categories in the competitive section.

● The Golden Knight: Slavic and Orthodox People's Film Festival

Festival screens films which are in accordance with the Slavonic and Orthodox Christian cinematographic tradition. The Festival's slogan is "For the virtuous Christian values, For the elevation of the human soul."

FESTIVAL DATES
  May 27- June 1, 1998 (tbc)
SUBMISSION DATES
  March 30, 1998
ADDRESS
  17 Vasiilyevskaya Street
  Moscow 123825
  Russia

TEL: 7-095-254 2646
FAX: 7-095-117 2264
ENTRIES: 120
ATTENDEES: 100,000
CONTACT: **Nikolai Burlyaev**

FILM TYPE
  Feature, Documentary, Animation, TV and student
COMPETITIVE
  Yes
LANGUAGE
  Any
COUNTRY
  Slavonic and Orthodox countries
ENTRY FEES
  Various

AWARDS
  The Gold, Silver and Bronze Knights.

● Yorkton Short Film and Video Festival

Yorkton showcases short films through recognition, promotion and education. The films available for admission to this festival must be Canadian.

FESTIVAL DATES
  May 28-30, 1998 (tbc)
SUBMISSION DATES
  April 3, 1998
ADDRESS
  49 Smith Street East
  Yorkton, Saskatchewan S3N 0H4
  Canada

TEL: 306-782 7077
FAX: 306-782 1550
E-MAIL: yorkton.filmfest@sk.sympatico.ca
WEB SITE: http://www.hmtnet.com/yorkton-shortfilm/
ENTRIES: 450
ATTENDEES: 2,000+
CONTACT: **Fay Kowal**

FILM TYPE
  Short
COMPETITIVE
  Yes
LANGUAGE
  Any
COUNTRY
  Canada
ENTRY FEES
  $75

AWARDS
  The Golden Sheaf Award

International Film Festival Guide   83

● Hudson Valley Film Festival

May

The Hudson Valley Film Festival celebrates the art and craft of the screen-writer. The festival is a nine-day event featuring screenings, script readings, panel discussions and culminating with a gala tribute party to honor one of the nation's leading screenwriters.

FESTIVAL DATES
May 29-June 6, 1998 (tbc)
SUBMISSION DATES
February 20, 1998
ADDRESS
40 Garden St.
Poughkeepsie, NY 12601
USA

TEL: 914 473-0318
FAX: 914 473-0082
E-MAIL: hvfo@vh.net
WEB SITE: http://www.sandbook.com/hvfo/
ENTRIES: 500
ATTENDEES: 7,000+
CONTACT: **Denise Kasell**

FILM TYPE
All (including screenplays)
COMPETITIVE
Yes
LANGUAGE
Any (with translation)
COUNTRY
Any
ENTRY FEES
$15-25US

AWARDS
The chosen screenwriter for the year's festival is given an award and tribute gala party.

● Atlanta Film & Video Festival

Atlanta showcases films from around the world. A focus of this festival is the acceptance and suppport of experimental and student films. The festival was created for " a means of fostering independent film and videomaking in Atlanta and the Southeast". In the upcoming year Atlanta will have more screenings, workshops, and opportunities to meet fellow artists.

FESTIVAL DATES
May/June, 1998
SUBMISSION DATES
January 30, 1998
ADDRESS
75 Bennett St., Suite N-1
Atlanta, GA 30309
USA

TEL: 404 352 4225
FAX: 404 352 0173
E-MAIL: afvf@imagefv.org
WEB SITE:
http://www.imagefv.org/festival.html
ENTRIES: 90-100 screened (600+ submitted)
ATTENDEES: 50,000+
CONTACT: **Charity Ellis**

FILM TYPE
All (including student and experimental)
COMPETITIVE
Yes
LANGUAGE
Any (English subtitles)
COUNTRY
Any
ENTRY FEES
Contact festival

AWARDS
The awards include grand jury, southeastern film & videomakers, "Best Student Film", "Best Documentary Film", "Best Documentary Video", "Best Narrative Short", "Best Narrative Feature", "Best Experimental Film", "Best Experimental Video", "Best Animated Film", "Best Animated Video" and honorable mentions.

● International Short Film Festival (Krakow)

The aim of the Festival is to present and review short films, including films dealing with the changes occurring at the close of this century in Europe and the world.

FESTIVAL DATES
May 31- June 4, 1998 (tbc)

SUBMISSION DATES
February 15, 1998

ADDRESS
c/o Apollo Film
ul Pychowicka 7
30-364 Krakow
Poland

TEL: 48-12-67 13 55/67 23 40
FAX: 48-12-67 15 52
ENTRIES: 2500
ATTENDEES: over 10,000
CONTACT: **Renata Puchaez**

FILM TYPE
Short (35 min. max.)

COMPETITIVE
Yes

LANGUAGE
Any

COUNTRY
Any

ENTRY FEES
None

AWARDS
The Grand Prix as well as the Golden, Silver, and Bronze Dragons.

● Brighton Arts Festival

ADDRESS	TEL:	44-1273-713 875
21-22 Old Steine	FAX:	44-1273-622 453
Brighton, East Sussex BN1 1EL	CONTACT:	**Christopher Barron**
UK		

● Edmonton Jewish Film Festival

ADDRESS	TEL:	403 444 8129
15301 Rio Terrace Drive	FAX:	403 444 5238
Edmonton, AL T5R 5M6	CONTACT:	**Shoshana Pollack**
Canada		

● Ethnogenre African American Film Festival

ADDRESS	TEL:	716-232 7100
c/o 55 Exchange Boulevard	FAX:	716-258 2237
Rochester, NY 14614	CONTACT:	**Robin Wilson Glover**
USA		

● Golden Prague International TV Festival

ADDRESS	TEL:	42-2-6121 2882
Czech TV, International Relations	FAX:	42-2-6121 2891
Kaveci Hory 140 70	CONTACT:	**Blanka Pavelkova**
Prague 4		
Czech Republic		

● Open Russian Film Festival Kinotaur (Sochi)

ADDRESS	TEL:	7-095-248 0911
35 Arbat	FAX:	7-095-248 0966
Moscow 121835	CONTACT:	**Alfred Eshtrem**
Russia		

● Prix Danube International TV Festival for Children

ADDRESS	TEL:	42-7-727 448
Mlynska dolina	FAX:	42-7-729 440
845 45 Bratislava	CONTACT:	**Jela Kezmoanova**
Slovakia		

● Royal Television Society Awards

ADDRESS	TEL:	44-171-430 1000
Holbom Hall	FAX:	44-171-430 0924
100 Gray's Inn Road	CONTACT:	**Nicky Harlow**
London WC1X 1AL		
UK		

● TV-QUIP East (Lithuania)

ADDRESS	TEL:	33-46 20 17 30
3 rue Herni Martin	FAX:	33-46 21 14 14
92100 Boulogne		
France		

● Anteprima Film Festival

Anteprima focuses on independent Italian film and video productions from around the world. Of the over 250 films screened a small percentage are in competition. The rest make up the the the other sections of Anteprima.

FESTIVAL DATES
First week of June, 1998
SUBMISSION DATES
April 15, 1998
ADDRESS
Viale Paolo Guidi 108
47041 Bellaria
Italy

TEL: 39-541 347 186
FAX: 39-541 347 186
ENTRIES: 273 screened
ATTENDEES: 5,000
CONTACT: **Antonio Costa**

FILM TYPE
All, but animation
COMPETITIVE
Yes
LANGUAGE
Italian
COUNTRY
Any (must be made by Italian)
ENTRY FEES
None

AWARDS
Award include the "Gabbiano D'oro" worth10 million lira and the "Gabbiano D'argento" worth 5, 000, 000 lira.

● Troia International Film Festival & Market (FILMERCA)

The Troia International Film Festival is the leading cultural event of its kind in Portugal.This festival devotes its Official Section (competitive) to the promotion of films coming from countries with a limited annual production (less than 20 films per year).

FESTIVAL DATES
Beginning of June, 1998
SUBMISSION DATES
March, 1998
ADDRESS
Troia
2902 Setubal Codex
Portugal

TEL: 351-65-44 121/44 127
FAX: 351-65-44 123
CONTACT: **Femanda Silva**

FILM TYPE
All, but animation
COMPETITIVE
Yes
LANGUAGE
Any
COUNTRY
Any
ENTRY FEES
None

AWARDS
The Golden and Silver Dolphin are awarded by an international jury. Other awards are also given out to entries in different sections such as First Works and American Independents.

● US International Film and Video Festival (Chicago)

The Festival offers the opportunity for filmmakers to showcase their work, as well as earning recognition and the possibility of many different awards. The festival organizers also run The Mobius Advertising Awards. The festival consists of day-long screenings concluding with an awards banquet where each entry screened is an award winner.

FESTIVAL DATES
June 3-4, 1998
SUBMISSION DATES
March 1, 1998
ADDRESS
The US Festivals Association
841 N Addison Avenue
Elmhurst, IL 60126-1291
USA

TEL: 630-834 7773
FAX: 630-834 5565
E-MAIL:
FILMFESTIVALandMOBIUSAWARDS@compuserve.com
ENTRIES: 100+
ATTENDEES: 350+
CONTACT: **JW Anderson**

FILM TYPE
All areas of advertising
COMPETITIVE
Yes
LANGUAGE
Any (with English translation)
COUNTRY
Any
ENTRY FEES
Various (from $125-$200)

AWARDS
Entries are grouped in 32 subject categories or 10 production techniques where they are judged in a two-tier system. Awards include the Golden Camera and Silver Screen, as well as certificates and industry sponsored awards.

● La Prix Jeunesse

Prix Jeunesse is the world's foremost conference on children's programming. It seeks to promote and recognize quality television programs for children and young people. Prix Jeunesse especially encourages programs which help children understand their role as citizens of a culturally diverse world, which challenge and invigorate children while entertaining them.

FESTIVAL DATES
June 4-10, 1998
SUBMISSION DATES
January, 1998
ADDRESS
c/o Bayerischer Rundfunk
D-80300 Munich
Germany

TEL: 49-89 5900 2058
FAX: 49-89 5900 3053
E-MAIL: prixjeunesse@papyrus.de
ENTRIES: 300
CONTACT: **Ursula von Zallinger**

FILM TYPE
Worldwide telecasters
COMPETITIVE
Yes
LANGUAGE
Scripts in German, English, French and Spanish
COUNTRY
Any
ENTRY FEES
Contact Festival

AWARDS
This festival's awards include certificates given for certain themes (e.g. Innovation, "Bread and Butter" Programming and Children's Voice) as well as the Prix Jeunesse prize-globe.

● Montreal International Festival of Cinema and New Media

New Media programs almost 400 differents works, and screens films in seven venues in Montreal. These include regular theatres, outdoor theatres as well as street venues. The names of the open-air theatres (Le Prince, Cassavetes and Fellini) get one into the spirit of independent film. A goal of this festival is to "discover the film and video directors of tomorrow and the creators of new electronic images." Special events, retrospectives, tributes and four competitions make up this 11-day event.

FESTIVAL DATES
June 4-14, 1998 (tbc)

SUBMISSION DATES
March, 1998

ADDRESS
3668 Boulevard St-Laurent
Montréal, Québec H2X 2V4
Canada

TEL: 514-843 4725
FAX: 514-843 4631
E-MAIL: montrealfest@fcmm.com
WEB SITE: http://www.fcmm.com/
ENTRIES: 200 screened
ATTENDEES: 100,000
CONTACT: **Claude Chamberlan**

FILM TYPE
All

COMPETITIVE
Yes

LANGUAGE
Any (French or English subtitles)

COUNTRY
Any

ENTRY FEES
$50 features; $20 short film & video

AWARDS
International Section: Public's Choice for fiction feature ($3,000), Public's Choice for Canadian films ($10,000 in production or development costs), Critic's Prize, Best Documentary Prize ($2,000). Video: Grand Prize ($2,000), Telefilm Canada Prize ($10,000 towards production or development). Short film: Grand Prize ($2,000) and the Broadcast Prize. Animation: the Softimage Grand Prize ($2,000).

● New York Gay & Lesbian Film Festival

This festival showcases films & videos by, about and of, interest to lesbians, gay men, bisexuals and transgendered people.

FESTIVAL DATES
June 4-14, 1998 (tbc)

SUBMISSION DATES
Early February, 1998

ADDRESS
47 Great Jones St., 6th Floor
New York, NY 10012
USA

TEL: 212 254 7228
FAX: 212 254 8655
E-MAIL: newfest@gramercy.ios.com
WEB SITE: http://www.newfestival.com/
ENTRIES: 400(150 screened)
ATTENDEES: 15,000
CONTACT: **Michael Peyton**

FILM TYPE
All

COMPETITIVE
Yes

LANGUAGE
Any

COUNTRY
Any

ENTRY FEES
$15US (after Dec. '97, free otherwise)

AWARDS
Awards are given out to Best Feature, Documentary and Short Film.

● Shots in the Dark International Mystery and Thriller Festival (Nottingham)

This festival showcases thrillers, mysteries and crime films. It is one of a small number of festivals that devotes its entire program to this specific genre. It takes place on the first Thursday in June and runs for 10 days.

FESTIVAL DATES
June 4-14, 1998

SUBMISSION DATES
March 1, 1998 (three months prior to festival)

ADDRESS
Broadway Media Centre
14 Broad Street
Nottingham NG1 3AL
UK

TEL: 44-115-952 6600
FAX: 44-115-952 6622
ENTRIES: 40 (screened)
ATTENDEES: 6,000
CONTACT: **Sofia Nazar**

FILM TYPE
All

COMPETITIVE
No

LANGUAGE
Any (English subtitles)

COUNTRY
Any

ENTRY FEES
None

● Toronto Worldwide Short Film Festival (TWSFF)

TWSFF's mandate is to help expose and educate the culturally diverse audi-ence to the short film genre and to create a market where filmmakers and buyers can meet. This is the only short film festival with a marketplace for its films in North America. It screens over 1,500 tapes for buyers and distributors from around the world. The festival also includes a workshop/symposium set up for professionals of the industry and filmmakers to facilitate discussions and debates. The festival also assists in promoting contacts within the various film communities from around the world.

FESTIVAL DATES
June 4-10, 1998

SUBMISSION DATES
March 1, 1998

ADDRESS
60 Atlantic Ave., Suite 110
Toronto, Ontario M6K 1X9
Canada

TEL: 416 535 4457/8506
FAX: 416 535 8342
E-MAIL: twsff@idirect.com
WEB SITE:
http://www.torontoshort.com/film/festival/
ENTRIES: 120 screened (1,400 submitted)
ATTENDEES: 8,000
CONTACT: **Brenda Sherwood**

FILM TYPE
Short (40 mins. or under)

COMPETITIVE
Yes

LANGUAGE
Any (English subtitles)

COUNTRY
Any

ENTRY FEES
None

AWARDS
The awards for International shorts include: Best Direction, Best Drama, Best Animation, Best Experimental and Best Documentary. For Canadian shorts they are: Best Direction, Best Canadian Film and Best Cinematography. An award is also given out to the best Short and best Children's short of the festival. Prize-winning films will be screened in Famous Players Canada theatres

● Cinevision International Film Festival Cinematograph (Innsbruck)

Cinevision screens films that are from, or about Africa, Asia or America. The program is selected strictly by invitation only. The festival is either a 5 or 10 day event that takes place at the beginning of June. The length of the 1998 festival will be decided in autumn of 1997.

FESTIVAL DATES
June 5-9, 1998 (tbc)

ADDRESS
Museumstrasse 31
A-6020 Innsbruck
Austria

TEL:	43-512-580723
FAX:	43-512-581762
ENTRIES:	40 screened
ATTENDEES:	3,000+
CONTACT:	**Helmut Groschup**

FILM TYPE
All

COMPETITIVE
Yes

LANGUAGE
Any

COUNTRY
Any

ENTRY FEES
Contact festival

AWARDS
This festival awards the Audience Award.

● Connecticut Gay & Lesbian Film Festival

Connecticut presents films by gay & lesbian filmmakers and films of interest to the gay community. This is a 9-day event which screens all genres of film that deal with gay topics. Aside from the regular screenings filmmakers will be present to answer questions. There will also be benefits as well as parties.

FESTIVAL DATES
June 5-13, 1998

SUBMISSION DATES
March 1, 1998

ADDRESS
Alternatives, Inc.
PO Box 231191
Hartford, CT 06123
USA

TEL:	860 586 1136
FAX:	860 793 2973
E-MAIL:	Leedml@aol.com
WEB SITE:	http://www.trincoll.edu/~cstudio/
ENTRIES:	38 screened
ATTENDEES:	2,300
CONTACT:	**Dan Millett**

FILM TYPE
All

COMPETITIVE
Yes

LANGUAGE
Any

COUNTRY
Any

ENTRY FEES
$10

● Sydney Film Festival

Sydney is a broad-based festival with a loyal public following and good international reputation. The festival showcases new features (about 70), documentaries (about 50) and shorts (about 50). Further programs include a retrospective, restorations and experimental works. In a past retrospective, the festival had the grandson of Rosselini introduce his grandfather's work. This event is also well attended by Australian distributors.

FESTIVAL DATES
June 5-19, 1998 (tbc)
SUBMISSION DATES
February 20, 1998
ADDRESS
PO Box 950
Glebe, NSW 2037
Sydney, NSW
Australia

TEL:	61-2-9660 3844
FAX:	61-2-9380 5972
E-MAIL:	info@sydfilm-fest.com.au
WEB SITE:	http://www.sydfilm-fest.com.au/
ENTRIES:	200 screened
ATTENDEES:	140,000
CONTACT:	**Jenny Neighbour**

FILM TYPE
All
COMPETITIVE
Yes (Australian Shorts only)
LANGUAGE
Any (English subtitles)
COUNTRY
Any
ENTRY FEES
$15

AWARDS
The awards include The Dendy Awards for Australian Short Films, The Yoram Gross Animation Award, The EAC Award and The New South Wales Film and Television Office Rouben Mamoulian Award. Each award winner receives $2,500 Australian dollars.

● Banff TV Festival

The Banff Television Festival is an annual, international, competitive event dedicated to the recognition and celebration of excellence in television programs.

FESTIVAL DATES
June 7-13, 1998 (tbc)
SUBMISSION DATES
February 24, 1998
ADDRESS
1516 Railway Ave.
Canmore, Alberta T1W 1P6
Canada

TEL:	403-678 9260
FAX:	403-678 9269
E-MAIL:	banff@bowest.awinc.com
WEB SITE:	http://www.banfftvfest.com/
ENTRIES:	600
ATTENDEES:	1200 (delegates)
CONTACT:	**Jerry Ezekiel**

FILM TYPE
Programs,made specifically for TV
COMPETITIVE
Yes
LANGUAGE
Any (English or french subtitles)
COUNTRY
Any
ENTRY FEES
$250

AWARDS
This TV festival has 12 separate categories. The "Banff Rockie" goes to the producer whose work is judged the best in each particular category. The grand prize is given to the program judged as the best of the festival. Programs by independent Canadian producers are eligible for one of two $20,000 Telefilm Canada Prizes, for English and French languages productions.

● Huesca International Short Film Festival

This event is one of the very few film festivals in Spain that focuses its program on short films. An important goal of the "Ciudad De Huesca" "is the diffusion of image as a contribution to the better knowledge and fraternity among the nations of the world."

FESTIVAL DATES
June 9-17, 1998
SUBMISSION DATES
April 1, 1998 (tbc)
ADDRESS
C/Villhermosa 21
Ciudad Ed Huesca
22001 Huesca
Spain

TEL:	34-74 21 25 82
FAX:	34-74 21 00 65
ENTRIES:	400+
ATTENDEES:	14,600

FILM TYPE
Short
COMPETITIVE
Yes
LANGUAGE
Any
COUNTRY
Any
ENTRY FEES
None

AWARDS
This festival awards various prizes to films judged the best in particular categories. These include the "Golden Danzante" (500 000plas), "Silver Danzante", "Bronze Danzante", and the "Cacho Pallero".

● International Festival of Animated Film, Zagreb

Zagreb is one of the world's four largest festival of animation and is held biennially. It focusing on the presentation and evaluation of the last two years of animation. This festival tries to avoid the general commercialization of animation, although it opens a space for exhibitors and product presentations.

FESTIVAL DATES
June, 1998
SUBMISSION DATES
March 1, 1998
ADDRESS
Koncertna Direckcija Zagreb, Animafest, 10000 Zagreb
Kneza Nislava 18
Croatia

TEL:	385 1 410 134/410 128
FAX:	385 1 410 134/443 022
E-MAIL:	ANIMAFEST.Z@CARNet.hr
WEB SITE:	http://animafest.hr/
ENTRIES:	600
ATTENDEES:	1300/screening
CONTACT:	**Margit Antauer**

FILM TYPE
Animation
COMPETITIVE
Yes
LANGUAGE
Any
COUNTRY
Any
ENTRY FEES
None

AWARDS
Jury Awards include; Grand Prix (Best film-5,000 German Marks), First Prize in category A and B (3,000 German Marks each), and the "Zlatko Grgic" Award for Best First Production in a Film Debut (5,000 German Marks).

● Midnight Sun Film Festival

Midnight Sun is split into three sections: "films by the great directors", "pearls of the new cinema" and silent films with live music. Films are screened at three separate venues (one being a circus tent). Traveling to the festival town of Sodankyla is its own mini film festival because the train is outfitted as a real cinema. No wonder this festival is meant for people who truly love the art of cinema.

FESTIVAL DATES
June 10-14, 1998 (tbc)
SUBMISSION DATES
March 31, 1998
ADDRESS
Malminkatu 36
00100 Helsinki
Finland

TEL: 358-0-685 2242
FAX: 358-0-694 5560
WEB SITE:
http://www.kaapeli.fi/~lumo/English/Festivals
/Sodankyla/
ENTRIES: 80
ATTENDEES: 18,000-20,000
CONTACT: **Peter von Bagh**

FILM TYPE
Feature
COMPETITIVE
No
LANGUAGE
Any
COUNTRY
Any
ENTRY FEES
None

● Florida Film Festival

Florida is a 10-day event that is hosted by the Enzian Theatre, in Maitland. Programs include studio premieres; feature, documentary, and short film competitions; celebrity guests, parties, an awards gala at Universal Studios, Florida and seminars featuring film industry professionals. A works-in-progress program offers early previews of new films. A goal of this festival is to showcase film as an art form.

FESTIVAL DATES
June 12-21, 1998 (tbc)
ADDRESS
Enzian Theater
1300 S. Orlando Avenue
Maitland, FL 32751
USA

TEL: 407-629 1088
FAX: 407-629 6870
E-MAIL: filmfest@gate.net
WEB SITE: http://www.enzian.org/fff.html
ENTRIES: 100+
ATTENDEES: 25,000+
CONTACT: **Mike Monello/Sigrid Tiedike**

FILM TYPE
All
COMPETITIVE
Yes
LANGUAGE
Any
COUNTRY
Any

AWARDS
The awards include an Honourary Award, Grand Jury, and Audience Award. There is an American Feature, Independent and Documentary Film Competition as well as a Student Competition that awards $1,000 to the winning film.

● Pesaro Film Festival

The Italian name for this festival is "Mostra Internazionale del Nuovo Cinema" which means "International Exhibition of the New Cinema". Its focuses on unusual and innovative films and videos of high stylistic quality. Pesaro is an excellent place to experience "new cinema". The festival takes place each year in the middle of June.

FESTIVAL DATES
June 12-20, 1998 (tbc)
SUBMISSION DATES
April 30, 1998
ADDRESS
Via Villafranca 20
00185 Rome
Italy

TEL: 39-6-445 66 43/49 11 56
FAX: 39-6-491 163
ENTRIES: 200+
ATTENDEES: 1000/day
CONTACT: **Adriano Apra**

FILM TYPE
All but animation
COMPETITIVE
No
LANGUAGE
Any
COUNTRY
Any
ENTRY FEES
None

● Oslo Gay and Lesbian Film Festival

"Skeive Filmer" is a non-profit festival. It is financed partly by its own surplus and partly by public funding. The festival always takes place in connection with Gay Pride week in Oslo.

FESTIVAL DATES
June 13-17, 1998 (tbc)
SUBMISSION DATES
May 1, 1998
ADDRESS
PO Box 6838
St. Olavs Plass
N-0130 Oslo
Norway

TEL: 47-22 34 50 71/22 57 25 04
FAX: 47-22 36 28 03
E-MAIL: sfilmer@sn.no
ENTRIES: 15
ATTENDEES: 3,000
CONTACT: **Anne Mette Hohnsen**

FILM TYPE
All
COMPETITIVE
No
LANGUAGE
Any (Norwegian, Danish, Swedish,English subtitles)
COUNTRY
Any

● International French Film Festival of Tuebingen

This festival focuses on the presentation of recent feature and short films from all francophone countries. The special themes include a homage and a retrospective.

FESTIVAL DATES
Mid-June, 1998

SUBMISSION DATES
April 30, 1998

ADDRESS
Frienchstrasse 11
D-72005 Tuebingen
Germany

TEL: 49-70-71 328 28
FAX: 49-70-71 310 06
ENTRIES: 80
ATTENDEES: 17 000 (13 000 open air)
CONTACT: **Michael Friederci**

FILM TYPE
All

COMPETITIVE
Yes

LANGUAGE
Any

COUNTRY
All countries with a francophone population

ENTRY FEES
None

AWARDS
The "Fliegende Kamera" is awarded to one of the 6 first films in competition.

● London Jewish Film Festival

The London Jewish Film Festival accepts all types of films from around the world that deal with the Jewish identity and experience.

FESTIVAL DATES
Mid-June, 1998

SUBMISSION DATES
March 15, 1998

ADDRESS
National Film Theatre
South Bank, Waterloo
London SE1 8XT
UK

TEL: 44-171-815 1323/4
FAX: 44-171-633 0786
E-MAIL: jane.ivey@bfi.org.uk
ENTRIES: 50+
ATTENDEES: 15,000
CONTACT: **Jane Ivey**

FILM TYPE
All

COMPETITIVE
No

LANGUAGE
Any (English subtitles)

COUNTRY
Any

ENTRY FEES
None

● Norwegian Short Film Festival

The Norwegian Short Film Festival is now the most important short film festival in Norway. It prides itself on being a national festival with a competition for Norwegian short films. It also has an international program of contempary shorts as well as special programs. One of its goals is to promote the distribution and production of Norwegian short films.

FESTIVAL DATES
June, 1998
ADDRESS
Storengvenlen 8B, 1342 Jar
Grimstad
Norway

TEL: 67 12 20 13
FAX: 67 12 48 65
E-MAIL: kortfilm@nfi.no
WEB SITE:
http://www.dnfi.no/krtf/1996/Welcome.html
ENTRIES: 500
ATTENDEES: 10,000+

FILM TYPE
Short
COMPETITIVE
Yes
LANGUAGE
Any
COUNTRY
Any

● Nantucket Film Festival

The Nantucket Film Festival is a screenwriter's festival presenting features, short films, documentaries, staged readings, and panel discussions. The festival is non-competitive with the exception of the screenplay competition. Writers are encouraged to present their films and works-in-progress to receive feedback from other writers and filmmakers.

FESTIVAL DATES
June 16-21, 1998 (tbc)

SUBMISSION DATES
April 16, 1998

ADDRESS
P.O. Box 688 Prince Street Station
New York, NY 10012
USA

TEL: 212 642 6339
E-MAIL: ackfest@aol.com
WEB SITE:
http://www.nantucketfilmfestival.org/
ENTRIES: 200 submitted
ATTENDEES: 5,000
CONTACT: **Jonathan Burkhart**

FILM TYPE
All (VHS, NTSC format preferred)
COMPETITIVE
Only screenwriting section
LANGUAGE
Screenplays must be written in English
COUNTRY
Any
ENTRY FEES
$20 short (35 minutes or less), $35 feature (add $5 for video return)

AWARDS
The Jury will award a prize to the winner for Best Screenplay at the Awards Presentation during the festival.

● International Hamburg Short Film Festival

The Festival is a forum for presenting the diversity of internationally produced short films and a place to meet filmmakers from Germany and around
the world. The three separate competitions held at this festival are: the
International short film competition, the No Budget competition and the
Three-minute Quickie. The first two competitions are open to any short film
that falls within its guidelines. The only films entered into the final competition, the Three-minute Quickie, are made by filmmakers chosen by the festival
to reflect a certain theme. The prize-winning film in this category receives the
Viewer's Award.

FESTIVAL DATES
June 17-21, 1998 (tbc)

SUBMISSION DATES
March 1, 1998

ADDRESS
KurzFilmAgentur Hamburg e.V.
Filmhaus Friedensallee 7
D-22765 Hamburg
Germany

TEL: 49-40-398 26 122
FAX: 49-40 398 26 123
ENTRIES: 2300
ATTENDEES: 17 ,000
CONTACT: **Birgit Kaemper**

FILM TYPE
Short

COMPETITIVE
Yes

LANGUAGE
Any (English or German subtitles)

COUNTRY
Any

ENTRY FEES
None

AWARDS
The awards in the International short film competition are: the Francois Ode (special jury) prize,
the Hamburg Short Film Award, the Premiere
Prize and the Viewers Award. In the "No Budget
competition" an award is given to the best film
which lacked public or private sponsorship.

● Newark Black Film Festival

The Newark Black Film Festival is a summer festival of films by black filmmakers and films featuring the history and culture of black people in America
and elsewhere. Every year this festival runs on the last two Wednesdays in
June, then skips a week and runs for the remaining Wednesdays in July.

FESTIVAL DATES
June 17, 24 ; July 8, 15, 22, 29, 1998

ADDRESS
The Newark Museum
49 Washington St., P.O. Box 540
Newark, NJ 07101-0540
USA

TEL: 201-596 6550
FAX: 201-642 0459
ENTRIES: 20+
ATTENDEES: 4,000+
CONTACT: **Jane Stein**

FILM TYPE
All

COMPETITIVE
Yes (in 1997)

LANGUAGE
Prefers English

COUNTRY
African & its Diasporant countries eg. US,
Canada

● San Francisco Lesbian and Gay Film Festival

The San Francisco Gay and Lesbian Film Festival is the largest and oldest festival of its kind in the world. It showcases the best and most diverse work by or about lesbians and gay men. Women as well as people of colour are particularly encouraged to participate. This festival always closes on San Francisco Gay Pride day.

FESTIVAL DATES
June 19-28, 1998 (tbc)
SUBMISSION DATES
February 24, 1998
ADDRESS
346 Ninth Street
San Francisco, CA 94102
USA

TEL:	415-703 8650
FAX:	415-861 1404
E-MAIL:	frameline@aol.com
WEB SITE:	http://www.frameline.org/
ENTRIES:	550 (received) 200 (in festival)
ATTENDEES:	53,000+
CONTACT:	**Michael Lumpkin**

FILM TYPE
All (by or relating to gay men or lesbians)
COMPETITIVE
No
LANGUAGE
Any (English script)
COUNTRY
Any
ENTRY FEES
$10 ($20-35, if late)

● Mystfest - International Mystery Film Festival

Mystfest is an event that showcases a significant panorama on films that belong to the mystery genre. Through this showcase, the commonalites between these films are shown.The festival, generally, takes place in the last week of June on an annual basis.

FESTIVAL DATES
June 21-27, 1998 (tbc)
SUBMISSION DATES
May 10, 1998
ADDRESS
Centro Culturale Polivalente Piazza
Della Repubblica 31
47033 Cattolica
Italy

TEL:	39-541-967802
FAX:	39-541-967803
ENTRIES:	20,000
ATTENDEES:	12,000
CONTACT:	**Marcello Di Bella**

FILM TYPE
All but animation
COMPETITIVE
Yes
LANGUAGE
Any
COUNTRY
Any
ENTRY FEES
None

AWARDS
Awards for best film and director.

● Prague International Film Festival

Prague has nine separate programs that show a wide variety of different films. These programs include: "Czech Cinema", "Panorama of World Cinema", 'Maverick', retrospectives and The International Competition, which a film can only enter if it has not competed in any other international competition. A goal of this festival is "to stimulate the Czech film culture as well as raise the Czechs' profile internationally."

FESTIVAL DATES
  June 21-29, 1998 (tbc)

ADDRESS
  c/o Bohemia Promotion, V haji 15
  170 00 Prague 7
  Czech Republic

TEL: 420-2-66795 421 3
FAX: 420-2-66795 405
WEB SITE:
http://www.filmfestivals.com/prague/index.ht
m
ENTRIES: 120
ATTENDEES: 100 000
CONTACT: **Katerina Rihova**

FILM TYPE
  All but short

COMPETITIVE
  Yes

LANGUAGE
  Any

COUNTRY
  Any

ENTRY FEES
  None

AWARDS
  Prizes awarded are the Golden Golem, Best Director, Best Acting Awards, Special Jury, Special Lifetime Achievement Awards and a Special Golden Golem Prize.

● International Animation Festival (Cardiff)

Cardiff is an international festival founded in 1965 that is run biennially. It features animated films, exhibitions, lectures, seminars, and is the only British festival dedicated to animation.

FESTIVAL DATES
  June 23-28, 1998

ADDRESS
  18 Broadwick Street
  London W1V 1FG
  UK

TEL: 44-171-494 0506
FAX: 44-171-494 0807
ENTRIES: 600
ATTENDEES: 2,250
CONTACT: **Fran Barlow**

FILM TYPE
  Animation

COMPETITIVE
  No

LANGUAGE
  English entries

COUNTRY
  Any

ENTRY FEES
  None

● La Rochelle International Film Festival

La Rochelle shows over 130 feature length films during a 10 day span in a friendly, non-competitive atmosphere. Its programs include: Tributes-works by certain actors or directors which have been unjustly forgotten- as well as "The World As It Is", Panoramas and Retrospective Celebrations. Each year the festival ends with an all-night program of 5 films, followed by breakfast in cafes overlooking the old port.

FESTIVAL DATES		**FILM TYPE**	
June 26-July 6, 1998 (tbc)		Feature	
ADDRESS		**COMPETITIVE**	
16 rue Saint Sabin		No	
75011 Paris		**LANGUAGE**	
France		Any	
		COUNTRY	
TEL:	33-1-48 06 16 66	Any	
FAX:	33-1-48 06 15 40	**ENTRY FEES**	
ENTRIES:	130	None	
ATTENDEES:	60,000		
CONTACT:	**Jean-Loup Passek**		

● Filmfest Munchen

Filmfest Munchen focuses on new full length international feature films and documentaries. The majority of the entrants are German, Austrian and Swiss premieres, as well as American independents and international TV movies.

FESTIVAL DATES		**FILM TYPE**	
June 27-July 4, 1998		Feature, Documentary and Animation	
SUBMISSION DATES		**COMPETITIVE**	
January-April, 1998		No	
ADDRESS		**LANGUAGE**	
c/o IMF GmbH		Any	
Kaiserstrasse 39		**COUNTRY**	
D-80801 Munich		Any	
Germany		**ENTRY FEES**	
		None	
TEL:	49-89 38 19 040		
FAX:	49-89 38 19 04 27		
ENTRIES:	150		
CONTACT:	**Eberhard Hauff**		

● Mostra Internazionale del Cinema Libero/Il Cinema Retrovato

The is a festival of film archives from all over the world, organized by the Bologna Film Archive and the Netherlands Film Museum.

FESTIVAL DATES
End of June, 1998

SUBMISSION DATES
April, 1998

ADDRESS
via Galliera
8-40121 Bologna
Italy

TEL: 39-51-228 975/237 068
FAX: 39-51-26 16 80
CONTACT: **Gian Luca Farinelli**

FILM TYPE
All

COMPETITIVE
No

LANGUAGE
Any

COUNTRY
Any

ENTRY FEES
None

● Vila do Conde Short Film Festival

Vila do Conde boasts an international as well as national short film competition. At the 1997 festival, the featured special programs included Music on Short Film and Music Videos. In addition to these two programs, other events related to the subject of music were included.

FESTIVAL DATES
June 30-July 5, 1998 (tbc)

SUBMISSION DATES
April, 1998

ADDRESS
Auditorio Municipal de Vila do Conde
4450 Vila de Conde
Portugal

TEL: 351 52 641644
FAX: 351 53 642871/53 648871
ENTRIES: 800 submitted
ATTENDEES: 14,000
CONTACT: **Miguel Dies**

FILM TYPE
Short

COMPETITIVE
Yes

LANGUAGE
Any

COUNTRY
Any

ENTRY FEES
None

AWARDS
The prizes awarded in this festival include the Great Prize City of Vila do Conde, a fiction prize, Prize Manoel De Oliveira for Documentary, an animation prize, Prize Cottinelli Telmo, Prize for a Young Portuguese Filmmaker and the Audience Award.

Brief Entries

● Cinema Expo International (Amsterdam)

ADDRESS
244 West 49th Street #200
New York, NY 10019
USA

TEL: 212-246 6460
FAX: 212-265 6428
CONTACT: **Jimmy Sunshine**

● Cologne Conference

ADDRESS
Im Mediapark 5b
50670 Cologne
Germany

TEL: 49-221-454 3280
FAX: 49-221-454 3289
CONTACT: **Lutz Hachmeister**

● Euro Aim Donostia Screenings (San Sebastian)

ADDRESS
Euro Aim
210 Avenue Winston Churchill
B-1180 Brussels
Belgium

TEL: 32-2-346 1500
FAX: 32-2-346 3842
CONTACT: **Nicolas Steil**

● Kalingrad Film Festival

ADDRESS
1 Ploshchad Pbedy
Kaliningrad 236000
Russia

TEL: 7-0112 21 89 26
FAX: 7-0223-21 16 77
CONTACT: **Alexandra Yakovleva-Aasmyae**

● Marketskaya

ADDRESS
c/o Seineva Organisation
10 rue la Boatie
75008 Paris
France

TEL: 33-1-53 76 16 28
FAX: 33-1-45 61 94 27
CONTACT: **Gerard Dijoud**

● St. Petersburg International Film Festival

ADDRESS
10 Kamennoostrovsky Ave.
197101 St. Petersburg
Russia

TEL: 812-238 5811
FAX: 812-238 5811
CONTACT: **Aleksander Manontov**

● Sunny Side of the Doc

ADDRESS
Doc Services
3 Square Stalingrad
13001 Marseille
France

TEL: 33-4-91 08 43 15
FAX: 33-4-91 84 38 34/91 52 26 65
CONTACT: **Olivier Masson**

● Bradford Animation Festival (BAF!)

The goal of this festival is to raise the profile of animation through its international film competition. It also displays the latest in animation, has seminars featuring well known animators and an exhibition of animation cells and puppets.

FESTIVAL DATES
July, 1998
SUBMISSION DATES
June, 1998
ADDRESS
National Museum Photography, Film and Television
Pictureville, Bradford BD1 1NQ
UK

TEL: 44-1274-727 488
FAX: 44-1274-723 155
WEB SITE:
http://nmsi.ac.uk/nmpt/animate.htm
ENTRIES: 250
ATTENDEES: 2,000
CONTACT: **Cary Sawhney**

FILM TYPE
All types of Animation
COMPETITIVE
Yes
LANGUAGE
Any
COUNTRY
Any
ENTRY FEES
None

AWARDS
The BAF! Awards are given out every year.

● INTERCOM International Communication Film & Video Festival

Intercom is an awards competition which "rewards technical excellence, creativity, and vision for film and video productions produced on video, as well as interactive multimedia". There are no public screenings and once the winners are chosen ,by a qualifed jury, they are notified within 2 months of the submission date

FESTIVAL DATES
August, 1998
SUBMISSION DATES
May, 1998
ADDRESS
32 West Randolph St., Suite 600
Chicago, IL 60601
USA

TEL: 312-425 9400
FAX: 312-425 0944
E-MAIL: filmfest@wwa.com
WEB SITE:
http://www.chicago.ddbn.com/filmfest/
ENTRIES: 400
CONTACT: **Jim Healy**

FILM TYPE
All (only on video)
COMPETITIVE
Yes
LANGUAGE
Any (English subtitles)
COUNTRY
Any
ENTRY FEES
$35-$250

AWARDS
The top award for each category is the Hugo. A Gold or Silver Hugo is presented to the best entry and second best entry in each category. Gold and Silver plaques are presented to entries that are judged to have "superior quality". Certificates of Merit are presented to entries which "deserve recognition".

● Jerusalem Film Festival

Jerusalem screens all types of films from all over the world. The prizes given out are for films that either focus on human rights or that of peace and tolerance. Even though this festival attracts the attention of at least 50,000 people per year, it still is able to keep an intimate feel, which is very unique for a festival of this size.

FESTIVAL DATES
July, 1998

SUBMISSION DATES
May, 1998

ADDRESS
Israel Film Archive, Jerusalem Cinematheque
Hebron Rd., PO Box 8561
Jerusalem 91083
Israel

TEL: 972 2 724 131
FAX: 972 2 733 076
WEB SITE:
http://www.qrd.tau.ac.il/israel_update.html#jer
usalem
ENTRIES: 165
ATTENDEES: 50,000
CONTACT: **Lia van Leer**

FILM TYPE
All

COMPETITIVE
Yes

LANGUAGE
Any (Engllish subtitles)

COUNTRY
Any

ENTRY FEES
None

AWARDS
The international competition is split into two categories: The Wim van Leer "In Spirit of Freedom" Award which is given to feature and documentary films that focus on human rights, and the Mediterranean Cinema "In Pursuit of Peace & Tolerance" award which is given to a feature or documentary film from the Mediterranean region that focus on peace and tolerance.

● L'Age d'Or Prize (Brussels)

The Age d'Or Prize is awarded by a jury to the best of the 5 award winning films chosen that year. It must have "originality, singularity of purpose and in style mark a deliberate break with cinematographic conformity". To enter the competition, a film must not have been released in Belgium or picked up by a distributor for the Belgian market. The goal of these awards are to "assist in the distribution of quality films in Belgium".

FESTIVAL DATES
First 2 weeks of July, 1998

SUBMISSION DATES
April 30, 1998

ADDRESS
Royal Film Archive
Rue Ravenstein 23
B-1000 Brussels
Belgium

TEL: 32-2-507 8370
FAX: 32-2-513 1272
ENTRIES: 25 screened
ATTENDEES: 6,000
CONTACT: **Ludo Bettens**

FILM TYPE
Feature (over 60 mins.), Documentary

COMPETITIVE
Yes

LANGUAGE
Any (English, French or Dutch subtitles)

COUNTRY
Any

ENTRY FEES
None

AWARDS
Every year the Film Museum grants 5 awards each amounting to 250,000BF. In addition, one award winning film will also be selected to receive the Age d' Or Prize. This prize has attached to it another 250,000BF (125,000BF to director; 125,000BF to producer and 125,000BF to distribution company who picks it up for release in Belgium).

● Karlovy Vary International Film Festival

Karlovy Vary is one of the oldest festival's in the world. It was founded in 1946 and held annually until 1958. Between 1957-1989 it alternated with the Moscow Film Festival. As of 1994 the festival started to run annually and is gaining back its excellent reputation for good films and beautiful surroundings. During the festival there are also parties, discussions, and the presence of many filmmakers, directors, celebraties, etc.

FESTIVAL DATES
July 3-11, 1998 (tbc)

ADDRESS
Valdstejnska 4
110 00 Prague 1
Czech Republic

TEL: 42-2-513 2473/513 2412
FAX: 42-2-520 542
E-MAIL: iffkv@tlp.cz
WEB SITE:
http://www.tlp.cz/internet/iffkarlovy_vary/
CONTACT: **Eva Zaoralova**

FILM TYPE
All

COMPETITIVE
Yes

LANGUAGE
Any

COUNTRY
Any

ENTRY FEES
None

AWARDS
Many prizes are awarded at this festival. They include the Grand Prix - Crystal Globe; Best Director, Actor (females & male); Special award for lifetime artistic contribution to world film; Special Award of the Jury; Special Jury Mention; Public Award for the best documentary (grant of $ 5000); Honourable mentions and The FIPRESCI jury award.

● The Masters of Animation-Seattle's International Animation Festival

Masters of Animation is a four day smorgasbord of animation from around the world. Over twenty artists representing many different types of animation come to this festival to enjoy each other's work. A major component to this festival are the discussions and tributes. In 1996 guests included Chuck Jones and Ray Harryhausen.

FESTIVAL DATES
July 3-6, 1998 (tbc)

ADDRESS
5030 Roosevelt Way
Seattle, WA
USA

TEL: 206 522 2853
E-MAIL: sca.crow@ix.netcom.com
WEB SITE: http://www.scarecrow.com/anima-
tio.htm
ENTRIES: 15+
CONTACT: **Norman Hill**

FILM TYPE
Animation

COMPETITIVE
No

LANGUAGE
Any

COUNTRY
Any

● Montevideo Festival for Children and Young People

The Festival's purpose is to present an overview of new film productions for children and adolescents, facilitating access to the best and most diverse material for children. This event also constitutes an attempt to encourage film distribution companies to purchase new films for children.

FESTIVAL DATES
July, 1998

ADDRESS
Cinemateca Uruguaya
Lorenzo Camelli 1311
Montevideo
Uruguay

TEL:	598-2-48 24 60/49 57 95
FAX:	598-2-49 45 72
ENTRIES:	8,000
ATTENDEES:	12,000
CONTACT:	**Ricardo Casas**

FILM TYPE
All

COMPETITIVE
Yes

LANGUAGE
Any

COUNTRY
Any

AWARDS
The Festival awards the "GURI" among others.

● Auckland International Film Festival

Auckland is organized by The New Zealand Film Festival, a charitable trust, this 29 year old Festival, along with its Wellington sibling, provides a non-competitive New Zealand premiere showcase for a striking diversity of film (and video) styles. An archival component, co-ordinated by Jonathan Dennis, also enjoys considerable prominence, as do the Moving Image Centre's programs of short films.

FESTIVAL DATES
July 10-25, 1998 (tbc)

SUBMISSION DATES
April 30, 1998

ADDRESS
PO Box 9544, Te Aro
Te Aro, Wellington 6001
New Zealand

TEL:	64-4-385 0162
FAX:	64-4-801 7304
E-MAIL:	enzedff@actrix.gen.nz
WEB SITE:	http://www.enzedff.co.nz/
ENTRIES:	900(120 feature and shorts screened)
ATTENDEES:	80,000+
CONTACT:	**Bill Gosden**

FILM TYPE
All

COMPETITIVE
No

LANGUAGE
Any (English subtitles)

COUNTRY
Any

ENTRY FEES
None

● Outfest: Los Angeles Gay & Lesbian Film Festival

Outfest premieres to the Los Angeles area the best new films and videos by, about or of interest to gay men and lesbians. In many cases this festival provides the only local opportunity to many of the chosen films. Outfest is sponsored by Out on the Screen a non profit organization which runs workshops, seminars and film screening during the festival as well as throught out the year.

FESTIVAL DATES
July 10-19, 1998 (tbc)
SUBMISSION DATES
Feb/March, 1998
ADDRESS
8455 Beverly Blvd., Suite 309
Los Angeles, CA 90048
USA

TEL:	213 951 1247
FAX:	213 951 0721
E-MAIL:	outfest@aol.com
WEB SITE:	http://www.outfest.com/
ENTRIES:	220 screened
ATTENDEES:	15,000+
CONTACT:	**Kelsey Bray**

FILM TYPE
All
COMPETITIVE
Yes
LANGUAGE
Any
COUNTRY
Any
ENTRY FEES
Contact festival

AWARDS
Juries select three winners in the Outfest '98 Film Competition for excellence in filmmaking. Six audience awards are also selected by post-screening ballots. Cash awards accompany the prize for each winning filmmaker.

● Wellington Film Festival

Wellington is non-competitive and extremely diverse in its selection of films. It maintains a good relationship with its sister film festival, in Auckland, as they combine to draw over 100,000 New Zealanders and international guests to their theatres in July.

FESTIVAL DATES
July 10-25, 1998 (tbc)
SUBMISSION DATES
April 30, 1998
ADDRESS
PO Box 9544
Te Aro, Wellington 6001
New Zealand

TEL:	64 4 385 0162
FAX:	64 4 801 7304
E-MAIL:	enzedff@actrix.gen.nz
WEB SITE:	http://www.enzedff.co.nz/
ENTRIES:	100-120 screened (500 submitted)
ATTENDEES:	49,000
CONTACT:	**Bill Gosden**

FILM TYPE
All
COMPETITIVE
No
LANGUAGE
Any (English subtitles)
ENTRY FEES
None

● Cambridge International Film Festival

Cambridge presents new British films, national premieres, and previews of major releases together with other programs including Retrospectives, Innovative documentaries and the best of Cannes, Berlin and Sundance.

July

FESTIVAL DATES
July 12-26, 1998
SUBMISSION DATES
May 1, 1998
ADDRESS
Cambridge Arts Cinema
8 Market Passage
Cambridge CB2 3PF
UK

FILM TYPE
All
COMPETITIVE
No
LANGUAGE
Any
COUNTRY
Any
ENTRY FEES
None

TEL: 44-1223-578 944
FAX: 44-1223-578 929
WEB SITE: http://www.gold.net/camfest/
ENTRIES: 150
ATTENDEES: 15,000
CONTACT: **Francois Ballay**

● Wine Country Film Festival

Wine Country "promotes the development and appreciation of fine film and the arts and stimulates cultural exchange". Contributing to this festival's atmosphere are actors, directors, producers and professionals from the world of entertainment who meet in a close, intimate environment, providing festival goers with a rich and diverse experience. It has five categories in which films are accepted for screening at the festival. They include international films, film that makes a social statement and films about the arts and enviroment. Workshops, seminars and demonstrations of new technologies are also part of this festival.

FESTIVAL DATES
July 16-August 9, 1998
SUBMISSION DATES
May 1,1998
ADDRESS
12000 Henno Road, P.O. Box 303
Glen Ellen, CA 95442
USA

FILM TYPE
All
COMPETITIVE
Yes
LANGUAGE
Any (English subtitles)
COUNTRY
Any
ENTRY FEES
$25

TEL: 707-996 2536/935-3456
FAX: 707-996 6964
E-MAIL: wcfilmfest@aol.com
WEB SITE: http://www.winezone.com/
ENTRIES: 100-200
ATTENDEES: 10 000+/-
CONTACT: **Stephen Ashton**

AWARDS
Their is a competition in the categories of Best First Feature Film and Best Short Film.

International Film Festival Guide   109

● Asian American International Film Festival

This festival is the oldest showcase of Asian and Asian-American cinema in North America. It has proved to be an invaluable exhibition opportunity for filmmakers and distributors on a variety of different levels. After its New York premiere, the festival travels on a 10-month national tour. Every year it runs on the last two weekends in July.

FESTIVAL DATES
July 17-19 and July 24-26, 1998

SUBMISSION DATES
March 15, 1998

ADDRESS
32 East Broadway, 4th Floor
New York, NY 10002
USA

TEL:	212-925 8685
FAX:	212-925 8157
E-MAIL:	ACVinNYC@aol.com
WEB SITE:	http://www.asiancinevision.org/
ENTRIES:	200 screened
ATTENDEES:	15,000
CONTACT:	**Vivian Huang**

FILM TYPE
All

COMPETITIVE
No

LANGUAGE
Any (English subtitles)

COUNTRY
Any (filmmaker must be of Asian heritage)

ENTRY FEES
None

● Vevey International Comedy Film Festival

There are many sections to this festival including a retrospective, an open air cinema, and a young people's jury. They all share a similar goal which unites the festival, "to present the best comedy films of the day and to offer the public a week of laughter and relaxation."

FESTIVAL DATES
July 17-25, 1998 (tbc)

SUBMISSION DATES
Beginning of June, 1998

ADDRESS
Cinema Rex, J-J Rousseau 6
1800 Vevey
Switzerland

TEL:	41-21-925 8899/8888
FAX:	41-21-921 7416
ENTRIES:	100+
ATTENDEES:	10,000
CONTACT:	**Yves Moser**

FILM TYPE
All, but Documentary

COMPETITIVE
Yes

LANGUAGE
Any

COUNTRY
Any

ENTRY FEES
Transportation only

AWARDS
The Canne d'Or for Best Film

● Moscow International Film Festival

Moscow's goal is to "develop cultural exchanges, to reach mutual understanding between nations, and encourage collaboration between cinematographers from around the world". The programs include an international competitive that only can include features that have not participated in other competitive international programs; non-competitive screenings, retrospectives, discussions and a Special Screening Youth Program. The aim of this program "...is to attract the attention of professionals to the work of young cinematographers."

FESTIVAL DATES
 July 18-28, 1998 (tbc)
SUBMISSION DATES
 May 14, 1998
ADDRESS
 Interfest
 10 Khohlovski Pereulok
 Moscow 109028
 Russia

TEL: 7 095 917 2486
FAX: 7 095 916 0107
WEB SITE: http://www.mmkf.com/
ENTRIES: 12 in competition (at least)
ATTENDEES: 100,000+
CONTACT: **Alexander Atanesyan**

FILM TYPE
 Features in competition
COMPETITIVE
 Yes
LANGUAGE
 Any
COUNTRY
 Any
ENTRY FEES
 None

AWARDS
 A Statuette of Saint George will be awarded to the following prizes: main prize to the director & producer of the Best Film; Special Jury Prize; Best Director and Best Actor (female & male). Other awards are the Christian Jury Award; Kodak St Anna Award; Andrei Tarkovsky Award; Russian Critics Award and a Special Prize for the contribution to the world of cinematography.

● Giffoni Children's Film Festival

Giffoni is the best known festival in Italy after the Venice Film Festival. It is a place where good cinema ,for the young, is presented to the young. Giffoni is interested in films "for the young which go beyond the canons of what is conventionally considered suitable material", so it includes films with "strong themes that are complex and at times problematic".

FESTIVAL DATES
 July 19-26, 1998 (tbc)
SUBMISSION DATES
 June, 1998
ADDRESS
 Piazza Umberto 1
 84095 Giffoni
 Valle Piana (SA)
 Italy

TEL: 39-89-868 544
FAX: 39-89-866 111
E-MAIL: gff@pn.itnet.it
WEB SITE:
http://www.starnet.it/gff/giffoni.news.html
ENTRIES: 14/for competiton
ATTENDEES: 2,000+
CONTACT: **Claudio Gubitosi**

FILM TYPE
 All
COMPETITIVE
 Yes
LANGUAGE
 Any (with English or French spot list)
COUNTRY
 Any
ENTRY FEES
 None

AWARDS
 There are 14 feature films chosen to take part in the competition at this festival. They are selected from the best world-wide productions of the last year. They compete for the "Gryphon" awards for best film (Silver), best actor and actress (Bronze) and best story/screenplay (Domenico Meccoli). The competition is also linked to the Italian Government, which will award 2 billion Lira to the ticket holder linked to the winning film.

● Taormina International Film Festival

Taormina's competitive section which is reserved for feature length films " reflects new expressive tendencies (new authors, new schools, countries with less frequent international programming)". These films must not have been commerically released in Italy or received any prizes from "recognized international events". It also includes tributes, retrospectives and a program of premieres that are to be released publicly in Italy.

FESTIVAL DATES
July 22-28, 1998

SUBMISSION DATES
July 1, 1998

ADDRESS
c/o Palazzo dei Congress
98039 Taormina
Italy

TEL: 39 942 21142/637 28195
FAX: 39 942 23348
ENTRIES: 100 screened
ATTENDEES: 40,000
CONTACT: **Stefano Francia**

FILM TYPE
Feature, Short and Documentary

COMPETITIVE
Yes

LANGUAGE
Any (Italian subtitles in competition; English or French in other sections)

COUNTRY
Any

ENTRY FEES
None

● Melbourne International Film Festival

Melbourne aims to screen an eclectic mix of outstanding filmmaking from around the world. It is a showcase for the latest developments in Australian and international filmmaking, offering audiences a wide range of features and shorts, encompassing fiction, documentaries, animation and experimental films. The films are screened in some of Melbourne's most celebrated inner city cinemas and theatres.

FESTIVAL DATES
July 23-August 9, 1998 (tbc)

ADDRESS
PO Box 2206
Fitzroy Mail Centre
Melbourne 3065
Australia

TEL: 61-3-9417 2011
FAX: 61-3-9417 3804
E-MAIL: miff@netspace.net.au

WEB SITE:
http://www.cinemedia.net/MIFF/miffhome.htm
ENTRIES: 200+
ATTENDEES: 55,000
CONTACT: **Sandra Sdraulig**

FILM TYPE
All

COMPETITIVE
Yes

LANGUAGE
Any (English subtitles)

COUNTRY
Any

ENTRY FEES
$25US (Amex Money Order) or $30AUS (Bank Draft)

AWARDS
City of Melbourne prizes - Grand Prix, Best Film ($5,000), Best Experimental Film ($2,000), Best Animated Film ($2,000), Best Fiction Film ($2,000), Beyond Award - Best Australian Short Comedy ($5,000), Film Victoria Erwin Rado Award - Best Australian Film 9$2,000) and Kino Cinemas Award-Creative Excellence in Australian Short Filmmaking ($2500).

● Rio Cine Festival

Rio Cine is an international film, television, video and publicity festival, as well as a Latin American showcase. Aside from film screenings, this festival also includes industry forums for film, TV and video, meetings, seminars, networking and contact with the Brazilian general public. In its international section it has screened "Trainspotting" (which was a Brazilian premiere), "Angel Baby", "The Celluloid Closet", "Safe" as well as many other well known films. Rio Cine is that rare event that has a real impact on the region's community.

FESTIVAL DATES
July 23-29, 1998 (tbc)
SUBMISSION DATES
April-May, 1998
ADDRESS
Rua Das Laranjeiras 219
Rio De Janeiro -RJ- 22410-001
Rio de Janeiro
Brazil

TEL: 55-21-553 2118
FAX: 55-21-553 0130
E-MAIL: cima@visualnet.com.br
WEB SITE:
http://www.visualnet.com.br/riocine/
ENTRIES: 300
ATTENDEES: 80,000
CONTACT: **Vilma Lustosa**

FILM TYPE
All
COMPETITIVE
Yes/No
LANGUAGE
Any
COUNTRY
Any
ENTRY FEES
None

AWARDS
Rio Cine has a Brazillian short's competition for film and video. In the former prizes awarded are the Best Short (Official Jury), Best Short (Popular Jury), Critics Prize, Best direction, Special Jury Prize, Best Actor (female & male) and Best Screenplay. In the latter they are Best Video, Best Video Clip, Best Documentary, Best direction, Best Video-art, Special Jury Prize, Special Jury Prize (Video Clip) and Ed Wood Prize.

● Fantasy Filmfest - International Film Festival for Science Fiction, Fiction, Horror and Thriller

Fantasy Filmfest is a unique genre festival that runs in six major German cities. In 1995, the Deutscher Fernsehdienst selected it as "one of the six most important film festivals in Europe." It's also the only worldwide touring independent film festival. In contrast to many European festivals, it is made possible, largely, by industry sponsors as opposed to governmental funding.

FESTIVAL DATES
July 29-September 2, 1998
SUBMISSION DATES
May 29, 1998
ADDRESS
Wittlesbacher Str. 26
10707 Berlin
Germany

TEL: 49 30 861 4532
FAX: 49 30 861 4539
ENTRIES: 50
ATTENDEES: 52,000-60,000
CONTACT: **Schorsch Muller**

FILM TYPE
All, but documentary
COMPETITIVE
No
LANGUAGE
English or German subtitles
COUNTRY
Any
ENTRY FEES
None

● Cinedecouvertes (Brussels)

ADDRESS
Rue Ravenstein 23
1000 Brussels
Belgium

FESTIVAL DATES
First two weeks in July, 1998
TEL: 32-2-506 8370
FAX: 32-2-513 1272

● Diamond Film Experience

ADDRESS
Boulevard de Centemaire 20
1020 Brussels
Belgium

TEL: 32-2-478-0450
FAX: 32-2-478-7840

● International Animation Expo (AnimExpo)

ADDRESS
45-11, Yeoido-Dong
Youngdeungpo-Ku
Seoul,
Korea

FESTIVAL DATES
July/August, 1999
TEL: 82-2-785 6855
FAX: 82 2 789 3968
E-MAIL: AnimExpo@ako.net
CONTACT: Hee-Soek Lee

● Philafilm

ADDRESS
IAMPTP
215 South Broad Street
Philadelphia, PA 19107
USA

TEL: 215-545 4862
FAX: 215-546 8055
CONTACT: Larry Smallwood Jr.

● The Gramado Film Festival of Latin and Brazilian Cinema

Since 1991, this festival has had a Latin and a Brazilian competition with a separate jury for each one. They also have a competition for short length Brazilian films.

FESTIVAL DATES
August, 1998
SUBMISSION DATES
June, 1998
ADDRESS
Av. das Hortensias,2029
Gramado, RS-95670.000
Brazil

TEL: 55-54-286-2335
FAX: 55-54-286-2335
E-MAIL: viadigital@pro.via-rs.com.br
WEB SITE: http://www.viadigital.com.br/gramado/cinema/
ENTRIES: 1,200
ATTENDEES: 100,000+
CONTACT: **Enoir Antonio Zorzanello**

FILM TYPE
Feature, Short
COMPETITIVE
Yes
LANGUAGE
Any Latin language
COUNTRY
Any Latin language country
ENTRY FEES
None

AWARDS
This festival awards the "Kikito Award"

● Locarno International Film Festival

Locarno aims to promote personal filmmaking of artistic merit by the promotion of new filmmakers. The New Cinema section showcases emerging directors whose work displays the innovative trends in style and content to the film industry. Other programs include the "International competition"; the "Piazza Grande" (at the largest open-air cinema in the world) evening outdoor screenings, "Retrospectives", "Leopards of Tomorrow", "Swiss Perspectives" and "Critics' Week".

FESTIVAL DATES
August 5-15, 1998 (tbc)
SUBMISSION DATES
May 31, 1998
ADDRESS
Via della Posta 6
CH-6600 Locarno
Switzerland

TEL: 41-91-751 02 32
FAX: 41-91-751 74 65
WEB SITE: http://www.pardo.ch/
ENTRIES: 350+ screened
ATTENDEES: 150,000
CONTACT: **Marco Muller**

FILM TYPE
All, but animation
COMPETITIVE
Yes
LANGUAGE
Any
COUNTRY
Any
ENTRY FEES
None

AWARDS
The festival's jury awards many prizes including;the Golden Leopard (30,000 to 50,000 Swiss Francs) for best film, the Silver Leopard (15,000 to 20,000 Swiss Francs) for best director in the "New Cinema" category and the best first or second feature of a director, and a Bronze Leopard (10,000 Swiss Francs) to an actress and actor,respectively.

• Palm Springs International Short Film & Video Festival

This is the largest competitive short film festival in North America. It includes a student and international competition, seminars, workshops, cash awards as well as an opportunity to network with individuals involved with the creation of a short film.

FESTIVAL DATES
August 5-9, 1998

SUBMISSION DATES
June 1, 1998

ADDRESS
1700 East Tahquitz Way, Suite 6
Palm Springs, CA 92262
USA

TEL: 619-322 2930
FAX: 619-322 4087
E-MAIL: filmfest@ix.netcom.com
WEB SITE: http:/psfilmfest.org/
ENTRIES: 1,500 (submitted)
ATTENDEES: 5,000+
CONTACT: **J.P. Allen**

FILM TYPE
All types of short film

COMPETITIVE
Yes

LANGUAGE
Any, English subtitles

COUNTRY
Any

ENTRY FEES
$20 US

AWARDS
Cash prizes awarded to best film in the Animation, Comedy, Documentary, Drama and Experimental categories.

• Edinburgh International Film Festival

Edinburgh is the longest continually running film festival in the world celebrating its 52nd year in 1998. The different programs include "Galas' (feature premieres); "Rosebud" (premieres of innovative drama or documentary films): "Scene by Scene" (lectures by film-makers); "Retrospectives" and "Documentaries". Special activities include "Mirrorball" (music videos and related projects), "The Best Of The Fest", the "Surprise Film" and "Cinema Under The Stars". Each year they run the "New British Expo (NBX)" - an industry market place for every one of last year's UK productions.

FESTIVAL DATES
August 9-23, 1998

SUBMISSION DATES
May 22, 1998

ADDRESS
Filmhouse, 88 Lothian Road
Edinburgh EH3 9BZ
Scotland

TEL: 44-1-31-228-4051
FAX: 44-1-31-229-5501/6621
E-MAIL: info@edfilmfest.org.uk
WEB SITE: http://www.edfilmfest.org.uk/
ENTRIES: 250
ATTENDEES: 30,000
CONTACT: **Lizzie Francke**

FILM TYPE
All

COMPETITIVE
Yes

LANGUAGE
Any

COUNTRY
Any

ENTRY FEES
15 or 80 Pounds (also delegate fees)

AWARDS
The Best British Feature, Best Animation and Best New Film prizes are awarded each year.

● Odense International Film Festival

Odense is an independent short film festival with an international and national competition. Its goal is to showcase short films "with an original and imaginative sense of creative delight as found in the works of Hans Christian Andersen" (who was born in Odense). Admittance to the competitive films, as well as the retrospectives, are free to the public. After the festival's completion, certain films will be included in the "Best of Odense" programme which tours Denmark at non-commerical engagements.

FESTIVAL DATES
August 11-15, 1998 (tbc)
SUBMISSION DATES
May 1, 1998
ADDRESS
Vindegade 18
DK-5000 Odense C
Denmark

TEL: 45-6-613-1372 ext. 4044
FAX: 45-6-591-4318
E-MAIL: mag4kult@inet.uni-c.dk
CONTACT: **Helle Nielson**

FILM TYPE
Short (45 mins. or less)
COMPETITIVE
Yes
LANGUAGE
Any
COUNTRY
Any
ENTRY FEES
None

AWARDS
The jury awards include the Grand Prix for best film in the international competition (35 000 DKK), 2nd prize for most imaginative production (15,000 DKK), 3rd prize for Festival's most surprising film (15,000 DKK), 4th to 6th prizes are The Special Prizes of the Jury (5,000 DKK each) and they also award Diplomas of Merit.

● Chicago Underground Film Festival

Chicago Underground screens films that "should be" considered controversial by mainstream society. Aside from the "regular" films this event also includes special programs, parties, live entertainment and the Pink Flamingos panel discussion.

FESTIVAL DATES
August 12-16, 1998 (tbc)
SUBMISSION DATES
May 15, 1998
ADDRESS
2501 N. Lincoln Ave., Suite 278
Chicago, IL 60614
USA

TEL: (773) 866 8660
FAX: (773) 275 8313
E-MAIL: cuff@ripco.com
WEB SITE: http://www.deafear.com/cuff/
CONTACT: **Bryan Wendort**

FILM TYPE
All
COMPETITIVE
Yes
LANGUAGE
Any (English subtitles)
COUNTRY
Any
ENTRY FEES
$25 (60 min. or less); $35 (over 60 min.)

● Chichester Film Festival (UK)

This Festival has a wide-ranging program that was constructed to be attractive, not only to a core group of supporters, but also to the tourists in the Chichester area. There will be a strong European content in a mix of films from Great Britain, America and around the world. Every year this festival starts on the second Thursday in August and continues for 17 days ending on a Sunday.

FESTIVAL DATES
August 13-30, 1998 (tbc)
SUBMISSION DATES
June 30, 1998
ADDRESS
New Park Film Centre
New Park Road
Chichester, West Sussex PO 19 1XN
UK

FILM TYPE
All
COMPETITIVE
Yes
LANGUAGE
Any
COUNTRY
Any
ENTRY FEES
None

TEL:	44-1243-784 881
FAX:	44-1243-539 853
ENTRIES:	50-60
ATTENDEES:	3,000+
CONTACT:	**Roger Gibson**

● Weiterstadt Open Air Filmfest

This annual filmfest clearly sees its atmosphere and surroundings as its greatest asset. The festival takes place in the middle of a small forest where they show different short films on a 60 m outdoor screen. During the day, films and discussions also take place inside.

FESTIVAL DATES
August 13-17, 1998 (tbc)
SUBMISSION DATES
June 15, 1998
ADDRESS
Filmfest c/o J.Poliltt
Bahnhofstr 70
D-64331 Weiterstadt
Germany

FILM TYPE
All
COMPETITIVE
Yes
LANGUAGE
Any
COUNTRY
Any

TEL:	49-6150-12185/6
FAX:	49-6151-719721
ATTENDEES:	1,000/day
CONTACT:	**Mario Rempp**

● Norwegian International Film Festival (Haugesund)

This is an extremely popular and Norwegian film festival heavily attended by people involved in the film industry as well as international guests. Apart from the the films screened during the festival, it also boasts a Nordic Film Market.

FESTIVAL DATES
  August 14-22, 1998
ADDRESS
  P.O. Box 145
  5501 Haugesund
  Norway

TEL:	47-52 73 44 30
FAX:	47-52 73 44 20
E-MAIL:	haugfest@online.no
WEB SITE:	
ENTRIES:	1,500
ATTENDEES:	10,000
CONTACT:	**Gunmar Johan Lowik**

FILM TYPE
  Feature and Documentary
COMPETITIVE
  Yes
LANGUAGE
  Any
COUNTRY
  Any
ENTRY FEES
  $150

AWARDS
  Awards are called the "Amanda Statuettes".

● Denver Jewish Film Festival

The Denver Jewish Film Festival is a 5-day event that showcases films which contain Jewish themes or would be of interest to the Jewish people. Aside from the film screenings and discussions afterward, the festival also features a filmmaker's forum with industry members, critics etc.

FESTIVAL DATES
  August 15-19, 1998 (tbc)
SUBMISSION DATES
  June 15, 1998
ADDRESS
  350 South Dahlia Street
  Denver, CO 80206
  USA

TEL:	303-399-2660
FAX:	303-320-0042
E-MAIL:	jewishfilm@sni.net
WEB SITE:	http://www.sni.net/film/
ENTRIES:	12-14 (screened)
CONTACT:	**Evan Dechtman**

FILM TYPE
  All(must have jewish theme)
COMPETITIVE
  No
LANGUAGE
  Any (English subtitles)
COUNTRY
  Any
ENTRY FEES
  None

● International Animation Festival in Japan, Hiroshima

This biennial animation festival is one one the largest in the world. It is a competitive festival that accepts film/video only under 30 minutes. It also consists of special programs, exhibitions, a symposium, and a conference.

FESTIVAL DATES
August 20-24, 1998
SUBMISSION DATES
March 21, 1998
ADDRESS
4-17 Kako-machi,Naka-ku
Hiroshima 730
Japan

TEL:	81-82-245 0245
FAX:	81-82 245 0246
E-MAIL:	hiroanim@urban.or.jp
WEB SITE:	http://www.urban.or.jp/ home/hiroanim
ENTRIES:	1,000
ATTENDEES:	30,000
CONTACT:	**Sayoko Kinoshita**

FILM TYPE
Animation
COMPETITIVE
Yes
LANGUAGE
Any (English or Japanese subtitles)
COUNTRY
Any
ENTRY FEES
None

AWARDS
The official prizes of this festival are as follows: Grand Prize (1,000,000 yen), Hiroshima Prize (1,000,000 yen), Debut Prize (500,000 yen), Special International Jury Prize, and prizes for outstanding work.

● Austin Gay & Lesbian International Film Festival (aGLIFF)

aGLIFF showcases film & videos that must have lesbian, gay, bisexual or transgender subject matter. They encourage submissions from women, people of color as well as southwest regional filmmakers. The festival also includes a symposium on evolving gay & lesbian images in mainstream and independent films as well as a regional showcase of film and videos by filmmakers from the Southwest.

FESTIVAL DATES
August 21- Sept. 3, 1998 (tbc)
SUBMISSION DATES
July 19, 1998
ADDRESS
P.O. Box L
Austin, TX 78713
USA

TEL:	512 476-2454
FAX:	512 477-7982
E-MAIL:	AusGLFilm@aol.com
WEB SITE:	http://www.agliff.org/
CONTACT:	**Scott Dinger**

FILM TYPE
All
COMPETITIVE
Yes
LANGUAGE
Any
COUNTRY
Any
ENTRY FEES
$15US ($20 if to return)

AWARDS
Awards will be given for best Regional Film, Documentary, Narrative, Music Video, Boys' Short, Girls' Short, Festival Mission, and Audience Favorite. The winners will be announced at the aGLIFF Awards Party on the concluding night of the festival. There will also be a $1000 cash award presented to a community organization.

● Espoo Cine

Espoo showcases feature length and documentary films from around the world. Its features usually include the best new European films of that year. Since Espoo has featured good quality films on a consisted basis it has received a good reputation for quality.

FESTIVAL DATES
August 21-30, 1998 (tbc)

ADDRESS
Ahertajankuja 4, P.O. Box 95
Espoo 02100
Finland

TEL: 358-0-466-599
FAX: 358-0-466-458
ENTRIES: 100+
ATTENDEES: 19,000
CONTACT: **Laura Manki**

FILM TYPE
Feature and Documentary

COMPETITIVE
No

LANGUAGE
Any

COUNTRY
Any

ENTRY FEES
None

● Sao Paulo International Short Film Festival

São Paulo is a non-competitive showcase for international short film production and a leading event for the short in Latin America. It is also an international gathering in which the "...aesthetic, political, economic and existential experiences related to the short format" are expoused. A selection of films from the festival will be screened in Rio de Janeiro at the end of the festival (from August 28th to September 4th in 1997)

FESTIVAL DATES
August 20-29, 1998 (tbc)

ADDRESS
Associacao Cultural Kinoforumatt
Rua Cristiano Viana 907
05411-001 Sao Paulo Sp
Brazil

TEL: 55-11-85 29601
FAX: 55-211 85 29601
E-MAIL: spshort@ibm.net

WEB SITE:
http://www.estacao.ignet.com.br/kinoforum/sa
oshortfest/

FILM TYPE
Short

COMPETITIVE
No

LANGUAGE
Any (English, Portugese or Spanish subtitles)

COUNTRY
Any

● Student Film & Video Festival

This festival takes place during the first five days of Montreal World Film Festival. Its goal is to help discover new talents by presenting films and videos made by students from Canadian schools and universities within the framework of an international event.

FESTIVAL DATES
August 22-26, 1998
SUBMISSION DATES
June 6, 1998
ADDRESS
1432 de Bleury Street
Montréal, Québec H3A 2J1
Canada

TEL: 514-848 7187
FAX: 514-848 3886
E-MAIL: ffm@interlink.net
WEB SITE: http://www.ffm-montreal.org/
ENTRIES: 100+ screened
CONTACT: **Daniele Cauchard**

FILM TYPE
All
COMPETITIVE
Yes
LANGUAGE
English or French
COUNTRY
Canada
ENTRY FEES
$25

AWARDS
Awards are given out to the best films in the animation, documentary, experimental and fiction categories. An award for best video are given to entrees in the same categories. The overall winner is presented with the Norman McLaren Award.

● International Short Film Festival of Santiago (FICS)

FICS' augural year is 1997. Its aim is to support the development of the new world wide short film production. To this end it screens the films for industry people including directors and TV reps to help find potencial investors. The festival also helps the filmmakers with the distribution and marketing of their films. FICS' long term goal is "to become an information centre focused on helping all new creators in the search for the best alternatives to perfect their productions".

FESTIVAL DATES
August 24-29, 1998 (tbc)
SUBMISSION DATES
July 28, 1998
ADDRESS
Avenida Vicuña Mackenna 836 of.
41Santiago
Chile

TEL: 56-2 665 2732
FAX: 56-2 635 5737
E-MAIL: santiago@fics.cl
WEB SITE: http://www.fics.cl/

FILM TYPE
Short
COMPETITIVE
Yes
LANGUAGE
Any
COUNTRY
Any

AWARDS
The best short-film of each gender both in the National and International categories will be awarded prizes in US dollars.

● Venice International Film Festival

Venice, also known as the "Mostra" (short for Mostra Internazionale d'arte Cinematografica-Venice), is the oldest film festival worldwide. In 1995, it celebrated (as did film) its 100th anniversary. Its international jury is made up of industry professsionals that will judge and then present chosen films with awards. It is considered one of the four top festivals worldwide.

FESTIVAL DATES
August 26-September 5, 1998

ADDRESS
La biennale di Venezia, Ca, Giustnian
S Marco, I-Venice 30124
Italy

TEL: 39-41-521 8860
FAX: 39-41-520 0569
WEB SITE:
http://www.worldmedia.fr/cine/venice96/
ENTRIES: over 140 films screened
ATTENDEES: 100,000
CONTACT: **Dario Ventimiglia**

FILM TYPE
Feature, Short

COMPETITIVE
Yes

LANGUAGE
Any (Italian subtitles)

COUNTRY
Any

ENTRY FEES
None (film transportation)

AWARDS
The awards include the Golden Lion for best picture, Silver Lion, Grand Special Jury Prize, Golden Lion for Life Time Achievement and awards for best actor, actress, supporting actor and supporting actress.

● International Film Festival of Québec City

This festival screens films for a week at the end of the summer. Its films reflect various trends in worldwide production and are screened in theatres located in Québec City. Seminars, short film presentations and many other activites take place during the event.

FESTIVAL DATES
August 27-September 2, 1998

SUBMISSION DATES
July 3, 1998

ADDRESS
14 St. Denis St.
Office Building 3
Québec City, Québec G1R 4B5
Canada

TEL: 418-694 9920
FAX: 418-694 7290
ENTRIES: 50 screened
CONTACT: **Natasha Messier**

FILM TYPE
Feature

COMPETITIVE
No

LANGUAGE
Any (French & English subtitles)

COUNTRY
Any

ENTRY FEES
Contact festival

● Montreal World Film Festival

The goals of this festival are to encourage understanding among nations, to foster the art of cinematography, promote meetings in North America between cinema professionals from around the world, and to stimulate the development of the motion picture industry.

FESTIVAL DATES
August 27-September 7, 1998
SUBMISSION DATES
July 3, 1998
ADDRESS
1432 de Bleury Street
Montréal, Québec H3A 2J1
Canada

TEL: 514-848 3883
FAX: 514-848 3886
E-MAIL: ffm@Interlink.net
WEB SITE: http://www.ffm-montreal.org/
ENTRIES: 200+
ATTENDEES: 350,000
CONTACT: **Serge Losique**

FILM TYPE
All
COMPETITIVE
Yes
LANGUAGE
Any (French or English subtitles)
COUNTRY
Any
ENTRY FEES
None

AWARDS
The awards given to feature films include Grand Prix of the Americas (best film), "Prix de Montreal" (director of a first feature film), Best Director, Actress, Actor, Screenplay and Best Artistic Contribution (awarded to technician). The short film competition awards first and second prizes.

● 1 Reel Film Festival

1 Reel draws on the works of national independent artists working in short format. It showcases artists' talents as emerging filmmakers. Its goal is to pro-vide a unique arena in which to explore the collective vision of the art of film-making. It is part of Bumbershoot, the Seattle Arts Festival, which presents more than 500 artists in music, theatre, dance, visual and the literary arts. In 1997, Bumbershoot will be celebrating its 27th year and is expecting over 200,000 visitors. The festival runs every labour day long weekend.

FESTIVAL DATES
August 28-31, 1998
SUBMISSION DATES
May 5, 1998
ADDRESS
Bumbershoot 1998, PO Box 9750
Seattle, WA 98109-0750
USA

TEL: 206 622 5123
FAX: 206 281 7799
WEB SITE: http://www.onereel.org/film/
ENTRIES: 70 screened (300 submitted)
ATTENDEES: 10,000
CONTACT: **Corey Win**

FILM TYPE
Short(40 mins. or less)
LANGUAGE
English
COUNTRY
USA
ENTRY FEES
US$10

● Telluride Film Festival

Telluride is world-renowned for innovative programming of all film disci-
plines-past, present and future. It has the reputation as a friendly gathering
with close filmmaker contact in a spectacular setting. Its programs include a
tribute and students film section. It takes place each year over the Labour day
weekend.

FESTIVAL DATES
September 4-7, 1998
SUBMISSION DATES
June 1- July 31, 1998
ADDRESS
PO Box B1156
53 S. Main Street, Suite 212
Hanover, NH
USA

TEL: 603-643 1255
FAX: 603-643 5938
E-MAIL: Tellufilm@aol.com
WEB SITE:
http://www.telluridemm.com/filmfest.html
ENTRIES: 400+
ATTENDEES: 3,000
CONTACT: **Stella Pence**

FILM TYPE
All
COMPETITIVE
No
LANGUAGE
Any (English subtitles)
COUNTRY
Any
ENTRY FEES
Student $25; $35 (over 20 min); $55 (20-40 min);
$75 (over 40 min)

● Australian Film Festival
(Canberra, Hobart, Sydney, Melbourne, Brisbane, Adelaide, Perth)

The focus of this festival is to judge all nominated films for the annual AFI
awards. AFI members in the seven capitol cities attend screenings and vote
for their favorites.

FESTIVAL DATES
August-October, 1998 (national tour)
SUBMISSION DATES
June 31, 1998
ADDRESS
c/o Australian Film Institute
49 Eastern Road,3205
South Melbourne, Victoria
Australia

TEL: 61-3-9696 1844
FAX: 61-3-9696 7972
ENTRIES: 3,500-4,000
CONTACT: **Lindsay van Niekerk**

FILM TYPE
All
COMPETITIVE
Yes
LANGUAGE
Any
COUNTRY
Australia only
ENTRY FEES
$25 for AFI members

AWARDS
35 Film & TV awards

● Rio de Janeiro Film Festival (Mostra Rio)

Mostra Rio - Rio de Janeiro Film Festival (previously Banco Nacional Film Festival) has been, ever since its first year, 1989, the city's biggest cinematic event, and one of the most important in Brazil.

FESTIVAL DATES
Late August, 1998

ADDRESS
Rua Vluntarios da Patria 97
Rio de Janeiro 22270-000
Brazil

TEL: 55-21-286 8505
FAX: 55-21-286 4029
WEB SITE:
http://ibase.org.br/~estacao/tabu.htm
ENTRIES: 200
ATTENDEES: 70,000
CONTACT: **IIda Santiago**

FILM TYPE
All

● Cinecon

Cinecon was founded in 1964, and its emphasis is on film appreciation and restoration of silent and golden age films of Hollywood. Each year silent and golden age film features, shorts and/or newsreels are retrieved and restored. In 1997, Cinecon assisted the Library of Congress with "His Glorious Night" starring John Gilbert (the film that supposedly ruined his career),and "Wild Bill Hickok" starring William S. Hart. Neither film had previously been seen by the public since its original release.Cinecon runs every year during the labour day weekend.

FESTIVAL DATES
August 28-September 1, 1997
September 3-7, 1998

SUBMISSION DATES
August 14, 1998

ADDRESS
P. O. BOX 418
Rancho Mirage, CA 92270
USA

TEL: 760 770 9533
E-MAIL: cinecon@aol.com
WEB SITE:
http://www.mdle.com/ClassicFilms/Cinecon/33/
ENTRIES: 15+
ATTENDEES: 500+
CONTACT: **Kevin John Charbeneau**

FILM TYPE
All
COMPETITIVE
No
LANGUAGE
Any ("talkies" are always in english)
COUNTRY
Any
ENTRY FEES
$100 (membership fee for all events)

AWARDS
The festival honours actors and technical personnel, as well as film historians/archivists with the "Film Career Achievement Award". The film historians/archivists award (same is design)is called the "William K. Everson Award".

---

126   *Festival Products*

Brief Entries

● Asia Pacific International Film Festival

ADDRESS
c/AFC GPO Box 3984
Sydney, NSW 2001
Australia

TEL: 61-2-9951 6413
FAX: 61-2-9954 4001
CONTACT: **Peter Page**

● Brisbane International Film Festival

ADDRESS
Level 3, Hoyts Regent Building
167 Queen St. Mall, GPO Box 990
Brisbane Qld 4001
Austraila

FESTIVAL DATES
July/August, 1998
TEL: 61-7-3220-0333
FAX: 61-7-3220-0400
E-MAIL: brisfilm@thehub.com.au
CONTACT: **Anne Demy-Geroe**

● Children's International Film Festival in Artek

ADDRESS
8 Eisenshtein Street, Suite 204
Moscow 129226
Russia

TEL: 7-095-181 0451
FAX: 7-095-181 1841
CONTACT: **Marlen Knutziev**

● European Cinema Congress (Wiesbaden)

ADDRESS
D-65019, Wiesbaden, PO Box 2927
Wiesbaden
Germany

TEL: 49-611-72 34 48
FAX: 49-611-72 34 03
CONTACT: **Joachim Sperner**

● Johannesburg Film Festival

ADDRESS
8th Floor, Hallmark Towers
54 Siemert Road, PO Box 16427
Doornfontein 2028 Johannesburg
South Africa

TEL: 27-11-402 5477
FAX: 27-11-402 6646
CONTACT: **Len Davis**

● Window Into Europe in Vyborg

ADDRESS
15 Druzhinnikovskaya Street
Moscow 123242
Russia

TEL: 7-095-255 9647
CONTACT: **Marlen Khutziev**

● Australian International Film Festival

This festival takes place in Canerra each year in September. In showcases International and Australian feature films as well as Australian shorts. The latter must be on longer than 20 minutes. An award is given to the best short film voted on by the festival audience.

FESTIVAL DATES
September, 1997
September, 1998

SUBMISSION DATES
July 15, 1997
July 15, 1998

ADDRESS
PO Box 1
Belconnen ACT 2616
Australia

TEL:	61 6 201 2989
FAX:	61 6 201 5900
E-MAIL:	c.hope@students.canberra.edu.au
CONTACT:	**Cathy Hope**

FILM TYPE
Features and Australian shorts

COMPETITIVE
No

LANGUAGE
Any

COUNTRY
Any

ENTRY FEES
None

AWARDS
Best Short Film award voted on by the audience.

● Prix Italia (Bologna)

In 1998 Prix Italia will still be a competitive festival, but will take place for the first time in September. Music is important to this festival, and therefore one of the categories in the competitive secton deals strictly with music.

FESTIVAL DATES
September, 1998

SUBMISSION DATES
July, 1998

ADDRESS
Viale Mazzini 14
1-00195 Rome
Italy

TEL:	39-6-37 51 49 96
FAX:	39-6-361 3401
ENTRIES:	700
CONTACT:	**Diana Palma**

FILM TYPE
Documentary, Music, Fiction

COMPETITIVE
Yes

LANGUAGE
English, French or Italian

COUNTRY
Any

ENTRY FEES
2,550,000 Italian Lire

● Oldenburg International Film Festival

September

The OIFF is dedicated to showcasing a wide range of versatile and individual filmmaking. The different sections include the International Section (with grand premieres in the presence of internationally celebrated guests),Retrospective (honouring female directors with a distinctive voice and vision), Short Films (preceding the prime time screenings in the International Section), Spotlights (in 1997, The Netherlands), and Sidebars (showcasing the unexpected). In 1997, the sidebar section will be called "Dark Drives - Under the Seal of Suburbia."

FESTIVAL DATES
September 3-7, 1997
September 9-13, 1998
SUBMISSION DATES
June 30, 1997
June 30, 1998
ADDRESS
Gottorpstr. 626122
Oldenburg
Germany

FILM TYPE
All, but animation
COMPETITIVE
No
LANGUAGE
Any (German or English subtitles)
COUNTRY
Any
ENTRY FEES
None

TEL: 49 441 256 27/59
FAX: 49 441 261 55
E-MAIL: ritter@filmfest-oldenburg.de
WEB SITE: http://www.filmfest-oldenburg.de/
ENTRIES: 150 (50 screened)
ATTENDEES: 12,000
CONTACT: **Thorsten Ritter**

● Festival Internacional de Cinema (Figueria da Foz)

In 1997, the Figueira Da Foz festival will be celebrated its 26th year. The festival's two sections are the Official Section and Special Programmes. The former is competitive for all categories of film whereas the latter, in 1997, presented a homage to directors Werner Schroeter and Robert Guediguian as well as showcased Films from Japan. The jury is selected from the festival audience plus six directors and celebrities. Its films are chosen on the "criteria of expressive and aesthetic values and favors films with social, progressive themes".

FESTIVAL DATES
September 4-14, 1997
September 3-13, 1998

SUBMISSION DATES
July 5, 1997
July 5, 1998

ADDRESS
Apartado dos Correios 50407
1709 Lisboa Codex
Portugal

TEL:	351-1-812-6231
FAX:	351-1-812-6228
E-MAIL:	jose.marques@ficff.pt
WEB SITE:	http://www.ficff.pt/
ENTRIES:	500 (250 screened)
ATTENDEES:	20,000
CONTACT:	**Jose Vieira Marques**

FILM TYPE
All

COMPETITIVE
Yes

LANGUAGE
Any (Portuguese, English, French, Spanish or Italian subtitles)

COUNTRY
Any

ENTRY FEES
None

AWARDS
The Official Section has five competitive categories: Fiction Films, Images and Documents, Short Films (15 min. max.), Films for Children and Video. Grand Prizes are given out to a feature as well as a film in the Images and Documents category.

● Toronto International Film Festival

Toronto's reputation is second only to Cannes in the field of international film festivals. It also has the reputation of being attended by the highest number of non-industry film-goers of any festival. During the festival, a very well-attended media and industry symposium takes place, showcasing items related to the film industry. Other Toronto programs include Perspective Canada, Galas, Special Presentations, Contemporary World Cinema, Discovery, Planet Africa, Real to Reel , Midnight Madness, Dialogues, the Director's Spotlight and The Masters (new for 1997). Dialogues, which combines the screening of favorite films of well-known filmmakers with their own in-person discussions, has included David Cronenberg, Jonathan Demme, Hal Hartley, John Woo and Gena Rowlands in the past.

FESTIVAL DATES
September 4-13, 1997
September 3-12, 1998

SUBMISSION DATES
June 30, 1997
June 30, 1998

ADDRESS
2 Carlton St., Suite 1600
Toronto, Ontario M5B 1J3
Canada

TEL:	416-967 7371
FAX:	416 967 9477
WEB SITE:	http://www.bell.ca/filmfest/
ENTRIES:	300+ (screened)
ATTENDEES:	250,000+
CONTACT:	**Piers Handling**

FILM TYPE
All

COMPETITIVE
Yes (for Canadian features and shorts)

LANGUAGE
Any (English subtitles)

COUNTRY
Any

ENTRY FEES
None

AWARDS
The awards at Toronto include the NFB John Spotten Award for Best Canadian Short Film, Toronto -CITY Award for Best Canadian Feature Film, Air Canada Peoples Choice Award, Metro Media Award and the FIPRESCI Critics Award.

● Boston Film Festival

Boston is a non-competitive festival that runs for two weeks at the beginning of September. All films screened during the festival receive reviews that run the day of its festival screening as well as when the film is released theatrically.

FESTIVAL DATES
  September 5-18, 1997
  September, 1998
SUBMISSION DATES
  July 7, 1997 (2 months before festival)
  July, 1998
ADDRESS
  Box 516
  Hull, MA 02045
  USA

TEL: 617 925 1373
FAX: 617 925 3132
EENTRIES: 50+
ATTENDEES: 25,000+
CONTACT: **Susan Fraine**

FILM TYPE
  All
COMPETITIVE
  No
LANGUAGE
  Any
COUNTRY
  Any
ENTRY FEES
  $60 features, $30 shorts

● Deauville Festival of American Films

Deauville is a showcase for American feature-length studio films, focusing on summer releases and European premieres. It also includes a "panorama of U.S. productions", a competition, tributes, discussions, and parties. Many distributors and filmmakers frequent this 10-day festival.

FESTIVAL DATES
  September 5-14, 1997
  September 4-13, 1998 (tbc)
SUBMISSION DATES
  August 14, 1997
ADDRESS
  c/o Le pubilc Systeme Cinema, 36 rue Pierret
  F-92200 Neuilly-sur-Seine
  France

TEL: 33-1-46 40 55 06
FAX: 33-1-46 40 55 39
E-MAIL: publics@imaginnet.fl
WEB SITE: http://www.imaginet.fr/deauville-fest
ENTRIES: 35-40
ATTENDEES: 45,000
CONTACT: **Daniel Benzakein**

FILM TYPE
  Feature
COMPETITIVE
  Yes
LANGUAGE
  Any (must be made in U.S.)
COUNTRY
  USA
ENTRY FEES
  None

AWARDS
  Deauville awards the Grand Prix Spécial Deauville, Prix du Jury Spécial Deauville, Prix de la Critique, Prix du Public and Trophée Fun Radio.The competition includes at least 10 independent films.

● Festival of Fantastic Films (Manchester)

September

Fantastic Films is a "fun-packed" weekend of 35 films spanning 100 years. There is an Independent Film Competition and advice from some of the industry's best directors. There is also interview/signing sessions for guests, an all-weekend video show, a Breakfast "Serial", panel discussions, 3D films, a magician and an F/X model & miniature exhibition. In 1997 a series has been put together with the Vampire Society "to celebrate the centenary of the publication of Dracula & the 40th anniversary of the Hammer Dracula Movie".

FESTIVAL DATES
  September 5-7, 1997
  September 4-6, 1998 (tbc)
SUBMISSION DATES
  July 31, 1997
  July 31, 1998
ADDRESS
  33 Barrington Road
  Altrincham, Cheshire WA14 1HZ
  UK

FILM TYPE
  Fantasy based films
COMPETITIVE
  Yes
LANGUAGE
  Any (English subtitles)
COUNTRY
  Any

TEL: 44-161-929 1423
FAX: 44-161-929 1067
E-MAIL: 101341.3352@compuserve.com
ENTRIES: 4 new/ 35 overall
ATTENDEES: 1,000+
CONTACT: **Gil Lane-Young**

● Tacoma Tortured Artists Film Festival

Tortured Artists is designed to nurture and support independent filmmakers by giving their work a place to be seen and by thus supplying needed feedback from audiences and members of the film industry.

FESTIVAL DATES
  September 6,12-13, 1997
  September, 1998
SUBMISSION DATES
  July 31, 1997
  July 31, 1998
ADDRESS
  Club 7 Productions
  728A Pacific Ave
  Tacoma, WA 98402
  USA

FILM TYPE
  All
COMPETITIVE
  Yes
LANGUAGE
  Any
COUNTRY
  Any
ENTRY FEES
  $20 (30 mins. or less); $30 (over 30 mins.)

AWARDS
  The festival awards a trophy and accommodations.

TEL: 206 5915894
FAX: 206 5912013
E-MAIL: C7P@aol.com
CONTACT: **Courtney Ferguson/ James Hume**

● Focus on Asia Fukuoka International Film Festival

The goal of this festival is to deepen citizens' understanding towards other Asian countries and to promote cultural and international exchange at the civilian level through excellent Asian films. This cultural event occurs every year in September.

FESTIVAL DATES
September 12-21, 1997
September 11-20, 1998
SUBMISSION DATES
May 1, 1997
May 1, 1998
ADDRESS
Executive Committee Office, 1-8-1 Tenjin
Chuo-ku, Fukuoka 810
Japan

FILM TYPE
Feature
COMPETITIVE
No
LANGUAGE
Asian and English subtitles
COUNTRY
Asian countries and regions
ENTRY FEES
None

TEL: 81-92-733 5170
FAX: 81-92-733 5595
ENTRIES: 20
ATTENDEES: 20,000
CONTACT: **Tadao Sato**

● Gladys Crane Mountain Plains Film Festival

The Gladys Crane Mountain Plains Film Festival is a new festival and will feature a new theme each year. In 1997, the theme is new films that deal with contemporary western themes and/or modern western landscapes which fall into the category of "Expanding the Western Vision". This event will also include guest artists, book and autograph signings, a discussion with old Cowboys talk about making movies, and "Hazard of the Game", a short section on stunt men.

FESTIVAL DATES
September 12-14, 1997
September 11-13, 1998 (tbc)
SUBMISSION DATES
March 1, 1997
March 1, 1998
ADDRESS
PO Box 3951
Laramie, WY 82071
USA

FILM TYPE
Feature, Documentary
COMPETITIVE
No
LANGUAGE
Any
COUNTRY
Any
ENTRY FEES
Contact festival

TEL: 307 766 6666
FAX: 307 766 2197
WEB SITE:
http://www.uwyo.edu/a&s/th&d/uwfilmfesti-val.html
CONTACT: **Harry Woods**

● The British Short Film Festival

A competitive festival for all British and International short films (up to 40 mins.) in all categories. There will also be a selection of films from Scandinavia, classic work from Australian directors and a display of the latest experimental work for France.

FESTIVAL DATES
September, 1997
Mid-September, 1998

SUBMISSION DATES
June 9, 1997
June 9, 1998

ADDRESS
Room 313, BBC Threshold House
65-59 Shepherd's Bush Green
London W12 7RJ
UK

TEL:	44-181-743 8000 ext. 62222
FAX:	44-181-740 8540
ENTRIES:	2,000+
CONTACT:	**Sophie Djian**

FILM TYPE
Short

COMPETITIVE
Yes

LANGUAGE
Any (English subtitles)

COUNTRY
Any

ENTRY FEES
None

● Cinefest - The Sudbury Film Festival

Since its inception in 1989, Cinefest has been able to stay true to its mandate of programming a wide range of Canadian and international films. Each year the festival has grown in popularity and size; this year, over 100 films will be screened in 6 days.

FESTIVAL DATES
September 16-21, 1997
September 15-20, 1998

SUBMISSION DATES
August 30, 1997
August 30, 1998

ADDRESS
218-40 Elm Street
Sudbury, Ontario P3C 1S8
Canada

TEL:	705-688 1234
FAX:	705-688 1351
E-MAIL:	cinefest@vianet.on.ca
WEB SITE:	http://www.cinefest.com/
ENTRIES:	100
ATTENDEES:	20,000
CONTACT:	**Tammy Frick**

FILM TYPE
All

COMPETITIVE
Yes

LANGUAGE
Any (English subtitles)

COUNTRY
Any

AWARDS
Awards given for Best Canadian Feature Film, Best Ontario Feature Film, Best Canadian Short Film, and Best International Feature Film.

● LUCAS - International Children and Young People's Film Festival (Frankfurt & Main)

LUCAS focuses on cinema for children and young people. Their discussion tables, evening meeting and,more importantly, the possibility for informal talks with experienced members of the film industry are turning this festival into a world renowned industry event.

FESTIVAL DATES
  Mid-September, 1997
  Mid-September, 1998

ADDRESS
  Deutsches Filmmuseum
  Schaumainkai 41
  D-60596 Frankfurt am Main
  Germany

TEL: 49-69-2123 88 35
FAX: 49-69-21 23 78 81
ENTRIES: 15 (in competition)
ATTENDEES: 5,000
CONTACT: **Walter Schobert**

FILM TYPE
  Feature
COMPETITIVE
  Yes
LANGUAGE
  Any
COUNTRY
  Any
ENTRY FEES
  None

● Umea International Film Festival

Umea is the largest film festival in Northern Scandinavia. It has also gained a considerable international reputation as a gateway for film distribution to Sweden and the Nordic countries.

FESTIVAL DATES
  September 17-24, 1997
  September 16-23, 1998

ADDRESS
  PO Box 43
  S-90102 Umea
  Sweden

TEL: 46-90-13 33 56/13 33 88
FAX: 46-90-77 79 61
ENTRIES: 250
ATTENDEES: 25,000-30,000
CONTACT: **Thom Palmen**

FILM TYPE
  All
COMPETITIVE
  Yes
LANGUAGE
  Any (English subtitles)
COUNTRY
  Any
ENTRY FEES
  None

● Breckenridge Festival of Film

A notable part of Breckenridge's charm is the relaxed atmosphere between guests and film-goers. This is largely achieved by the access film-goers have to the writers, directors, producers, actors and actresses at informal sessions after screenings, at receptions, and at outdoor film forums.

FESTIVAL DATES
September 18-21, 1997
September 17-20, 1998 (tbc)
SUBMISSION DATES
June 30, 1997
ADDRESS
Riverwalk Centre
150 W Adams, PO Box 718
Breckenridge, CO 80424
USA

TEL: 970-453 6200
FAX: 970-453 2692
E-MAIL: filmfest@brecknet.com
WEB SITE:
http://www.brecknet.com/bff/home.html
ENTRIES: 35-55
ATTENDEES: 2,500+
CONTACT: **Julie Bullock**

FILM TYPE
All
COMPETITIVE
No
LANGUAGE
Any
COUNTRY
Any
ENTRY FEES
$35 US

● International Student Animation Festival of Ottawa (SAFO)

In 1997, the first International Student Animation Festival, a biennial event, will be held in Ottawa. Aside from film screening, the festival's programmes will include: an official competition, school retrospectives and tribute screenings, professional development workshops and panels, an animarket trade fair, Chez-Ani (the animator's rendez-vous and informal screening room), special events, and opening and closing ceremonies.

FESTIVAL DATES
September 18-21 1997
ADDRESS
2 Daly Ave., Suite 120
Ottawa, Ontario K1N 6E2
Canada

TEL: 613 232 8769
FAX: 613 232 6315
E-MAIL: oiaf@ottawa.com
WEB SITE: http://oiaf.ottawa.com/
CONTACT: **Chris Robinson**

FILM TYPE
Student animation
COMPETITIVE
Yes
LANGUAGE
Any (English & French offical languages)
COUNTRY
Any

AWARDS
Cash prizes will be awarded to the prizewinners.

● San Sebastian International Film Festival

Twenty films take part in the official section's competition. Only films that have not been screened at another IFFPA recognized festival can be entered. The festival "aims at promoting better understanding between nations and making a positive contribution to the development of culture and the moving image industries". Other sections of competition include one for best Spanish and South American films of the year as well as one for new directors. The winner of the New Director's Prize is awarded 25 million pesetas (approx. US$200,000), which is split between the director and producer.

FESTIVAL DATES
  September 18-27, 1997
  September 17-26, 1998 (tbc)

SUBMISSION DATES
  July 30, 1997
  July 30, 1998

ADDRESS
  Plaza de Oqendo s/n
  20004 San Sebastian
  Spain

TEL: 34-43-48 12 12
FAX: 34-43-48 12 18
E-MAIL: ssiff@mail.ddnet.es
WEB SITE: http://www.ddnet.es/san_sebast-
ian_film_festival/
ENTRIES: 200+ screened
ATTENDEES: 125,000
CONTACT: **Diego Galan**

FILM TYPE
  All

COMPETITIVE
  Yes

LANGUAGE
  Any (Spanish subtitles)

COUNTRY
  Any

ENTRY FEES
  None

AWARDS
  The prizes include the Concha de Oro for the best film; Special Jury Prize; Concha de Plata to the best director; Concha de Plata to the best actor (female & male); Jury Prize to the best photography; Jury Prize to highlight any other technical or artistic aspect considered deserving by the Jury, and the New Directors' Prize.

● Atlantic Film Festival (Halifax)

Atlantic premieres new work from the Atlantic region and Canada. Other programs include International Perspectives (a selection of fine films from Celtic and Nordic countries as well as the US), Canadian Perspectives; Different Takes: The Industry Series, The Late Shift and the special children's series, ScreenScene, which presents quality films for children and teens as well as presenting seminars and workshops on film production and media education.

FESTIVAL DATES
  September 19-27, 1997
  September 18-26, 1998 (tbc)
SUBMISSION DATES
  June 13 , 1997
  Mid-June, 1998
ADDRESS
  PO Box 36139
  Halifax, Nova Scotia B3J 3E9
  Canada

TEL: 902-422 3456
FAX: 902-422 4006
E-MAIL: aff@screen.com
WEB SITE: http://www.screen.com/atlantic-film.html
ENTRIES: 200
ATTENDEES: 12,000
CONTACT: **Gord Whittaker**

FILM TYPE
  All
COMPETITIVE
  Yes
LANGUAGE
  Any (English subtitles)
COUNTRY
  Any (mainly Atlantic Canada & North Atlantic rim)
ENTRY FEES
  $25-$95 (discounts for members)
AWARDS
  The Movie Network's People's Choice Award for Best Feature; Best Canadian film or video over 60 minutes ($2,500) and under 60 minutes ($1,000); Best Atlantic Short Film or Video under 60 mins. ($10,000); The William F. Moonsnail Awards ($1,000 each to chosen director, cinematographer, writer, editor, art director, sound and actor-female, male); Casablanca sound prize; the Rex Tasker Award for best documentary ($1,500); the Margaret Perry Award for Best Nova Scotia Produced Film ($2,500); the Linda Joy Busby Media Arts Society Awards and the Gordon Parsons Children's Choice Awards.

● Cheyenne Western Film Festival

Cheyenne's mandate is to showcase American Westerns as well as to preserve old Western films and serials. The festival is a three-day event which features film screening at different theatres, talks and autograph sessions with actors, western activities (gun tricks, roping, etc.), musical entertainment, an exhibit with various trade tables, and an authentic western shoot-out performance. In 1997, there will also be an auction for lunch with visiting celebrities.

FESTIVAL DATES
  September 19-21, 1997
  September 18-20, 1998
ADDRESS
  PO 1941
  Cheyenne, WY 82003
  USA

TEL: 307-635 4646
FAX: 307-638 7419
WEB SITE: http://www.wyoming.com/~western/festival.htm
ENTRIES: 4-6
ATTENDEES: 1,000
CONTACT: **Wendy Pette**

FILM TYPE
  US Westerns
LANGUAGE
  English
COUNTRY
  USA

● Festival international du cinema francophone en Acadie

The main goal of this festival is the promotion of new francophone productions from Canada and around the world. This festival showcases as many short films as feature in any one category. The festival's 10th anniversary in 1996 has resulted in the broadening of the entire festival's programming.

FESTIVAL DATES
September 19-25, 1997
September 18-24, 1998 (tbc)
SUBMISSION DATES
July 5, 1997
July 5, 1998
ADDRESS
140 Botsford Street, Suite 28
Moncton, New Brunswick E1C 4X4
Canada

FILM TYPE
All
COMPETITIVE
Yes
LANGUAGE
French
COUNTRY
Any Francophone production from around the world

TEL:	506-855 6050
FAX:	506-857 8002
E-MAIL:	filmzone@istar.ca
ENTRIES:	1,000 submitted (130 screened)
ATTENDEES:	8,000
CONTACT:	**Judith Hamel**

● Helsinki Film Festival - Love and Anarchy

Love and Anarchy's goal is to screen quality controversial films from around the world to Finnish audiences, distributors and visitors. The most important factors in the selection procedure for this festival are "unconventional concepts and daring cinematographic execution" . In 1996, over 80 Scandinavavian and/or Finnish premieres took place in five downtown venues, thus turning the capitol of Finland into a film lovers paradise.

FESTIVAL DATES
September 19-25, 1997
September 25-Oct. 1, 1998 (tbc)
SUBMISSION DATES
June 30, 1997
June 30, 1998
ADDRESS
Unioninkatu 10
SF-00130 Helsinki
Finland

FILM TYPE
All
COMPETITIVE
No
LANGUAGE
Any (English subtitles)
COUNTRY
Any
ENTRY FEES
None

TEL:	358-9-639 528
FAX:	358-9-631 450
E-MAIL:	la@cultnet.fi
WEB SITE:	http://love_and_anarchy.cultnet.fi/
ENTRIES:	300 submitted (95 screened)
ATTENDEES:	25,000
CONTACT:	**Jaana Siltala**

● Carrousel International du Film de Rimouski

Carrousel is a cornerstone of international exchange in youth cinema. With thousands of spectators from around the world, this festival is able to carry out its mission of "initiating young people into cinema".

FESTIVAL DATES
September 21-28, 1997
September 20-27, 1998

SUBMISSION DATES
May 19, 1997
May 19, 1998

ADDRESS
10 Eveche East, PO Box 1462
Rimouski, Québec G5L 8M3
Canada

TEL: 418-722 0103
FAX: 418-724 9504
ATTENDEES: 20,000
CONTACT: **Sylvie Blanchette**

FILM TYPE
All, documentary

COMPETITIVE
Yes

LANGUAGE
Any

COUNTRY
Any

ENTRY FEES
None

AWARDS
This festival awards the "Camèrio" in six different categories. These are for best short, feature and animatied film as well as for best actor, actress and best film.

● Aspen Filmfest

Aspen Filmfest is now a six day event which takes place the last Tuesday-Sunday of the month of September. Its focus is on American Independents, foreign features, and documentaries as well as in- person tributes and special presentations. Its mandate is to present the latest narrative and documentary features.

FESTIVAL DATES
September 23-28, 1997
September 22-27, 1998

SUBMISSION DATES
July 11, 1997
July 10, 1998

ADDRESS
110 E Hallam, Suite 102
Aspen, CO 81611
USA

TEL: 970-925 6882
FAX: 970-925 1967
E-MAIL: geldred@aspenfilm.org
WEB SITE: http://www.aspen.com/filmfest/
ENTRIES: 375 (25 screened)
ATTENDEES: 6,000+
CONTACT: **George Eldred**

FILM TYPE
Feature, documentaries

COMPETITIVE
No

LANGUAGE
Any (English subtitles)

COUNTRY
Any

ENTRY FEES
$20

● Films From The South

Films From the South considers itself an audience festival with a combined approach to distribution. Its goal "is to broaden the filmgoing habits of Norwegian audiences beyond productions from Europe and the US, to include films of high artistic standards from other parts of the world."

FESTIVAL DATES
Last week in September, 1997
Last week in September, 1998
SUBMISSION DATES
July 15, 1997
July 15, 1998
ADDRESS
Fredensborgveien 39
N-0177 Oslo
Norway

FILM TYPE
All
COMPETITIVE
No
LANGUAGE
English, Danish, Norwegian or Swedish subtitles
COUNTRY
Africa, Asia or Latin America
ENTRY FEES
None

TEL:	47-22 36 07 18
FAX:	47-22-36 22 80/85 76 98
ENTRIES:	35
ATTENDEES:	4,000
CONTACT:	**Brynjar Bjerkem**

● International Children Animation Festival "Goldfish"

Goldfish screens animated films by children and professional studios. The former must be no longer than 30 minutes whereas the latter can be up to 60 minutes. Its goal " is to further contacts between the childrens animation artists from different countries". The festival is frequented by Russian film directors and animators.

FESTIVAL DATES
September, 1998
SUBMISSION DATES
May 10, 1998
ADDRESS
Ulitsa Koroleva 12, Office 3-6
Moscow 127 000
Russia

FILM TYPE
Animation
COMPETITIVE
Yes
LANGUAGE
Any
COUNTRY
Any

TEL:	7 095 217 71 09
FAX:	7 095 217 76 36/978 54 16
WEB SITE:	

http://www.awn.com/goldfish/index.html

CONTACT:	**Lorna Gauthier-Villars**

● Riminicinema Mostra Internazionale

September

The festival focuses its attention on displaced,wandering filmmakers and con-
taminated cinema,originating from the relationships and the exchanges
between different cultures and peoples. In 1998 there may be a major change
in the festivals size, focus as well as date.

September 23-28, 1997

SUBMISSION DATES
August 10, 1997

ADDRESS
Via Gambalunga 27
I-47037 Rimini
Italy

TEL: 39-541-26399/22627
FAX: 39-541-24227
ENTRIES: 60 (selected)
ATTENDEES: 10,000
CONTACT: **Gianfranco Miro Gori**

FILM TYPE
Feature

COMPETITIVE
Yes

LANGUAGE
Any (English or French subtitles)

COUNTRY
Any

ENTRY FEES
None

AWARDS
The Golden and Silver "R" worth
15,000,000 Lira and 5,000,000 Lira, respectively.

142   *Festival Products*

● Dutch Film Festival (Utrecht)

This is one of the most important annual film events in the Netherlands. Simultaneous to this festival, the Holland Film Meeting (three days) is scheduled which showcases to an international audience of professionals the recent Dutch film and TV productions. The programs featured at the Dutch Film Festival include Retrospectives, Seminars, live TV talk-shows and the "Cinema Militans Leature".

FESTIVAL DATES
  September/October, 1997
  September/October, 1998

ADDRESS
  Hoogt 4
  NL-3512 GW Utrecht
  The Netherlands

TEL:	31-30-322 684
FAX:	31-30-313 200
E-MAIL:	nedfilmfest@artnet.intouch.nl
WEB SITE:	http://www.dru.nl/nedfilmfest/
CONTACT:	**Jacques van Heyningen**

FILM TYPE
  Feature and Short film (in competition)

COMPETITIVE
  Yes

AWARDS
  The Golden Calf awards are out in eleven different categories.

● FilmFest Hamburg

FilmFest Hamburg is an important meeting point for distributors and exhibitors from all over the world. It screens the best of any given year's international films from Europe, Asia, Hollywood, and US Independents. It is also a popular festival for art-house exhibitors and is a perfect venue for launching an independent project. Its films are screened in five theatres on a total of ten screens.

FESTIVAL DATES
  September 25-October 2, 1997
  September 24-Oct. 1, 1998

SUBMISSION DATES
  July 1, 1997
  July 1, 1998

ADDRESS
  Friedensalee 1
  D-22765 Hamburg
  Germany

TEL:	49-40-39826 210
FAX:	49-40-39826 211
E-MAIL:	Filmfest-Hamburg@t-online.de
WEB SITE:	http://www.filmfesthamburg.de/
ENTRIES:	120-150
ATTENDEES:	30,000
CONTACT:	**Josef Wutz**

FILM TYPE
  All

COMPETITIVE
  No

LANGUAGE
  Any (German or English subtitles)

COUNTRY
  Any

AWARDS
  The Douglas Sirk Lifetime Award is given to honour a member a the film industry who has made a genuine contribution to international film.

● Black Filmworks Festival of Film and Video

Black Filmworks opening and closing nights are usually held in the historic Paramount theatre which holds over 2,700 people. Since this event is also a competition and awards ceremony, only the present year's award winners are screened. Their mandate is "to discover, encourage and assist in expanding opportunities for Black filmmakers who address the rich complexity and variety of Black culture". To enter a film into this festival a black person must be either the producer, director or writer.

FESTIVAL DATES
September 26-27; October 3-4, 1997
September/October, 1998 (tbc)

SUBMISSION DATES
July 23, 1997 (early); August 1, 1997 (late)
July 23, 1997 (early); August 1, 1997 (late)

ADDRESS
Black Filmmakers Hall of Fame
405 14th Street, Suite 515
Oakland, CA 94612
USA

TEL:	510-465 0804
FAX:	510-839 9858
WEB SITE:	http://www.pagelist.com/bfhfi/
ENTRIES:	33-50
ATTENDEES:	5,000+
CONTACT:	**Dorothy Karvi**

FILM TYPE
All

COMPETITIVE
Yes

LANGUAGE
Any (English subtitles)

COUNTRY
Any

ENTRY FEES
$25-32

AWARDS
In each of over 10 categories their are 3 prizes awarded. These categories include Feature, Documentary, Comedy, Short, Animation, Health, Student, etc. The 1st, 2nd, and 3rd place film, overall, will receive a cash prize of $1,500, $750 and $500 dollars, respectively.

● Central Florida Film & Video Festival

The Central Florida Film & Video Festival will be celebrating its 16th year in 1997, making it the oldest festival of its kind in the state of Florida. Its goal is to "'showcase the discovery of new and emerging artists from the United States and around the world". This eleven day festival also presents art exhibitions which include performances by local artists, musicians, as well as fashion shows, and film related seminars.

FESTIVAL DATES
September 26-Oct 3, 1997
September 25-Oct 2, 1998 (tbc)

SUBMISSION DATES
June 9, 1997 (late entries by July 1 add $15)

ADDRESS
15 1/2 N. Eola Dr., Suite 5
Orlando, FL 32801
USA

TEL:	407 839 6045
FAX:	407 839 6045
E-MAIL:	jneff@magicnet.net
WEB SITE:	http://www.cffvf.org:/
ENTRIES:	140+ screened
ATTENDEES:	2,000+
CONTACT:	**Brenda Joyner**

FILM TYPE
All

COMPETITIVE
Yes

LANGUAGE
Any (English subtitles)

COUNTRY
Any

ENTRY FEES
$20US (Florida filmmakers); $30 (under 30 mins.); $35 (30-60 mins.); $40 (over 60 mins.)

AWARDS
Awards will be given to top finishers in the categories of narrative, experimentals, documentaries, animation, music video and features. Additional awards may be presented outside a particular category if the judges see fit to do so. The film/video awarded Best of the Show will receive the HammerCam Award. Cash prizes ranging from $100-$500US dollars will be presented to each winning filmmaker who attends the festival as well as hotel accommodation for two days. Unattending award winners will be sent award and cash equivalent.

● Cinesation

Cinesation is a non-profit organization for the presentation and preservation of vintage motion pictures. It shows 25 hours of movies, 1/2 of them silent and 90% of the show is 35mm. The films screened are from 1915 to the1950's.

FESTIVAL DATES
September 26-28, 1997
September 25-27, 1998 (tbc)
ADDRESS
PO Box 352
Frankenmuth, MI 48734
USA

TEL: 517-652 8881
FAX: 517-652 9699
E-MAIL: Cinesation@aol.com
WEB SITE:
http://www.mdle.com/ClassicFilms/Cinesation
ENTRIES: 25 hours
ATTENDEES: 200+
CONTACT: **Dennis Atkinson**

FILM TYPE
All (primarily feature & short)
COMPETITIVE
No
LANGUAGE
Any (primary English)
COUNTRY
Any
ENTRY FEES
$45 (for the weekend)

● Festival International du Film Francophone (Namur)

During its eight days, the Festival attracts film professionals, cinemaphiles and many other spectators. Included are symposiums, animation, and premiers from the four corners of La Francophonie. This event occurs each year at the end of September.

FESTIVAL DATES
September 26-Oct. 4, 1997 (tbc)
End of September, 1998
SUBMISSION DATES
September 1, 1997
September 1, 1998
ADDRESS
175 Rue des Brasseurs
B-5000 Namur
Belgium

TEL: 32-64-22-48 28/45 04
FAX: 32-81 22 43 84
WEB SITE: http://www.ciger.be/namur/evenements/fiff95/index.html
ENTRIES: 150
ATTENDEES: 28,000
CONTACT: **Andre Ceuterick**

FILM TYPE
All
COMPETITIVE
Yes
LANGUAGE
French (or member of "L'Espace Francophone")
COUNTRY
Member of "L'Espace Francophone" (47 countries)
ENTRY FEES
None

AWARDS
14 films compete for the Bayards d'Or awarded to writers as well as actors.

● New York Film Festival

New York is over thirty years old with an excellent reputation of screening international films of high quality. Interestingly enough, New York does not screen a large amount of films like other festivals(i.e., Cannes and Toronto screen over 200 films any given year), but prefers to keep the number down to around thirty. This presents the opportunity to showcase the films chosen for the festival, and gives them extensive media coverage. In the past this festival has screened Bernardo Bertolucci's LAST TANGO IN PARIS(1972), Akira Kurosawa's RAN (1985), Quentin Tarantino's PULP FICTION (1994), SECRETS & LIES and THE PEOPLE VS LARRY FLYNT (1996). It has spotlighted such acclaimed directors as Jean-Luc Godard, the Taviani Brothers, David Mamet, Martin Scorsese and Krzysztof Kieslowski.

FESTIVAL DATES
September 26-Oct. 12, 1997
September 25-Oct. 11,1998
SUBMISSION DATES
June, 1997 (approx.)
June, 1998 (approx.)
ADDRESS
70 Lincoln Centre Plaza
New York, NY 10023-6595
USA

FILM TYPE
All
COMPETITIVE
Yes
LANGUAGE
Any
COUNTRY
Any
ENTRY FEES
None

TEL:	212-875 5610
FAX:	212-875 5636
E-MAIL:	FSLCPress@aol.com
ENTRIES:	1300 (approx. 30 screened)
ATTENDEES:	55,000
CONTACT:	**Richard Pena**

● University Film & Video Assosiation Student Film & Video Festival-UFVA

The mandate of the UFVA Film & Video Festival is to exhibit the very best in current student film & video worldwide, emphasizing independence, creativity, and new approaches to visual medium. The Festival has grown to become the largest student festival in the world and the only student festival in the USA which is truly international in scope, and features a traveling exhibition. Its annual conference takes place in August where the films chosen for that year are previewed. The premiere occurs in September at the International House in Philadelphia and the International

FESTIVAL DATES
September 26-28, 1997
September, 1998
SUBMISSION DATES
May 31, 1997
May 31, 1998
ADDRESS
Department of Film & Media Arts
Temple University 011-00
Philadelphia, PA 19122
USA

FILM TYPE
All
COMPETITIVE
Yes
LANGUAGE
Any (English subtitles)
COUNTRY
Any
ENTRY FEES
$15-20 (US school); $10-15 (outside US or member)
AWARDS
UFVA will award 1st, 2nd, and 3rd prize and honorable mentions in each of four categories, as well as, a Directors Choice award. First prize winners in each category: $1000 product grant from Kodak Worldwide Student Program.

TEL:	215-923-3532 ; 800-499-UFVA (in US)
FAX:	215-204-6740
E-MAIL:	ufva@vm.temple.edu
WEB SITE:	thunder.ocis.temple.edu/~ddoyon/
ENTRIES:	37 screened
CONTACT:	**Denis Doyon**

● Vancouver International Film Festival

The programs that this festival focuses on are "Dragons & Tigers: Cinema of East Asia", Canadian Images, Non-Fiction features (documentaries) and the Annual Film & Television Trade Forum. This forum lasts 4 days and is attended by professionals in the industry from all over the world.

FESTIVAL DATES
September 26-October 12, 1997
September 25-October 11, 1998 (TBC)
SUBMISSION DATES
July 2 (Canadian), July 15 (International), 1997
Mid-July, 1998
ADDRESS
1008 Homer Street, Suite 410
Vancouver, British Columbia V6B 2X1
Canada

TEL:	604-685 0260
FAX:	604-688 8221
E-MAIL:	viff@viff.org
WEB SITE:	http://viff.org/viff/
ENTRIES:	300 screened
ATTENDEES:	125,000
CONTACT:	**Alan Franey**

FILM TYPE
All
COMPETITIVE
No
LANGUAGE
Any
COUNTRY
Any
ENTRY FEES
None

AWARDS
Awards include Most Popular Canadian Film, Dragon and Tiger Award for Young Cinema ($5,000), Best Canadian Screenplay ($3,000), as well as an award by the National Film Board for Best Documentary ($1,500) and Best Animation ($500).

● Neighbours Haifa International Film Festival

Haifa's goal is to promote cultural knowledge of cinema from the Mediterranean Basin. This event facilitates exchanges, symposia and studies of the common features linking these filmmaking traditions, in a spirit of tolerance and coexistence. Also, it promotes the acquisition of films for commercial distribution. Haifa's programs include a panorama, New Israeli Cinema, retrospectives, and Mute Cinema.

FESTIVAL DATES
September, 1997
September, 1998
SUBMISSION DATES
July, 1997
July, 1998
ADDRESS
142 Hanassi Boulevard
Haifa 34633
Israel

TEL:	972-4-838 3424
FAX:	972-4-838 4327
ATTENDEES:	25,000
CONTACT:	**Pnina Blayer**

FILM TYPE
All
COMPETITIVE
Yes
LANGUAGE
Any
COUNTRY
Any
ENTRY FEES
None

AWARDS
Haifa has the "Golden Anchor" competition which awards $25,000 to the film judged best by an international jury. The film must be feature length, produced during the two years previous to its entry date, the director or writer must be from the Mediterranean Basin and a country involved in the films production must lie along the Mediterranean Basin.

● Ottawa International Animation Festival

Ottawa is a biennial, competitive event held every even numbered year in Canada's national capital, Ottawa. The sections this festival includes are, retrospective programs, workshops, the World Famous Animators picnic, Chez-Ani, outdoor screenings and a mini-animation trade fair.

FESTIVAL DATES
September 29-Oct 4, 1998
SUBMISSION DATES
July, 1998
ADDRESS
2 Daly Avenue, Suite 140
Ottawa, Ontario K1N 6E2
Canada

TEL: 613-232 8769
FAX: 613-232-6315
E-MAIL: oiaf@ottawa.com
WEB SITE: http://oiaf.ottawa.com/
ENTRIES: 1,000
ATTENDEES: 30,000
CONTACT: **Chris Robinson**

FILM TYPE
Animation
COMPETITIVE
Yes
LANGUAGE
Any (English or French subtitles)
COUNTRY
Any
ENTRY FEES
None

AWARDS
The awards include a Grand Prize as well as a UNICEF Prize.

Brief Entries

● Arsenals International Film Forum (Riga)

ADDRESS
Marstalu 14, Box 626
Riga LV 1047
Latvia

TEL: 371-2-221620
FAX: 371-7-820445
E-MAIL: vaiva@krasta.org.lv
CONTACT: **Augusts Sukuts**

● Cartoombria International Festival of Animatied Film

ADDRESS
Umbria Spettacolo Foundation
25 via Bomtempi
06122 Perugia 288 Perugia-Centro
Italy

TEL: 39 75 57 26 76 4
FAX: 39 75 57 26 76 8

● Edinburgh Fringe Film and Video Festival

ADDRESS
29 Albany Street
Edinburgh EH1 3QN
Scotland

E-MAIL: ffvf@cityscape.co.uk
WEB SITE: http://www.gold.net/users/cp71
CONTACT: **David Cumings**

● EuropaCinema (Viareggio)

ADDRESS
Lungotovere Flamionio 46, Pal. XX1
I-Rome 196
Italy

TEL: 39-6- 3208334
FAX: 39-6 3202765
CONTACT: **Felice Laudadio**

● Festival Du Film Britannique de Dinard

ADDRESS
2 Boulevard Feart
35800 Dinard
France

TEL: 33-2-99 88 19 04
FAX: 33-2-99 46 67 15
CONTACT: **Sylvie Bautrel**

● Independent Feature Film Market (New York)

ADDRESS
IFP, 104 West 29th Street, 12th Avenue
New York, NY 10001
USA

FESTIVAL DATES
September 16-23, 1997
September 15-22, 1998
TEL: 212-465 8200
FAX: 212-465 8525
CONTACT: **Valerie Shepard**

● Latin American Film Festival

ADDRESS
79 Wardour Street
London W1V 3TH
UK

TEL: 44-171-434 3357
FAX: 44-171-287 2112
CONTACT: **Eva Tarr**

● Magdeburg International Film Festival

ADDRESS
Coquistrasse 18A
D-39104 Magdeburg
Germany

TEL: 49-39 14 86 68
FAX: 49-39 14 86 68
CONTACT: **Michael Blume**

September

● Rendez-vous: Finance and Co-production (Berlin)

ADDRESS	TEL:	32-2-346 1500
Euro Aim	FAX:	31-2-346 3842
210 Avenue Winston Churchill	E-MAIL:	EUROAIM@POPHOST.enet.BE
B-1180 Brussels	CONTACT:	**Daniel Zimmermann**
Belgium		

● Santa Fe de Bogota Festival

ADDRESS	TEL:	57-1 282 5196
Calle 26, No 4092	FAX:	57-1 342 2872
Santa Fe de Bogota	CONTACT:	**Henry Laguado**
Columbia		

Canadian International Annual Film / Video Festival

This Canadian festival focuses on amateur film and video. Its location changes thought out Canada, but its headquarters have been in Barrie for over 10 years. It accepts all types of entries including super 8, 16mm, Betacam, Video 8 etc. It is open to all non-professional productions as long as the filmmakers were not involved in film as a career at the time of the work's creation

FESTIVAL DATES
October, 1997 (tba)
October, 1998 (tba)

ADDRESS
25 Eugenia Street
Barrie, Ontario L4M 1P6
Canada

TEL: 705 737 2729
FAX: 705 737 2729
E-MAIL: andrewsb@bconnex.net
ciaff@iname.com
WEB SITE:
http://cn.camriv.bc.ca/~georg/CIAFF/Canadian.html
ENTRIES: 200+
ATTENDEES: 2,500
CONTACT: **Ben Andrews**

FILM TYPE
All

COMPETITIVE
Yes

LANGUAGE
Any (English subtitles)

COUNTRY
Any

ENTRY FEES
$20 Amateur, $25 Student, $40 Independent

AWARDS
Many awards are given out in three different categories. They include Best Canadian Entry, documentary, animation, experimental etc.

IndieQueens Independent and Student Film Showcase

The IndieQueens Independent and Student Film showcase is dedicated to giving filmmakers a screening oportunity. The are two separate events held monthly from October to May each year. The Independent Film Showcase takes place at Queens Theatre In The Park, a 500-seat performance arts theatre with 35mm and 16mm capabilities. The Student Film Showcase takes place at The Queens Museum of Art, a 100-seat screening room with 16mm and video capabilities. Both The Queens Museum and Queens Theatre In The Park are located in Flushing Meadows Park, In Queens, NY. The films are promoted in local newspapers, and trades, including both The Queens Museum and The Queens Theatre's newsletters. Included among the invited guests are distributors and acquisition executives.

FESTIVAL DATES
Oct-May, 1997-98 (monthly)

SUBMISSION DATES
submissions always encouraged

ADDRESS
82-66 172nd Street
Jamaica Hill, NY 11432
USA

TEL: 1 718 291 9513
FAX: 1 718 760 1972
E-MAIL: IndieQ@aol.com
WEB SITE: http://members.aol.com/Indie/
ATTENDEES: 500 per screening
CONTACT: **Christine Boose**

FILM TYPE
All (independent & student)

COMPETITIVE
No

LANGUAGE
Any (English subtiltles)

COUNTRY
Any

ENTRY FEES
None

● Isfahan International Festival of Film and Video for Children and Young Adults

Isfahan is a competitive event aimed at young people up to the age of 15. An international jury awards prizes for best short, medium-length and feature film. Also awarded are prizes for best direction and best performance by a young person.

FESTIVAL DATES
October, 1997
October, 1998

SUBMISSION DATES
August, 1997
August, 1998

ADDRESS
Farhang Cineman
Dr. Shariati Avenue
Gholhak, Tehran 191139
Iran

TEL: 98-212 65086/200 2088
FAX: 98-21-237 082
ENTRIES: 80-100
ATTENDEES: 100,000
CONTACT: **E. Zarghami**

FILM TYPE
All
COMPETITIVE
Yes
LANGUAGE
Persian, English and French
COUNTRY
Any (except Israel)
ENTRY FEES
None

AWARDS
This festival awards the Golden Butterfly.

● Austin Film Festival and Heart of Film Screenwriting Conference

Austin Film Festival as part of its program also runs The Austin Heart of Film Screenwriters Conference which takes place during the first four days of the festival. The festival's focus is on narrative films. Documentaries are not accepted into the competition, but can be screened in the regular program.

FESTIVAL DATES
October 2-9, 1997
October 1-8, 1998

SUBMISSION DATES
August 15, 1997
August 14, 1998

ADDRESS
1600 Nueces
Austin, TX 78701
USA

TEL: 800 310 3378
FAX: 512 478 6205
E-MAIL: Austinfilm@aol.com
WEB SITE: http://www.lnstar.com/austin-film/
CONTACT: **Barbara Morgan**

FILM TYPE
All (documentaries not in competition: must be NTSC)
COMPETITIVE
Yes
LANGUAGE
Any (English subtitles)
COUNTRY
Any
ENTRY FEES
$35

AWARDS
Austin has a competition for films and screenplays. The submission dates for screenplays are May the 15 and must be: feature length, cannot be under option and writer must not be making a living at writing.

● Feminale Women's Film Festival

Feminale Women's Film Festival will only screen film and video productions by women directors. It offers a film market, current productions from all over the world, discussion groups, a lesbian program, and youth forum.

FESTIVAL DATES
October, 1998
SUBMISSION DATES
June 1, 1998
ADDRESS
Hansaring 86
D-50670 Cologne
Germany

TEL: 49-221-130 0225
FAX: 49-221-130 028/417 568
ENTRIES: 200
ATTENDEES: 18,000
CONTACT: **Katja Mildenberger**

FILM TYPE
All
COMPETITIVE
No
LANGUAGE
Any
COUNTRY
Europe, special countries by invitation only
ENTRY FEES
None

● Film Camera Festival Manaki Brothers (Bitola)

The works at this festival stress the cinematographic elements of each film screened. The awards are given to the director of photography of each winning film. Because of the event's focus, a "special atmosphere" or feeling surrounds this festival. It is named after the two brothers who brought cinematography to the Bitola (in the Balkans) in 1905.

FESTIVAL DATES
October, 1997
October, 1998
ADDRESS
Vardar-Film 8Mart, No. 4a
91000 Skopje
Macedonia

TEL: 389-91-117527/116626
FAX: 389-91-211 811/116626
CONTACT: **Gorjan Tozija/Marcel Martin**

FILM TYPE
Feature in competition
COMPETITIVE
Yes
LANGUAGE
Any
COUNTRY
Any
ENTRY FEES
None

AWARDS
The awards are the The Golden, Silver and Bronze Camera 300.

● Mill Valley Film Festival

Mill Valley showcases a variety of different international films. Its programs include a Videofest, tributes, special events and seminars. The festival takes place in beautiful surroundings through out the entire event.

FESTIVAL DATES
October 2-12, 1997
October 1-11, 1998

SUBMISSION DATES
June 30, 1997
June 30, 1998

ADDRESS
Film Institute of Northern California
38 Miller Avenue, Suite 6
Mill Valley, CA 94952
USA

FILM TYPE
All

COMPETITIVE
No

LANGUAGE
Any

COUNTRY
Any

ENTRY FEES
$25, $30 international ($5 dollars less if submitted early)

TEL: 415-383 5256
FAX: 415-383 8606
E-MAIL: finc@well.com
WEB SITE: http://www.finc.org/
ENTRIES: 100+
ATTENDEES: 40,000
CONTACT: **Mark Fishkin**

● H.P. Lovecraft Film Festival

The H. P. Lovecraft Film Festival was established to promote the works of the great master of horror throught the film adaptions of student, amateur and professional filmmakers. Submissions need to be either a direct adaptation from one of the authors' stories or must be inspired by or relate to the Lovecraft/Cthulhu Mythos. It usually takes place the first weekend in October each year.

FESTIVAL DATES
October 3-5, 1997
October 2-4, 1998

SUBMISSION DATES
August 1, 1997
August 1, 1998

ADDRESS
610 SW Broadway, Suite 505
Portland, OR 97205
USA

FILM TYPE
All

COMPETITIVE
Yes

LANGUAGE
Any (English subtitles)

COUNTRY
Any

ENTRY FEES
None

FAX: (503) 243 2479
E-MAIL: festival@beyond-books.com
WEB SITE: http://www.beyond-books.com/~beyond/Festival/
ATTENDEES: 440+
CONTACT: **Andrew Migliore**

AWARDS
Each year an award for Best Student Adaptation and Best Amateur Adaption is awarded. They receive $100US and a plaque.

● lo-con Short Film Festival

lo-con is a short film festival that accepts film in two categories: Short (under 30 minutes) and Shorter (under 15 minutes). The films screened are made from any media including films, tape, animation and digital production. The festival receives press coverage from the Hollywood Reporter, Variety and LA Weekly.

FESTIVAL DATES
October 3-5, 1997
October, 1998 (tbc)
SUBMISSION DATES
September 1, 1997
September 1, 1998
ADDRESS
289 S. Robertson Blvd., Suite 270
Beverly Hills, CA 90210
USA

TEL: 310 888 3522
E-MAIL: lo-coninfo@lo-con.com
WEB SITE: http://lo-con.com/
ENTRIES: 25 screened
ATTENDEES: 600+
CONTACT: **Tammy Glover**

FILM TYPE
Short
COMPETITIVE
Yes
LANGUAGE
English
COUNTRY
Any
ENTRY FEES
$25

AWARDS
A plaque is presented to the winner of the Audience Award.

● Silence Elles Tournent

The goal of this festival is the presentation and promotion of films and videos directed by women or women/men teams. The festival is therefore able to contribute to the expansion of the distribution networks and to the advancement of film and video directed by women or women/men teams.

FESTIVAL DATES
October 3-12, 1997
October 2-11, 1998
SUBMISSION DATES
June 15, 1997
June 15, 1998
ADDRESS
Cinema Femmes Montreal
55 Avenue Du Mont-Royal West, Suite 211
Montréal, Québec H2T 2S6
Canada

TEL: 514-282 1240
FAX: 514-282 1440
E-MAIL: eltourne@Mlink.net
WEB SITE:
http://www.Mlink.NET/~eltourne/
ENTRIES: 200
ATTENDEES: 20,000
CONTACT: **Jocelyne Denault**

FILM TYPE
All
COMPETITIVE
Yes
LANGUAGE
Any (preferably French or English subtitles)
COUNTRY
Any
ENTRY FEES
$30 short & videos, $40 medium & feature length

AWARDS
Awards include best feature, documentary, short, video, actress, actor, first work, photography and the Public's Prize.

● Warsaw Film Festival

Warsaw is an audience geared event that screens quality feature films. It sections include a World Panorama, American Independents, European Cinema and a showcase of new Polish films.

FESTIVAL DATES
October 3-12, 1997 (tbc)
October, 1998

ADDRESS
Rynek Nowomiejski 5/7
00264 Warsaw
Poland

TEL: 48-2-635 9541
FAX: 48-2-635 9541
ENTRIES: by invitation only
CONTACT: **Stefan Laudyn**

FILM TYPE
Feature

COMPETITIVE
No

LANGUAGE
Any

COUNTRY
Any

● Prix Europa

As of 1997, Prix Europa will merge with Prix Futura Berlin and hold an annual double competition that will select the best European television and radio programs and support their distribution throughout Europe. A goal of the festival will still be "to enable (European Television producers) to overcome national, regional or local boundaries and to create a television community within the emerging Europe that expresses the richness and diversity of our cultural heritage."

FESTIVAL DATES
October 5-12, 1997
October, 1998

SUBMISSION DATES
June 1, 1997
June 1, 1998

ADDRESS
Competition Office, SFB
D-14046 Berlin
Germany

TEL: 49-30-30-31 16 10
FAX: 49-30-30-31 16 19
E-MAIL: Prix-EUROPA.@t-online.de
ENTRIES: 250
CONTACT: **Susanne Hoffmann**

FILM TYPE
Feature and Documentary TV productions

COMPETITIVE
Yes

LANGUAGE
Any (English subtitles)

COUNTRY
Any European country

ENTRY FEES
None

AWARDS
The prizes include the Prix Europa Television Programme of the Year, (6,250ECU), Special Prix Europa (6,250ECU), the Distribution Prize (10,000ECU), and the Viewer's Prize (10,000ECU).

● Taipei Golden Horse Film Festival

The goals of this festival are to contribute to a better understanding of the world cinema both as an art form and as an industry. The three sections that comprise this festival are as follows: a competition, an international film exhibition and a Chinese film exhibition.

FESTIVAL DATES
October, 1997
October, 1998

SUBMISSION DATES
August 31, 1997
August 31, 1998

ADDRESS
7F, No 45, Chilin Road
Taipei 104
Taiwan, R.O.C.

FILM TYPE
All

COMPETITIVE
Yes

LANGUAGE
Any

COUNTRY
Any

ENTRY FEES
None

TEL: 886-2-567 5861
FAX: 886-2-531 8966
E-MAIL: tghff@email.gcn.net.tw
WEB SITE: http://www.goldenhorse.org.tw/
ENTRIES: 80
CONTACT: **Jane Yu**

AWARDS
This festival has a prestigious competition designed to promote the production of Chinese-language cinema. The prizes given out are called the Golden Horse Awards.

● Flanders International Film Festival (Ghent)

Flanders is held in the ancient city of Ghent, Belgium and is the most prestigious film event of the year. Its official competition "The Impact of Music on Film" has 15 films competing for three major prizes and a large distribution grant. There is also a competition for Belgian shorts featuring prizes up to 1 million Belgian Francs. Other sections of the festival include "Filmspectrum" (showcasing films to be released in Belgium), "The Memory Of Film" (a film retrospective), which in 1997, will feature film & filmmakers blacklisted by HUAC, and a concert in the Flemish Opera House. During this festival the Joseph Plateau Awards, Belgium's annual film awards, are distributed at a celebratory gala event.

FESTIVAL DATES
October 7-18, 1997
October 6-17, 1998

SUBMISSION DATES
August 10, 1997
August 10, 1998

ADDRESS
1104 Kortrijksesteenweg
B-9051 Ghent
Belgium

FILM TYPE
Feature, Short

COMPETITIVE
Yes

LANGUAGE
Any

COUNTRY
Any

ENTRY FEES
None

TEL: 32-9-242 8060/221 8946
FAX: 32-9-221 9074
E-MAIL: filmfestival@glo.be
WEB SITE: http://www.rug.ac.be/filmfestival/Welcome.html
ENTRIES: 200+
ATTENDEES: 65,000+
CONTACT: **Jacques Dubrulle**

AWARDS
Flanders awards over $100,000US in prize money. The three main prizes are: The Gilded Spur (Best Film) worth $35,000 US approx., The Silver Spur (Best Director) worth $18,000 US approx. and The George Delerue Award (Best Composer) worth $25,000US approx. which all have a distribution grant attached to them.

● Chicago International Film Festival

This is the oldest competitive film festival in the US. It focuses on the search for new talents as well as honoring the history of cinema. The sections include The Feature Competition (20 films which must not have opened commercially in the US or have been in competition in any other US festival prior to its admittance), World Cinema (30 films), Explore: The USA, The Short Subject, The Documentary and Student Productions. The section entitled Exclusive Screenings showcases between six and eight they believe to have a "powerful impact on audiences in America and around the world". In 1996 they included "Shine", "Secrets and LIes" and "Breaking the Waves".

FESTIVAL DATES
October 9-19, 1997
October 8-18, 1998
SUBMISSION DATES
August 8, 1997
July 28, 1998
ADDRESS
32 West Randolph St., Suite 600
Chicago, IL 60601
USA

TEL: 312-425 9400
FAX: 312-425 0944
E-MAIL: filmfest@wwa.com
WEB SITE:
http://www.chicago.ddbn.com/filmfest/
ENTRIES: 2,000
ATTENDEES: 75,000
CONTACT: **Michael J. Kutza**

FILM TYPE
All (plus student films)
COMPETITIVE
Yes
LANGUAGE
Any
COUNTRY
Any
ENTRY FEES
$35-$150 (no fee for certain invited films)
AWARDS
The top award in the feature film competition is the Golden Hugo. It is presented,by an international jury, to the best film, director, lead actor and actress and best screenplay. A separate competition is held for first and second time filmmakers (called Premiering Filmmakers) and is judged by the International Film Critics Federation. Other awards include: Gold and Silver plaques which are presented to entries that are judged to have "superior quality" and Certificates of Merit which are presented to entries which "deserve recognition" and the Getz World Peace Award given to a filmmaker "whose work has best contributed to a better understanding among people".

Pittsburgh International Lesbian & Gay Film Festival (PILGFF)

PILGFF is an important arena for independent lesbian and gay film and video in the tri-state area. It also features educational programs, and talks by film-makers, video producers, and critics. The festival also premieres major releases of interest to the gay community. In the past these have included "Jeffrey", "My Own Private Idaho", and "Priscilla, Queen of the Desert."

FESTIVAL DATES
October 9-19, 1997
October 8-18, 1998 (tbc)

ADDRESS
P.O. Box 110224
Pittsburgh, PA 15232
USA

TEL: 412 232 3277
FAX: 412 327 1630
WEB SITE:
http://trfn.pgh.pa.us/orgs/pilgf/pilgf_home.ht
ml
ATTENDEES: 2,000
CONTACT: **Tom Deane**

FILM TYPE
All
COMPETITIVE
No
LANGUAGE
Any
COUNTRY
Any

Sitges International Fantasy Film Festival

Sitges has different sections to its festival that are all quite popular. These include the Official Section, which is competitive and the prized "Maria" (robot from Metropolis) which is the symbol of the festival. Other sections are; the Informative Section, "Anima't" and "Brigadoon" which concentrates fully on alternative and daring filmmaking. Only films which have not participated in other Spanish film festivals before can enter the Competitive Sections.

FESTIVAL DATES
October 9-19, 1997
October 8-18, 1998 (tbc)

SUBMISSION DATES
August 15, 1997
August 15, 1998

ADDRESS
c/o Rossello 257, 3-E
08008 Barcelona
Spain

TEL: 34-3-415 3938
FAX: 34-3-237 6521
E-MAIL: cinsit@arrakis.es
ENTRIES: 150
ATTENDEES: 28,500+
CONTACT: **Alex Gorina**

FILM TYPE
All, but Documentary
COMPETITIVE
Yes
LANGUAGE
Any
COUNTRY
Any
ENTRY FEES
None

AWARDS
The major prize awarded at this festival is the Maria.

● Chicago International Children's Film Festival

This is the largest competitive children's film festival in North America. It focuses on humanistic, nonviolent children's films and videos which celebrate a global culture.

FESTIVAL DATES
October 10-19, 1997
October, 1998
SUBMISSION DATES
June 1, 1997
June 1, 1998
ADDRESS
1517 W Fullerton Avenue
Chicago, IL 60614
USA

TEL: 773-281 9075
FAX: 773-929 5437
E-MAIL: kidsfest@facets.org
ENTRIES: 350
ATTENDEES: 10,000
CONTACT: **Elizabeth Shepherd**

FILM TYPE
All
COMPETITIVE
Yes
LANGUAGE
Any (English subtitles)
COUNTRY
Any
ENTRY FEES
$35 shorts, $75 features

● International Film Festival Mannheim-Heidelberg

Mannheim-Heidelberg is one of the oldest in the world. It has always been dedicated to the discovery of new talent. Many of today's well-known directors from all over the world began their international careers at this festival including; Truffaut (1959), Kieslowski (1975), and Atom Egoyan (1984).

FESTIVAL DATES
October 10-18, 1997
October 9-17, 1998
SUBMISSION DATES
August 1, 1997
August 1, 1998
ADDRESS
Collini- Centre, Galerie
D-68161 Mannheim
Germany

TEL: 49-621-152316/102943
FAX: 49-621-291564
E-MAIL: ifmh@mannheim-filmfestival.com
WEB SITE: http://www.mannheim-filmfesti-val.com/
ENTRIES: 100+
ATTENDEES: 40,000
CONTACT: **Dr. Michael Koetz**

FILM TYPE
All, animation
COMPETITIVE
Yes
LANGUAGE
Any
COUNTRY
Any
ENTRY FEES
None

AWARDS
An international jury awards prizes which include; the international independent award of Mannheim-Heidelberg for Best fiction feature (DM 30,000), Best Documentary (DM 10,000), and Best Short (DM 5,000).

● Israel Film Festival

October

The Israel Film Festival focuses on films and TV dramas that are made in the state of Israel. All works screened are personally chosen by the festival director. During the festival there are galas, parties and certain special events. The annual festival takes place in both Los Angeles and New York.

FESTIVAL DATES
L.A.: Nov. 5-20; N.Y. : Dec. 4-23, 1997
ADDRESS
6404 Wilshire Boulevard, Suite 1240
Los Angeles, CA 90048
USA

TEL: 213-966 4166
FAX: 213-658 6346
ENTRIES: By invitation only(15 screened)
ATTENDEES: 40,000
CONTACT: **Julie Friedman**

FILM TYPE
Feature, Documentary, TV drama and Short film
COMPETITIVE
No
COUNTRY
Israel
ENTRY FEES
None

● Native Americas International Film Exposition

NAIFE's goal is to "provide a focus to an emerging Native film movement that works to advance the making of films by about and with indigenous people of the Americas". The festival includes premieres, panel discussions, curated film series of the portrayal of native people in film, awards gala and educational workshops of which 700 people participated in 1996. It is an annual event that takes place every Columbus Day weekend.

FESTIVAL DATES
October 10-13, 1997
October 9-12, 1998 (tbc)
SUBMISSION DATES
August 25, 1997
July 31, 1998
ADDRESS
P.O. Box 5034
Sante Fe, NM 87502
USA

TEL: 505 983 5220
FAX: 505 983 7647
E-MAIL: natvfilm@numa.niti.org
WEB SITE: http://numa.niti.org/naife/
ENTRIES: 200(24 screened)
ATTENDEES: 4,000
CONTACT: **Virginia Manion**

FILM TYPE
All
COMPETITIVE
Yes
LANGUAGE
Any (English subtitles)
COUNTRY
Any
ENTRY FEES
$25 feature; $15 short; $10 video

AWARDS
Competition for feature, documentary,and short films.

● New Orleans Film and Video Festival

New Orleans' main two sections are "The Big House" and "Cinema16". The former is for features only and is non-competitive. It screens films with larger budgets which already have distribution. The latter is competitive and showcases independent works in 8 and 16mm, video and 35mm features either in limited distribution or lacking distribution. Many of the filmmakers in Cinema 16 attend and will be available after screening for Q&A sessions. This festival sees itself primarily as a big party. During the "party" their are also premieres; previews; workshops; panels; social events and receptions.

FESTIVAL DATES
New Orleans' main two sections are "The Big House" and "Cinema16". The
October 10-16, 1997
October   9-15,1998

SUBMISSION DATES
July 15 (early) 25 (late), 1997
July 15 (early) 25 (late), 1998

ADDRESS
New Orleans Film and Video Society
225 Baronne, Suite 1712
New Orleans, LA 70112
USA

TEL: 504-523 3818
FAX: 504-529 2430
E-MAIL: nofilm@nettown.com
WEB SITE:
http://www.neworleansfilmfest.com
ENTRIES: 250+(89 Cinema 16; 32 Big House
screened)
ATTENDEES: 7,000+
CONTACT: **Carol Gniady**

FILM TYPE
All

COMPETITIVE
Yes

LANGUAGE
Any

COUNTRY
Any

ENTRY FEES
$25/film or video (early); $35 (late) for US & Canada; overseas also includes half the return shipping cost of the print

AWARDS
"MovieMaker Breakthrough Award" $20,000+ worth of goods & services given to the winning filmmaker who has not had previous distribution, other sponsors award prizes, engraved awards and certificates.

● Raindance Film Showcase (London)

Raindance focuses on independently produced shorts and features. They are screened to an audience of industry professionals, acquisition executives, filmmakers and film lovers. Raindance always runs one week before Mifed in Milan.

FESTIVAL DATES
October 10-18, 1997
End of October, 1998

SUBMISSION DATES
September 1, 1997
September 1, 1997

ADDRESS
81 Berwick Street
London W1V 3PFF
UK

TEL: 44-171-287-3833
FAX: 44-171-439 2243
E-MAIL: indiefilm@easynet.co.uk
ENTRIES: 150 screened
ATTENDEES: 5,000
CONTACT: **Elliot Grove**

FILM TYPE
Feature, Short

COMPETITIVE
Yes (audience awards only)

LANGUAGE
Any

COUNTRY
Any

ENTRY FEES
50 Pounds/entry

AWARDS
The Raindance Awards for Short and Feature Films.

● Videonale - International festival for video art

The Videonale Festival is held biannually, and traditionally includes a comprehensive exhibition of video sculpture and installations, and includes a video tape competition preselected by a jury. Many of Bonn's art institutions contribute to the week-long festival with special programs and events. The Videonale Intermezzo(separate from the Videonale festival) presents video

FESTIVAL DATES
October 10-12, 1997 (Videonale Intermezzo)
September, 1998 (Videonale Festival)

ADDRESS
Hochstadenring 22
D-53119 Bonn
Germany

TEL: 49 0 228 692818
FAX: 49 0 228 654137
E-MAIL: videonal@viswiz.gmd.de
WEB SITE: http://viswiz.gmd.de/videoale/
ENTRIES: 100 screened (700 submitted)
ATTENDEES: 5,000+
CONTACT: **Rosanne Altstatt**

FILM TYPE
Any

COMPETITIVE
Yes

LANGUAGE
Any

COUNTRY
Any

ENTRY FEES
Contact festival

AWARDS
The Videonale Prize is awarded at every Videonale Festival.

● Austrian Film Days (Wels)

Austrian Film Days showcases European and Austrian films in Wels. It is a biennial festival which screens over 70 films in four days, and presents an award to a feature and documentary film.

FESTIVAL DATES
October 7-11, 1998

SUBMISSION DATES
July 1, 1998

ADDRESS
Austrian Film Office
Columbusgasse 2
A-1100 Vienna
Austria

TEL: 43-1-604 0126
FAX: 43-1-602 0795
ENTRIES: 70
ATTENDEES: 12,000
CONTACT: **Reinhard Pyrker**

FILM TYPE
All

COMPETITIVE
Yes

LANGUAGE
Any

COUNTRY
European

ENTRY FEES
None

● Cinekid: The International Film and Television Festival for Young Adults

In October , Cinekid showcases films and television productions for children. Its sections for admittance are: films for children, films for young people, an information program and TV productions. The first two sections are competitive. One of Cinekid's goals is to give "a survey of the best new international children's film and television productions" and "to motivate Dutch film distributors and television programmers {towards} qualified films."

FESTIVAL DATES
October 11-19, 1997
October 10-18, 1998 (tbc)
SUBMISSION DATES
July 31, 1997
July 31, 1998 (tbc)
ADDRESS
Weteringschaus 249
NL-1017 XJ Amsterdam
The Netherlands

TEL:	31-20-624 7110
FAX:	31-20-620 9965
E-MAIL:	engel2x@xs4all.nl
ENTRIES:	15
ATTENDEES:	10,000
CONTACT:	**Elly Engel**

FILM TYPE
Feature, Animation
COMPETITIVE
Yes
LANGUAGE
Any
COUNTRY
Any
ENTRY FEES
None

AWARDS
The Cinekid Award.

● Iowa Independent Film & Video Festival (IIFVF)

The IIFV seeks videos and films under 30 minutes in narrative, documentary, experimental, and animation categories. It highlights independent film and video from the 12-state Midwestern US region: Illinois, Indiana, Iowa, Kansas, Michigan, Minnesota, Missouri, Nebraska, North Dakota, Ohio, South Dakota, Wisconsin. Film and video makers must be living in, or originally from this region. Entries also qualify if they are produced in one of the above Midwestern states.

FESTIVAL DATES
October 11-12, 1997
October, 1998
SUBMISSION DATES
September 5, 1997
September 5, 1998
ADDRESS
University of Northern Iowa
Electronic Media Division
Cedar Falls, IA 50614-0139
USA

TEL:	319 273 2788/2217
FAX:	319 273 7356
E-MAIL:	martinc@uni.edu
WEB SITE:	http://www.uni.edu/~martin/iifv.html
ENTRIES:	15-20 screened
ATTENDEES:	500-600
CONTACT:	**Christopher Martin**

FILM TYPE
Short (under 30 mins.)
COMPETITIVE
Yes
LANGUAGE
English preferable
COUNTRY
12-state Midwestern US region
ENTRY FEES
$20 (one entry); $30 (two entries)

AWARDS
The awards include Best of Show, Golden Corn Award for Excellence and the Honorable Mention. Cash prizes are given out with awards.

● Cork International Film Festival

Cork is Ireland's oldest film event established in 1956 "to bring to Irish audiences the best of international cinema and to serve as a platform for Irish filmmaking". Cork's program includes feature films, a documentary section,a showcase of new Irish films, retrospectives, seminars and master classes. It also features the short film by screening over 100 contemporary shorts, in competition from around the world. Films are screened at the Cork Opera House, Triskel Arts Centre and the Kino, Cork's arthouse cinema.

FESTIVAL DATES
  October 12-19, 1997
  October 11-18, 1998
SUBMISSION DATES
  July 15, 1997
  July 15, 1998
ADDRESS
  Hatfield House, Tobin Street
  Cork
  Ireland

TEL:	353-21-271711
FAX:	353-21-275945
E-MAIL:	ciff@indigo.ie
WEB SITE:	http://www.corkfilmfest.org/
ENTRIES:	200
ATTENDEES:	15,000
CONTACT:	**Michael Hannigan**

FILM TYPE
  All
COMPETITIVE
  Yes
LANGUAGE
  Any
COUNTRY
  Any
ENTRY FEES
  None

AWARDS
  The prizes include Best European Short Film, Best First Film by an Irish Director, Best Irish Short Film and a Special Jury Commendation. Cork also awards prizes for black and white films that include Best Feature, Best Short, and Best Cinematography.

● Sheffield International Documentary Festival

This is the UK's only film festival dedicated to excellence in documentary film and television. The festival is non-competitive and includes themed screenings and filmmaker workshops for both the public and the professional.

FESTIVAL DATES
  October 13-19, 1997
  End of October, 1998
SUBMISSION DATES
  July, 1997
  July, 1998 (TBC)
ADDRESS
  The Workstation
  15 Patemoster Row
  Sheffield S1 2BX
  UK

TEL:	44-114-276 5141
FAX:	44-114-272 1849
E-MAIL:	shefdoc@fdgroup.co.uk
WEB SITE:	http://www.shef.ac.uk/city/sidf/
ENTRIES:	75 publically screened
ATTENDEES:	500
CONTACT:	**Kathy Loizou**

FILM TYPE
  Documentary
COMPETITIVE
  Yes
LANGUAGE
  Any
COUNTRY
  Any
ENTRY FEES
  None

● Hollywood Film Festival

Hollywood's mandate, with its 1997 inaugural festival, " is to bridge the gap between the established entertainment industry and the global creative community" and to "discover emerging filmmakers and multimedia artists". This 5-day event will include screenings by award finalists; galas; a live cybercast of the festival; panel discussions; seminars with topics such as pitching, screenwriting, financing, distribution and marketing. A tribute to Orson Welles will feature a Q&A session with his chief cinematographer, Gary Graver.

FESTIVAL DATES
October 14-19, 1997
October 13-18, 1998 (tbc)

SUBMISSION DATES
August 30, 1997
August 30, 1997

ADDRESS
433 N. Camden Dr., Suite 600
Beverly Hills, CA 90210
USA

FILM TYPE
All

COMPETITIVE
Yes

LANGUAGE
Any (English subtitles)

COUNTRY
Any

ENTRY FEES
$50

TEL: 310 288 1882
FAX: 310 475 0193
E-MAIL: awards@hollywoodawards.com
WEB SITE: http://www.hollywoodfilmfesti-val.com//
CONTACT: **Carlos de Abreu**

AWARDS
The awards include the Hollywood Discovery Award, Hollywood Young Filmmakers Award, Hollywood Cyberaward, and the Moviemaker Breakthrough Award. Over $20,000 US in prizes will be awarded as well as introductions to industry professionals (distributors, agents, producers, etc).

● Bite the Mango Film Festival

Bite the Mango seeks to raise the awareness of Black and Asian (including Indian,Pakistani and Middle Eastern) film and video in the Unitied Kingdom. It also seeks to create a platform to stimulate debate as well as screen global cinema not normally available in the U.K.

FESTIVAL DATES
October, 1997
October, 1998

SUBMISSION DATES
October, 1997
October, 1998

ADDRESS
National Museum of Photography, Film and Television
Pictureville, Bradford BD1 1NQ
UK

FILM TYPE
All, but animation

COMPETITIVE
No

LANGUAGE
Any (English subtitles)

COUNTRY
Any

ENTRY FEES
None

TEL: 44-1274-727 488
FAX: 44-1274-723 155

WEB SITE:
http://hmsi.ac.uk/nmpt/mango.htm
ENTRIES: 100
ATTENDEES: 2,000
CONTACT: **Cary Sawhney**

● British Film Festival (Cherbourg)

This festival showcases new British features and shorts as well as classics and lesser known films. Its program also includes tributes to major British film-makers.

FESTIVAL DATES
October, 1997
October, 1998

ADDRESS
8 Passage Digard
F-50100 Cherbourg
France

TEL: 33-33 93 38 94
FAX: 33-33 01 20 78
ENTRIES: 28
ATTENDEES: 6,500
CONTACT: **Yolande Forafo**

FILM TYPE
All

COMPETITIVE
Yes

LANGUAGE
Any (must be British)

COUNTRY
British countries

ENTRY FEES
None

AWARDS
This festival offers an audience award which includes 20,000 French francs and free French subtitling for film.

● Hamptons Film Festival (East Hampton)

Hamptons offers a wide range of premieres by well-known filmmakers, as well as showcasing new directors' work. Its mandate is to "support students and American independent filmmakers of outstanding promise by screening their work and providing grants." Aside from its regularly scheduled festival, Hamptons offers a continuous program dealing with film including screenings, workshops and seminars.

FESTIVAL DATES
October 15-19, 1997
October 14-18, 1998 (tbc)

SUBMISSION DATES
August 8, 1997
August 8, 1998

ADDRESS
3 Newtown Mews
East Hampton, NY 11937
USA

TEL: 516-324 4600
FAX: 516-324 5116
E-MAIL: filmfest@peconic.net
WEB SITE:
http://www.peconic.net/arts/hamptons/filmfestival/
ENTRIES: 40 screened
ATTENDEES: 20,000
CONTACT: **Bruce Feinberg**

FILM TYPE
All, but animation

COMPETITIVE
No

LANGUAGE
Any (English subtitles)

COUNTRY
Any

ENTRY FEES
$25 (30 min. or less)/ $50 (more then 30 min.)

AWARDS
Awards for Most Popular Film, Best Director, Best Documentary Feature and Best Short Film.

• The Moving Pictures Festival Of Dance on Film and Video

Moving Pictures is an annual event dedicated to "exploring the intersections of dance and the camera". The films are screened at three venues in the downtown Toronto area. The exhibit will also tour and visit different cities across Canada. Aside from regular festival screenings, Moving Pictures also presents panel discussions, free screenings and an awards presentation.

FESTIVAL DATES
  October, 1997
  October, 1998

SUBMISSION DATES
  May 30, 1997
  May 30, 1998

ADDRESS
  253 College St., Suite 102
  Toronto, Ontario M5T 1R5
  Canada

FILM TYPE
  All

COMPETITIVE
  Yes

LANGUAGE
  Any

COUNTRY
  Any

ENTRY FEES
  $20Cdn. ($25 for International entries)

TEL:	416 961 5424
FAX:	416 961 5624
E-MAIL:	movingpix@total.net
WEB SITE:	http://www.total.net/~moving-pix/
CONTACT:	**Kathleen M. Smith**

• AFI Los Angeles International Film Festival

AFI tries to find ways to put on acceptable, professionally curated shows that exhibit lower-cost production forms both domestically and internationally. AFI runs during the last two weeks of October.

FESTIVAL DATES
  October 16-31, 1997
  October 15-30, 1998

SUBMISSION DATES
  June 6 (early); August 29 (late), 1997
  June 6 (early); August 29 (late), 1998

ADDRESS
  2021 N. Western Avenue
  Los Angeles, CA 90027
  USA

FILM TYPE
  All

COMPETITIVE
  Yes

LANGUAGE
  Any

COUNTRY
  Any

ENTRY FEES
  $30

TEL:	213-856 7707
FAX:	213-462 4049
E-MAIL:	afifest@afionline.org
WEB SITE:	http://www.afionline.org/
ENTRIES:	400-700 (60 screened)
ATTENDEES:	40,000
CONTACT:	**Jon Fitzgerald**

● Leeds International Film Festival

Leeds is the third largest UK film festival. It includes premieres, previews of major international releases, a retrospective of shorts, and features from around the world.

FESTIVAL DATES
October 16-31, 1997
October 15-30, 1998
SUBMISSION DATES
August 1, 1997
August 1, 1998
ADDRESS
The Town Hall, The Headrow
Leeds LS1 3AD
UK

TEL:	44-113-247 8389
FAX:	44-113-247 8397
WEB SITE:	http://www.sensei.co.uk/films/
ENTRIES:	160-200 screened
ATTENDEES:	15-20,000
CONTACT:	**Liz Rymer**

FILM TYPE
All
COMPETITIVE
No
LANGUAGE
Any (English subtitles)
COUNTRY
Any
ENTRY FEES
5 pound administration fee

AWARDS
An audience award for best film.

● San Juan Cinemafest

San Juan Cinemafest occurs during the winter in the capitol of Puerto Rico. Its competitive section is for Caribbean films only, but screens a variety of international films including shorts, documentaries, animation etc.

FESTIVAL DATES
October 16-26, 1997
October 15-25, 1998 (tbc)
ADDRESS
PO Box 4543
San Juan, PR 00902
USA

TEL:	787-721 6125
FAX:	787-723 6412
CONTACT:	**Jose Artemio Torres**

FILM TYPE
All
COMPETITIVE
Yes
LANGUAGE
Any
COUNTRY
Any

AWARDS
The Pitirre Award is given out to fiction, documentary and animation films.

● St. John's Women's Film & Video Festival

St. John's s is a 4-day celebration of all types of films. This autumn festival showcases films that have been created by women. One of the goals of this international event is to screen and promote quality films that have been created by women and are of interest to women. Other events that occur during this festival include discussions and parties.

FESTIVAL DATES
October 16-19, 1997
October 15-18, 1998

SUBMISSION DATES
June 15, 1997
June 15, 1998

ADDRESS
PO Box 984
St. John's, Newfoundland A1C 6C2
Canada

FILM TYPE
All

COMPETITIVE
No

LANGUAGE
Any (English or French subtitles)

COUNTRY
Any

ENTRY FEES
$10 Cdn. (to cover shipping)

TEL: 709-754 3141
FAX: 709-754 3143
E-MAIL: daninef@plato.ucs.mun.ca
ENTRIES: 30-40 screened
CONTACT: **Danine Farquharson**

● Athens Film Festival

Athens' first festival takes place in October of 1997 and will showcase local and international independent films as well as a screenwriting contest. The three winning screenplays will be read by the Wind Dancer Production Company in Los Angeles as well as Lambart Production Company in Paris, France and will receive a monetary award.

FESTIVAL DATES
October 17-24, 1997
October 16-23, 1998 (tbc)
SUBMISSION DATES
July 1 (early) August 15 (late), 1997
July 1 (early) August 15 (late), 1998 (tbc)
ADDRESS
P.O.BOX 1631
Athens, GA 30603
USA

TEL:	706 613-7669
FAX:	706 613-0956
E-MAIL:	gafilm@negia.net
WEB SITE:	http://www.negia.net/~gafilm/
CONTACT:	**Juanita Giles**

FILM TYPE
All
COMPETITIVE
Yes
LANGUAGE
Any (English subtitles)
COUNTRY
Any
ENTRY FEES
$40 (early); $45 (late)

AWARDS
Athens has six prize categories for film as well as prizes for the screenwriting event. The prize categories include: Best Feature, Best Short, Best Documentary, Best Super 8, Best Local, and Festival Choice.

● ImageOut: The Rochester Lesbian and Gay Film & Video Festival

Image out screens all types of film and video that deal with the Lesbian & Gay experience.

FESTIVAL DATES
October 17-25, 1997
October 16-24, 1998 (tbc)
SUBMISSION DATES
Mid-June, 1997
Mid-June, 1998
ADDRESS
713 Monroe Ave.
Rochester, NY 14607
USA

TEL:	716 271-2640
E-MAIL:	imageout@ggw.org

WEB SITE:
http://www.ggw.org/freenet/i/imageout/index.html

ENTRIES:	60+
ATTENDEES:	3,000
CONTACT:	**Rachel Brister**

FILM TYPE
All
COMPETITIVE
No
LANGUAGE
Any
COUNTRY
Any
ENTRY FEES
None

● V'iennale - Vienna International Film Festival

The V'iennale is a non-competitive selective festival that screens films from around the world. The selection of contemporary world cinema is composed of influential features, documentaries and shorts. The Tributes ,in 1997, will honour the careers of the French actress Catherine Deneuve, the American director Albert Brooks and the Portuguese producer Paulo Branco. A special event will pay homage to the Hollywood legends Robert Mitchum and James Stewart. The theatres used will include the Gartenbau, Urania, Metro, Stadtkino and Knnstlerhaus.

FESTIVAL DATES
October 17-29, 1997
October 16-28, 1998 (tbc)
SUBMISSION DATES
August, 1997
August, 1998
ADDRESS
Stiftgasse 6
A-1070 Vienna
Austria

FILM TYPE
All, but animation
COMPETITIVE
No
LANGUAGE
Any (German or English subtitles)
COUNTRY
Any
ENTRY FEES
None

TEL: 43-1-526 5947
FAX: 43-1-523 4172
E-MAIL: office@viennale.or.at
WEB SITE: http://viennale.or.at/
ENTRIES: 130+
ATTENDEES: 48,000
CONTACT: **Alex Horwath**

● Valladolid International Film Festival

Valladolid is one of the major film festivals in Spain. It is over 40 years old and has a wide scope of films that are screened. Its main goal is to show and promote films of artistic quality which contribute to the knowledge of world-wide cinematography.

FESTIVAL DATES
October 17-25, 1997
October 16-24, 1998 (tbc)
SUBMISSION DATES
June 30, 1997
June 30, 1998
ADDRESS
PO Box 646
47003 Valladolid
Spain

FILM TYPE
All
COMPETITIVE
Yes
LANGUAGE
Any (Spanish subtitles)
COUNTRY
Any
ENTRY FEES
None

TEL: 34-83-305700/305777/305788
FAX: 34-83-309835
WEB SITE:
http://www.gui.uva.es/seminci/seminci-eng-lish.html
ENTRIES: 72 (for competition)
ATTENDEES: 80,000
CONTACT: **Denise O'Keefe**

AWARDS
The awards include, the Golden and Silver Spike for best two feature films and short films, an award for best new director, best actor, actress, and director of photography.

● Sao Paulo International Film Festival

Sao Paolo is a cultural, non-profit event of international films with two main sections; "The New Filmmakers Competition" and "International Perspective", respectively. The former is a competitive section for films by new filmmakers. The work must either be the 1st, 2nd or 3rd of the director, be produced after 1995, and not have been shown in Brazil. The latter must have been produced after 1995, be a short or feature as well as not have been shown in Brazil.

FESTIVAL DATES
October 18-31, 1997
October 17-30, 1998 (tbc)
SUBMISSION DATES
September 1, 1997
September 1, 1998
ADDRESS
Al. Lorena 937 cj.302
01424-001 Sao Paolo - SP
Brazil

TEL: 55-11-883 5137
FAX: 55-11-853 7936
E-MAIL: info@mostra.org
WEB SITE: http://www.mostra.org/
ENTRIES: 100+
CONTACT: **Leon Cakoff**

FILM TYPE
Feature, Short
COMPETITIVE
Yes
LANGUAGE
Any (Portuguese, English, Spanish or French subtitles)
COUNTRY
Any
ENTRY FEES
None

AWARDS
The prizes awarded include, Best Film, Special Prize Of The Jury, Critic's Prize and the Audience Prize (chosen from the 10 voted must popular by the audience). The winners are awarded with the "Bandeira Paulistatrophy", a flag of São Paulo stylized by the artist Tomie Ohtake.

● Uppsala International Short Film Festival

This is a competitive international short film festival in (6) separate categories. It is one of the more popular festivals in Sweden.

FESTIVAL DATES
October 21-26, 1997
End of October, 1998
SUBMISSION DATES
August, 1997
August, 1998
ADDRESS
PO Box 1746
S-751 47 Uppsala
Sweden

TEL: 46-18-12 00 25
FAX: 46-18 12 13 50
CONTACT: **Annette van der Maaul**

FILM TYPE
Short
COMPETITIVE
Yes
LANGUAGE
Any
COUNTRY
Any
ENTRY FEES
None

AWARDS
Uppsala Filmkay Award

● Hof International FilmDays

October

Hof FilmDays is over 25 years old and has an excellent repetition for showcasing quality international films. Instead of programming hundreds of films, Hof screens about 50 features and 30 shorts. Therefore a screening at Hof can definately help a film be seen by the "right" people. The festival is very popular with well-known independent filmmakers. Some of its regular visitors are Atom Egoyan, John Sayles and Henry Jaglom. Wim Wenders has "named" Hof the "Home of Films". It takes place annually the last week in October.

FESTIVAL DATES
  October 22-26, 1997
  October 28-Nov. 1, 1998 (tbc)
SUBMISSION DATES
  September 12, 1997
  September 15, 1998
ADDRESS
  Int. Hofer Filmtage
  Lothstrabe 28
  D-80335 Munich
  Germany

TEL:	49-89-1297422
FAX:	49-89-123 6868
E-MAIL:	hofer-filmtage@media-online.de
WEB SITE:	http://www.media-online.de/hofer-filmtage/
ENTRIES:	84 screened
ATTENDEES:	25,000
CONTACT:	**Heinz Badewitz**

FILM TYPE
  All
COMPETITIVE
  Yes
LANGUAGE
  Any
COUNTRY
  Any
ENTRY FEES
  None

AWARDS
  Hof awards the "Eastman Supporting Award for Young German Directors".

● Denver International Film Festival

Denver programs include new international feature releases, independently produced fiction films and documentaries, animation, experimental works, and children's programs. Furthermore, a number of acclaimed film artists from the US and around the world are honored with tributes.

FESTIVAL DATES
  October 23-30, 1997
  October 8-15, 1998
SUBMISSION DATES
  August 1, 1997
  July 15, 1998
ADDRESS
  1430 Larimer Square, Suite 201
  Denver, CO 80202
  USA

TEL:	303-595 3456
FAX:	303-595 0956
E-MAIL:	DFS@DenverFilm.org
WEB SITE:	http://www.DenverFilm.org/
ENTRIES:	400+
ATTENDEES:	25,000
CONTACT:	**Ron Henderson**

FILM TYPE
  All
COMPETITIVE
  No
LANGUAGE
  Any (English subtitles)
COUNTRY
  Any
ENTRY FEES
  $25, $10 students

AWARDS
  Denver awards the "MovieMaker Breakthrough Award" which is $1,000 in cash and $20,000 worth of goods & services given to the top winning feature filmmaker who has not had previous distribution.

174   *Festival Products*

● Cinema Mediterranean Montpellier

Cinema Mediterranean Montpellier showcases films that are about or related to the Mediterranean culture. It is a competitive festival that awards prizes to both short and feature films.

FESTIVAL DATES
  October 24-November 2, 1997
SUBMISSION DATES
  August 31, 1997
ADDRESS
  6 Rue Vielle-ai Guillerie
  F-34090 Montpellier
  France

TEL:	33-67 66 36 36
FAX:	33-67 66 36 37
ENTRIES:	150(Shorts) 40(Features)
ATTENDEES:	55,000
CONTACT:	**Pierre Pitiot**

FILM TYPE
  Feature, Short
COMPETITIVE
  Yes
LANGUAGE
  Any (French or English subtitles)
COUNTRY
  Any (related to Mediterranean culture/area)
ENTRY FEES
  Various

AWARDS
  This festival awards the Antigone d'Or for a feature film worth $20,000, and the Grand Prix for a short worth $4,000.

● International Film Festival in Abitibi - Temiscamingue

Abitibi-Temiscamingue runs for six days starting the last Saturday in October. It is becoming known for its quality programming, warmth of welcome and professionalism of its organization. Due to its increasingly good reputation, it has become an extremely popular event. It screens films in all categories from more than 20 countries around the world.

FESTIVAL DATES
  October 25-30, 1997
  October 30-November 4, 1998
SUBMISSION DATES
  September 1, 1997
  September 1, 1998
ADDRESS
  215 Mercier Avenue
  Rouyn - Noranda, Québec J9X 5W8
  Canada

TEL:	819-762 6212
FAX:	819-762 6762
ENTRIES:	200+ submitted (70-80 screened)
ATTENDEES:	10,000
CONTACT:	**Jacques Matte**

FILM TYPE
  All
COMPETITIVE
  Yes
LANGUAGE
  French or English subtitles
COUNTRY
  Any
ENTRY FEES
  None

AWARDS
  The three prizes awarded at this festival are a public prize for best feature (Grand Prix Hydo-Quebec), a jury prize for best short or medium length film (Prix Telebec) worth $1,000 dollars and a public's prize for best animation (Prix Anime`).

● Short Attention Span Film and Video Festival (SASFVF)

On opening night the SASFVF will screen two shows at the Victoria Theatre in San Francisco. Nearly 1,000 people will see these shows and another 1,000+ will see the show around the US on its tour of small venues. In 1996 the festival went on to: PFA, Berkeley; Cornell University, Ithaca; The Knitting Factory, NY; CalArts, Los Angeles and 911 Media Center, Seattle.

FESTIVAL DATES
  October 25, 1997
  End of October, 1998
SUBMISSION DATES
  August 15, 1997
  August 15, 1998
ADDRESS
  PO Box 460316
  San Francisco, CA 94146
  USA

TEL: 415 576 9335
E-MAIL: sasfvf@aol.com
WEB SITE: http://www.creative.net/~weath-er/
ENTRIES: 150 (60 screened)
ATTENDEES: 2,000+
CONTACT: **Sarah Anderson**

FILM TYPE
  Short (2 min. or shorter)
COMPETITIVE
  No
LANGUAGE
  Any
COUNTRY
  Any
ENTRY FEES
  $5US

AWARDS
  The Viewers' Choice Awards are given each year, based on audience vote. Last year's winners recieved subscriptions to MovieMaker Magazine, Film Threat Magazine, a festival T-shirt and video compilation tapes.

● The Drive-In; Independent Short Film & Video Exhibition

The Drive-In is designed to promote independent filmmaking and create relationships between industry professionals and emerging talent. Work submitted will be screened by a panel of industry professionals and if chosen for the an exhibition will be screened at an Off-Broadway theatre space in Times Square. It holds exhibitions of films at least twice a year and as many as four times (one in each season).

FESTIVAL DATES
  October, 1997 (tba)
  February, 1998 (tba)
SUBMISSION DATES
  August 1, 1997
ADDRESS
  c/o Stolen Car Productions
  928 Broadway, Suite 401
  New York, NY 10010
  USA

TEL: 212 677-1770
FAX: 212 677 1202
E-MAIL: stolencarp@aol.com
WEB SITE: http://members.aol.com/stolen-carp/DriveInHome/DriveIn1.html
CONTACT: **Lauren J. Pollack**

FILM TYPE
  Short
COMPETITIVE
  Yes
LANGUAGE
  Any
COUNTRY
  Any
ENTRY FEES
  $25

AWARDS
  Of the films viewed in the Fall Exhibition one wil be presented with the Stolen Car Best Short Film Award. If your film wins this award you qualify, along with the three other winners in the year's exhibitions, for the "Jump Start Filmmakers Grant". This grant is worth over $10,000 in production costs and is meant to help the indie filmmaker create their first feature-length film, or realize their next film project.

International Leipzig Festival for Documentary and Animated Film

Instead of screening the various types of films available, this competitive festival has decided to showcase only films of high caliber in the documentary and animation format.

FESTIVAL DATES
October 28-November 2, 1997
October/November, 1998
SUBMISSION DATES
September 5, 1997
September 5, 1998
ADDRESS
Elsterstra. 22-24
D-4109 Leipzig
Germany

TEL:	49-341-980 3921
FAX:	49-341-980 4828
ENTRIES:	1,000
ATTENDEES:	16,000
CONTACT:	**Fred Gehler**

FILM TYPE
Documentary, Animation
COMPETITIVE
Yes
LANGUAGE
Any
COUNTRY
Any
ENTRY FEES
20 DM for accreditation

AWARDS
The Golden and Silver Dove are awarded annually.

Fort Lauderdale International Film Festival

Since its inception in 1986, Fort Lauderdale has screened films of all types and genres. It has many programs which include a national student film competition, various gala events , seminars and short, documentary and feature film sections. One of its major sections is the awarding of Lifetime Achievement Awards presented to writers, directors, producers, actors and composers, respectively.

FESTIVAL DATES
October 29-Nov. 16, 1997
October 28-Nov. 15, 1998
SUBMISSION DATES
September 1, 1997
September 1, 1998
ADDRESS
2625 East Sunrise Boulevard
Fort Lauderdale, FL 33304
USA

TEL:	954-563 0500
FAX:	954-564 1206
E-MAIL:	brofilm@aol.com
WEB SITE:	http://www.filmmag.com/fliff/
ENTRIES:	100+
ATTENDEES:	34,000+
CONTACT:	**Greg Von Hausch**

FILM TYPE
All
COMPETITIVE
Yes
LANGUAGE
Any
COUNTRY
Any
ENTRY FEES
Contact festival

AWARDS
Awards include $1,000 to the winner of the National Student Film Competition and the Lifetime Acheivement Award.

● South Bay Jewish Film Series

The South Bay Jewish Film Series serves about 2600 film lovers in the San Jose area. Its focus is on full length films dramas, comedies, documentaries, musicals, animated etc from independent producers. Films from all over the world have been shown. The Series is made up of four films, each film is given 3 showings in a one-week period for four consecutive weeks screening films on Wednesdays, Thursdays and Sundays. Every effort is made to assure that the film will be reviewed by the San Jose Mercury News and other local publication film critics.

FESTIVAL DATES
October 29-30; November 5-6, 9, 12-13, 16, 19-20 and 23. 1997
October-November, 1998

SUBMISSION DATES
June, 1998

ADDRESS
c/o Greater San Jose Jewish Community Center
, 14855 Oka Rd
Los Gatos, CA 95030
USA

FILM TYPE
Feature length

COMPETITIVE
No

LANGUAGE
Any (English Subtitles)

COUNTRY
Any

ENTRY FEES
None

TEL:	408-358-3636 X64
FAX:	415-969-1085
E-MAIL:	sbjfs@best.com
WEB SITE:	http://www.best.com/~sbjfs/

ATTENDEES:	2,600+
CONTACT:	**Fagie Rosen**

● The Paris Lesbian Film Festival

This festival's mandate is "to enable the viewing of films about the lives of lesbians in all their diversity". It also aims to continue the feminist tradition by providing a forum for Lesbian culture and creativity encompassing film, painting, sculpture, music and debate". All films screened must be created by women as well as about topics that women, in particular, lesbians find of interest. It " is more than a celebration of women's cinema - it is also the assertion of lesbian visibility and feminist militancy at its best".

FESTIVAL DATES
October/November, 1997
October/November, 1998

ADDRESS
Cineffable
37 avenue Pasteur
93100 Montreuil
France

FILM TYPE
All

COMPETITIVE
No

LANGUAGE
Any (translated into French by festival)

COUNTRY
Any

ENTRY FEES
None

TEL:	33 1 48 70 77 11
FAX:	33 1 48 70 77 11
E-MAIL:	106370.1435@compuserve.com
WEB SITE:	http://www.ourworld.com-puserve.com/homespages/cineffable/lesbian.htm
ENTRIES:	100+ screened
ATTENDEES:	5,000+

● San Luis Obispo International Film Festival

San Luis Obispo seeks to promote the appreciation of classic films, and the film preservation movement, by showing select films of historic and cultural significance. In addition, this festival emphasizes the technical aspects of filmmaking with special screenings, seminars, workshops, and guest lectures. There are also showcases for independent filmmakers; a documentary and short film series and the exhibition of new works from around the globe. For 1997, the competition is for documentaries and in 1998 it will include features.

October

FESTIVAL DATES
October 30-Nov. 9, 1997
October 29-Nov. 8, 1998 (tbc)

SUBMISSION DATES
August 1, 1997
August 1, 1998

ADDRESS
P.O. Box 1449
San Luis Obispo, CA 93401
USA

TEL: 1 805 546-FILM (3456)
FAX: 1 805 781-6799
E-MAIL: slofilmfest@slonet.org
WEB SITE:
http://www.slonet.org/vv/ipsloiff/
ATTENDEES: 5,200
CONTACT: **Mary A. Harris**

FILM TYPE
All

COMPETITIVE
Yes

LANGUAGE
Any (English subtitles)

COUNTRY
Any

ENTRY FEES
$40US

AWARDS
The "King Vidor Memorial Award," an annual tribute honoring an individual or organization for significant contributions to the art of filmmaking. The George Sidney Independent Film Competition is a juried competition for independent filmmakers. The jury can award $500 for 1st place; an award of merit of 2nd & 3rd place and three honourable mention certificates.

Barcelona International Gay and Lesbian Film Festival

ADDRESS
Casal Lambda, Ample 5
08002 Barcelona
Spain

FESTIVAL DATES
October 27-Nov. 7, 1997
TEL: 34 3 412 72 72
FAX: 34 3 412 74 76
E-MAIL: lambda@pangea.org

Birmingham International Film & TV Festival

ADDRESS
Central Independent Television, Broad Street
Birmingham B1 2JP
UK

TEL: 44-121-634 4213
FAX: 44-121-634 4392
CONTACT: Sarah McKenzie

Brynmawr Film Festival

ADDRESS
Leisure Dept, Blaenau Gwent BC, Civic Centre
Ebbw Vale, Wales NP3 6XB
UK

TEL: 44-1495-308996
FAX: 44-1495-308 996
CONTACT: Geoff Cripps

Festival de L'image de Film (Chalon-sur- Saone)

ADDRESS
5 bis, Avenue Nicephore Niepce
71100 Chalon-sur-Saone
France

TEL: 33-85 42 52 00
FAX: 33-85 42 52 22
CONTACT: Marcel Lathiere

Festival Internazionale del cinema di Salerno

ADDRESS
Corso Vittorio Emmanuele 140
Casella Postale 137
I-84100 Salerno
Italy

TEL: 39-89-22 36 32
FAX: 39-89-22 36 32
CONTACT: Rossi Ignazio

Forum Festival (Bratislava)

ADDRESS
Groesslingova 32
81109 Bratislava
Slovakia

TEL: 421-7 37 88 29 0
FAX: 421-7 37 88 29 0
CONTACT: Mrs Filusova

International Documentary Congress (Los Angeles)

ADDRESS
8949 Wilshire Boulevard
Beverly Hills, CA 90211
USA

TEL: 310-247 3000 ext. 176
FAX: 310-785 9334
E-MAIL: idf@netcom.com
CONTACT: Tracy Fowler

Le Giornate del Cinema Muto (Pordenone)

ADDRESS
La Cineteca del Friuli
Via Osoppo 26
I-33013 Gemona
Italy

TEL: 39-432-980458
FAX: 39-432-970543
E-MAIL:
CONTACT: Linio Jacob

Brief Entries
● Mifed (Milan)

ADDRESS
EA Fiera Milano
Largo Domodossoia 1
I-20145 Milano
Italy

FESTIVAL DATES
October 19-24, 1997
TEL: 39-2-48 01 29 12/20/42
FAX: 39-2-49 97 70 20
CONTACT: Elena Lloyd

● Mostra de Valencia / Cinema de Mediterrani

ADDRESS
Plaza del arzpbispo, 2 Bajo
46004 Valencia
Spain

TEL: 34-96-392 1506
FAX: 34-96-391 15 56
CONTACT: Luis Fernandez

● Show East (Atlantic City)

ADDRESS
244 West 49th Street #200
New York, NY 10019
USA

TEL: 212-246 6460
FAX: 212-265 6428
CONTACT: Jimmy Sunshine

● The NYU International Student Film Festival

ADDRESS
New York University, Tisch School of the Arts,
721 Broadway
New York, NY 10003
USA

FESTIVAL DATES
October 25-31, 1997
TEL: 212 998 1795; 39-55-500-7203
(Florence)
E-MAIL: hwangd@is3.nyu.edu

October

● Tokyo International Film Festival

Tokyo screens the most eagerly awaited major international productions in the "Special Screening" section. Both "blockbuster" films and international film festival award winners are showcased from around the world. Other sections include "Cinema Prism" and "Nippon Cinema Classics". All films are to be entertaining, of high artistic value, and be released in Japan after autumn of the festival year. Aside from the films screenings, a symposium as well as various activities are scheduled for the festival.

FESTIVAL DATES
November 1-10, 1997
November, 1998 (tba)

SUBMISSION DATES
July 15, 1997
July, 1998

ADDRESS
4F Landic Ginza Building, 1-6-5 Ginza
Chuo-ku, Tokyo 104
Japan

TEL: 81-3-3563 6305
FAX: 81-3-3563 6310
WEB SITE: http://www.tokyo-filmfest.or.jp/index-e.htm
ENTRIES: 105
ATTENDEES: 100,000+
CONTACT: **Toshiyuki Hone**

FILM TYPE
Feature

COMPETITIVE
Yes

LANGUAGE
Any

COUNTRY
Any

ENTRY FEES
None

AWARDS
There are two competitions at this festival. The International Competition and the Young Cinema Competition. The former awards the Tokyo Grand Prix, Special Jury Prize, Best Director, Actress, Actor, Artistic Contribution and Best Screenplay. The latter awards the Tokyo Gold, Silver, and Bronze worth 20, 10 and 5 million Yen, respectively.

● Worldfest-Charleston

Worldfest Charleston was founded in 1993 and is a sister festival to Worldfest Houston. A selection of the award winners are screened at the 10-day event. Each November it attracts both filmmakers and film buffs from all over the USA and the world. It also features seminars and many other activities. In a field of almost 300 other events in South Carolina, Worldfest Charleston has won the Hodges Tourism Award at the Governor's Tourism Conference.

FESTIVAL DATES
November 1-9, 1997
November, 1998

SUBMISSION DATES
September 5, 1997
September 5, 1998

ADDRESS
PO Box 838
Charleston, SC 29402
USA

TEL: 1 800 501 0111
FAX: 1 713 965 9960
E-MAIL: Worldfest@aol.com
WEB SITE: http://www.sc.net/worldfest/
ENTRIES: 1,500 (screened by jury for awards)
ATTENDEES: 15,000
CONTACT: **J. Hunter Todd**

FILM TYPE
All

COMPETITIVE
Yes

LANGUAGE
Any (English subtitles)

COUNTRY
Any

ENTRY FEES
$50-$200

AWARDS
Worldfest has over 200 categories the nine major ones. There are Gold, Silver, Bronze and Certificates of Merit Awards in each sub-category as well as Special Jury Awards given out at the sole discretion of the jury. There is also one GRAND AWARD for each of the Major Category headings and the Best overall Student winner receives a Kodak Raw Stock award equivalent to $2,500.00.

● Film Art Fest (Ljubljana)

Film Art Fest is organized by the cultural and congress centre Cankariev dom in Ljubljana. The aim is to illustrate progress and continuity of film as an art form. Only films of a high artistic level will be invited to participate, consequently, an invitation is a tribute to the filmmaker. This event occurs every year at the beginning of November.

FESTIVAL DATES
  November 3-16, 1997
  November 2-15, 1998 (tbc)
SUBMISSION DATES
  September 1, 1997
  September 1, 1998
ADDRESS
  Presemova 10
  Cankarjev Dom
  Ljubljana 61000
  Slovenia

FILM TYPE
  Feature, Documentary
COMPETITIVE
  No
LANGUAGE
  Any
COUNTRY
  Any
ENTRY FEES
  None

TEL:	386-61-1767 100
FAX:	386-61-224 279
ENTRIES:	10,000
ATTENDEES:	8,000
CONTACT:	**Jelka Stergel**

● Cinanima-International Animation Film Festival (Espinho)

The main purpose of the festival is to celebrate the art of animation. Cinanima comprises a competitive and non-competitive program which includes retrospectives. Besides the exhibition of the films, some exhibitions, debates and animation workshops are also presented.

FESTIVAL DATES
November 4-9, 1997 (tbc)
Beginning of November, 1998
SUBMISSION DATES
August, 1997
August, 1998
ADDRESS
Apartado 43, Rua 62
251 4501Espinho
Portugal

TEL: 351-2-724 611/721 621
FAX: 351-2-726 015
ENTRIES: 500
ATTENDEES: 10,000
CONTACT: **Antonio Gaio**

FILM TYPE
Animation
COMPETITIVE
Yes
LANGUAGE
Any
COUNTRY
Any
ENTRY FEES
None

AWARDS
The awards include; the Cinanima 96 (trophy, certificate and approx. $3,200 US), Jury's Special Award (trophy, certificate and approx. $1,600 US) and the Best Film in each category (trophy, certificate).

● Mix - The New York Lesbian & Gay Experimental Film/Video Festival

MIX sees itself "as a place of innovation and inspiration for generations of first-time image makers". It accepts entries of any experimental film/video/cyber/performance and installation work which calls into question and attacks the mainstream, be it in regard to sexuality or media making. Shorts are encouraged, as is work by makers from under-represented communities.

FESTIVAL DATES
November, 1997
November, 1998
SUBMISSION DATES
August 1, 1997
July 1, 1998
ADDRESS
341 Lafayette St., Suite 169
New York, NY 10012
USA

TEL: 212 501 2309
FAX: 212 571 5155
E-MAIL: mix@echonyc.com
WEB SITE: http://www.echonyc.com/~mix/
ENTRIES: 400-500 (100-150 screened)
ATTENDEES: 2,000-3,000
CONTACT: **Rajendra Roy**

FILM TYPE
All
COMPETITIVE
No
LANGUAGE
Any (English subtitles)
COUNTRY
Any
ENTRY FEES
$10 US sliding-scale entry

● Shorts International Film Festival

In 1997, the Shorts International Film Festival will have its inaugural year. Its mandate is "to develop a platform completely dedicated to the art of the short film". Once the shorts have been screened at the festival, a national tour will be arranged for the category winners to travel and screen their films in several major U.S. cities. The films that are screened at the festival will be packaged as a special program for a cable television broadcast.

FESTIVAL DATES
    November 5-6, 1997
    November 4-5, 1998 (tbc)
SUBMISSION DATES
    September 15, 1997
    September, 15 1998
ADDRESS
    10 Columbus Circle , 10th Floor
    New York, NY 10019
    USA

TEL: 212 489 3648
FAX: 212 489 9462
E-MAIL: info@shorts.org
WEB SITE: http://www.shorts.org/

FILM TYPE
    Short
COMPETITIVE
    Yes
LANGUAGE
    Any (English subtitiles)
COUNTRY
    Any
ENTRY FEES
    $25

AWARDS
    The festival awards the Grand Prize($2,000) for best director in each category.

● London Film Festival

London is one of the largest and best known film festivals that take place in the U.K. Every year over 100,000 people frequent its many theatres for two weeks in November. Its focus is on a wide range of world cinema from all over the globe.The programs include British Cinema Now, Panorama France, US Independents, an Asian and Short Film Showcase and Out of Africa. It runs for eighteen days starting on the first Thursday in November.

FESTIVAL DATES
    November 6-23, 1997
    November 5-22, 1998
SUBMISSION DATES
    August 15, 1997
    August 15, 1998
ADDRESS
    National Film Theatre, South Bank
    Waterloo, London SE1 8XT
    UK

TEL: 44-171-815 1323/8151324
FAX: 44-171-633 0786
E-MAIL: jane.ivey@bfi.org.uk
WEB SITE:
http://www.ibmpcug.co.uk/IFF.html
ENTRIES: 200+
ATTENDEES: 100,000
CONTACT: **Adrian Wooten**

FILM TYPE
    All
COMPETITIVE
    Yes
LANGUAGE
    Any
COUNTRY
    Any
ENTRY FEES
    None

International Film Festival Guide   185

● Margaret Mead Film and Video Festival

This is the largest Documentary and Ethnographic film festival in the US. It focuses on a variety of non-fiction films and videos from around the world. Same of its sections include a retrospective and special focus. The special focus for 1996 was "fake documentary", "local television international" and "Pacific Islands".

FESTIVAL DATES
November 6-12, 1997
November 5-11, 1998

SUBMISSION DATES
May 3, 1997
May 3, 1998

ADDRESS
American Museum of Natural History
79th Street at Central Park West
New York, NY 10024-5192
USA

FILM TYPE
Documentary

COMPETITIVE
Yes

LANGUAGE
Any

COUNTRY
Any

ENTRY FEES
$30 Independent, $75 TV commericials

TEL:	212-769 5305
FAX:	212-769 5329
E-MAIL:	Charnov@amnh.org.
ENTRIES:	50
ATTENDEES:	6,000
CONTACT:	**Elaine Charnov**

● Nordic Film Days

Nordic Film Days is a "film-packed" long weekend which showcases a selection of Nordic and Baltic films. It's a competitive event for these films, the winners receiving monetary awards.

FESTIVAL DATES
November 6-9, 1997
November 5-8, 1998

ADDRESS
Nordische Filmtage
D-23552 Lubeck
Germany

FILM TYPE
All

COMPETITIVE
Yes

LANGUAGE
Danish, English and German

COUNTRY
Nordic and Baltic countries

ENTRY FEES
None

TEL:	49-451-1224105/1224109
FAX:	49-451-1224106
ENTRIES:	100
ATTENDEES:	8,000
CONTACT:	**Andrea Kunsemuller**

AWARDS
At this festival their are prizes awarded in 6 different categories. They include: feature, documentary, children's, social development and Baltic feature. The prize money ranges from 5,000- 25,000 DM.

● Northamptom Film Festival

In 1997, the festival expands to 4 full days in November. It also will accept submissions from the entire United States for the first time and have a competitive section. This expansion occured due to its popularity, but still promises to continue its "commitment to help showcase new artists". Northampton also features film workshops, seminars and parties. At previous festivals many directors were on hand to discuss their works and share their ideas.

FESTIVAL DATES
November 6-9, 1997
November 5-8, 1998 (tbc)
SUBMISSION DATES
June 30, 1997
June 30, 1998
ADDRESS
351 Pleasant St., Box 137
Northampton, MA   01060
USA

TEL:	413-586-3471
FAX:	413-584-4432
E-MAIL:	filmfest@nohofilm.org
WEB SITE:	http://www.nohofilm.org/
ENTRIES:	120 (30-40 screened)
ATTENDEES:	2,000+
CONTACT:	**Howard Polonsky**

FILM TYPE
Any
COMPETITIVE
Yes
LANGUAGE
Any (English subtitles)
COUNTRY
USA
ENTRY FEES
$25US

AWARDS
The awards include the "Best of the Fest", Best use of Film/Video for Journalism and the Kodak Vision Award.

● Amiens International Film Festival

In 1996, this festival's competition focused on films that deal with cultural identities. In 1997, part of its program will showcase a panorama of 90's South-African cinema, as well as, a theme about "European suburbs".

FESTIVAL DATES
November 7-16, 1997 (tbc)
November 6-15, 1998 (tbc)
SUBMISSION DATES
September 8, 1997
September 8, 1998
ADDRESS
39 rue de Noyou
F-80000 Amiens
France

TEL:	33-3-22 71 35 70
FAX:	33-3-22 92 53 04
ENTRIES:	220
ATTENDEES:	40,000
CONTACT:	**Jean-Pierre Garcia**

FILM TYPE
All, but animation
COMPETITIVE
Yes
LANGUAGE
Any
COUNTRY
Any
ENTRY FEES
None

AWARDS
This festival awards their Grand Prix to the best Feature and Short Film.

● Banff Festival of Mountain Films

Banff focuses on the best international films and videos on mountains and the spirit of adventure. This festival provides an opportunity for filmmakers to meet and exchange ideas in a relaxed environment through seminars, on-demand screening facilities and social gatherings.

FESTIVAL DATES
November 7-9, 1997
November 6-8, 1998
SUBMISSION DATES
Mid-September, 1997
Mid-September, 1998
ADDRESS
The Banff Centre
PO Box 1020, Stn. 38
Banff, Alberta TOL OCO
Canada

TEL: 403-762 6441
FAX: 403-762 6277
E-MAIL: Karen_Turnbull@BanffCentre.ab.ca
WEB SITE:
http://www.banffcentre.ab.ca/CMC/
ENTRIES: 150
ATTENDEES: 6,000
CONTACT: **Karen Turnbull**

FILM TYPE
All (regarding mountain culture)
COMPETITIVE
Yes
LANGUAGE
Any (English translation/subtitles)
COUNTRY
Any
ENTRY FEES
$50 Canadian

AWARDS
The awards include the Grand Prize, best film on climbing, on mountain sports, on mountain culture, and on mountain environment, all receiving a $2,000 cash prize. Other awards are the Bill Roberts Award for Young Filmmakers, People's Choice, and the Special Jury awards.

● Children's Film Festival (Augsburg)

Every year thousands of children and teenagers visit "their" film festival. Within this group are over 300 classes from the Augsburg region. Special programs are dedicated to certain topics and certain directors. Prior to the commencement of the festival, two school classes are chosen for a jury and will be specially trained to select the winning film for their age particular group. The festival also includes discussions with directors, seminars and workshops.

FESTIVAL DATES
November 7-16, 1997
November 6-15, 1998
SUBMISSION DATES
September 10, 1997
September 10, 1998
ADDRESS
Filmburo Augsburg
Schroeckstr.8
D-86152 Augsburg
Germany

TEL: 49-821-15 30 77
FAX: 49-821-34 95 21 8
ENTRIES: 15 screened (8 in competition)
ATTENDEES: 16,000
CONTACT: **Ellen Gratza**

FILM TYPE
All
COMPETITIVE
Yes
LANGUAGE
Any
COUNTRY
Any
ENTRY FEES
None

AWARDS
The Augsburg Children's Film Dragon is awarded at this festival.

● Cinemental 3; Le Festival de Films Francophones au Manitoba

This is the only Francophone film festival, with the exception of Moncton, outside of Quebec. The best French films of the year, in all categories, are shown at this festival.

FESTIVAL DATES
November, 1997
November, 1998

SUBMISSION DATES
August 1, 1997
August 1, 1998

ADDRESS
340 Provencher
Winnipeg, Manitoba R2H 0G7
Canada

TEL: 204-233-8972
FAX: 204-233-3324
ENTRIES: 40 screened
ATTENDEES: 2,000
CONTACT: **Marc Francois Trombley**

FILM TYPE
All

COMPETITIVE
Yes

LANGUAGE
French (English subtitles)

COUNTRY
French speaking countries

ENTRY FEES
None

AWARDS
Call in June 97 for new festival dates.

● Hawaii International Film Festival

Hawaii's goal is "to advance understanding and cultural exchange among the peoples of Asia, the Pacific and North America through the medium of film". The continuous theme of this festival, since its inception in 1981, is "When Strangers Meet". It also is the only major film festival in the world, where all screenings are absolutely free to the general public. The first week takes place in Honolulu, and the second week on the islands of Maui, Kauai, the Big Island of Hawaii, Molokai and Lanai. At least 26 screens are used during the festival and is the only statewide film festival in the U.S.

FESTIVAL DATES
November 7-20, 1997
November 6-19, 1998 (tbc)

SUBMISSION DATES
July 15, 1997
July 15, 1998

ADDRESS
700 Bishop Street, Suite 400
Honolulu, HI 96813
USA

TEL: 808-528 3456; in US 1 800 752-8193
FAX: 808-528 1410
E-MAIL: hiffinfo@hiff.org
WEB SITE: http://www.hiff.org/
ENTRIES: 1,000 (80 screened)
ATTENDEES: 65,000+
CONTACT: **Christian Gaines/ Lani Miyahara**

FILM TYPE
All

COMPETITIVE
Yes

LANGUAGE
Any (English subtitles)

COUNTRY
Asia, Pacific and North America

ENTRY FEES
$25(waived for Pacific and Hawaii-based film-maker)

AWARDS
This festival features"The Maile Awards" named after fragrant leaves that grow in Polynesia. The best feature and documentary film receive a Golden Maile. Other awards include the Eastman Kodak Cinematography Award and Special Jury Awards.

● Reeling '97: The Chicago Lesbian and Gay International Film Festival

Reeling's focus is to celebrate and present works by and about Lesbians, Gay Men, Bisexuals, and Transgendered People.

FESTIVAL DATES
  November 7-16, 1997
  November 6-15, 1998
SUBMISSION DATES
  July 15, 1997
  July 15, 1998
ADDRESS
  Reeling c/o Chicago Filmmakers
  1543 W. Division St.
  Chicago, IL 60622
  USA

TEL: 773 384 5533
FAX: 773 384 5532
E-MAIL: reeling@chicagofilmmakers.org
WEB SITE:
http://www.chicagofilmmakers.org/reeling/
ENTRIES: 150 screened
ATTENDEES: 8,000+
CONTACT: **Brenda Webb**

FILM TYPE
  All
COMPETITIVE
  Yes
LANGUAGE
  Any (English subtitlies)
COUNTRY
  Any
ENTRY FEES
  $15 (under 60 mins.); $20 (over 60 mins.)

AWARDS
  Prizes for 1st, 2nd and 3rd in the
catagories of: Documentary,
Animation/Experimental, and Narrative.

● Stockholm International Film Festival

The goal of this festival is to broaden the forum for innovative quality films in Scandinavia beyond what is currently available through commercial outlets and traditional film institutions.The non-competitive sections include Open Zone, American Independents, Twilight Zone, Collage, Tributes, Northern Lights and Short Films.

FESTIVAL DATES
  November 7-16, 1997
  November 6-15, 1998
SUBMISSION DATES
  September 12, 1997
  September 11, 1998
ADDRESS
  PO Box 7573
  10395 Stockholm
  Sweden

TEL: 46-8-20 05 50
FAX: 46-8-20 05 90
E-MAIL: info@filmfestivalen.se
WEB SITE: http://www.filmfestivalen.se/
ENTRIES: 120
ATTENDEES: 50,000
CONTACT: **Petter Mattsson**

FILM TYPE
  All
COMPETITIVE
  Yes
LANGUAGE
  Any
COUNTRY
  Any
ENTRY FEES
  None

AWARDS
  The Bronze Horse is awarded to the best film and Aluminium Horses are awarded to best screenplay, cinematography, actor, actress and best first feature film.

• Rassegna di Palermo International Sportfilmfestival

November

This festival is very specific in its focus. It aims to promote a stimulating comparison between film and video works exclusively about sports themes. It accepts entries from all over the world, but they must conform to the festival's main focus.

FESTIVAL DATES
November 10-14, 1997
November 9-13, 1998

SUBMISSION DATES
July 31, 1997
July 31, 1998

ADDRESS
Via Notarbartolo, 1g
I-Palermo 90141
Italy

TEL: 39-91-611 4968/625 1858
FAX: 39-91-611 4968/625 6256
E-MAIL: magg601@pn.itnet.it
ENTRIES: 100
ATTENDEES: 4,000
CONTACT: **Vito Maggio**

FILM TYPE
All

COMPETITIVE
Yes

LANGUAGE
Any

COUNTRY
Any

ENTRY FEES
None

AWARDS
The major award given out is the Premio Paladino d'Oro.

22nd san francisco international lesbian & gay film festival
june 1998

for information and entry forms:

F R A M E L I N E

346 ninth street
san francisco ca 94103
tel: 415 703-8650/fax: 415 861-1404/e: frameline@aol.com
www.frameline.org

setagte

● Arctic Light Film Festival

Kiruna is the main location of the Arctic Light Film Festival which covers a large area in northern Sweden by showing film and arranging activities in towns and villages like Gallivare, Malmberget, Vittangi, Pajala and Overkalix. Arctic Light is the largest film festival in the area, and screens films in both the largest igloo and the largest underground mine in the world. In 1996, pupils in groups of 15 where permitted to, free of charge and for half a day, get acquainted with filmmaking and video equipment in one of several film courses, that occur throughtout the festival.

FESTIVAL DATES
 November 12-18, 1997
 November 11-17, 1998, (tbc)
ADDRESS
 PO Box 234
 SE-981 24 Kiruna
 Sweden

FAX: 46 980 828 01
E-MAIL: Arcticlight.Filmfestival@kiruna.se
WEB SITE: http://www.kiruna.se/~alff/
ENTRIES: 45 approx.
ATTENDEES: 4-5,000
CONTACT: **Lena Bjerkesjo**

FILM TYPE
 All
COMPETITIVE
 Yes
LANGUAGE
 Any
COUNTRY
 Any

AWARDS
 A video competition for pupils in Primary, Secondary and Upper Secondary school in the county of Norrbotten. A theme is set and the maximum running time is 5 minutes. The prize is a video camera, value SEK 21,000 and cameras valued at SEK 1,000

● film+arc graz (International Festival of Film and Architecture)

film+arc graz is a biennial festival that focuses on the innovative treatment of topics related to architecture, city and space. Questions pertaining to the philosophical, political and social components of architecture and urbanism are among the central topics of the competition.

FESTIVAL DATES
 November 12-16, 1997
SUBMISSION DATES
 July 10, 1997
ADDRESS
 Hallerschloszstrasse 21
 A-8010 Graz
 Austria

TEL: 43 316 356 155
FAX: 43 316 356 156
E-MAIL: artimage@xarch.tu-graz.ac.at
WEB SITE: http://www.xarch.tu-graz.ac.at/fil-marc/
ENTRIES: 400
ATTENDEES: 10,000
CONTACT: **Charlotte Pochhacker**

FILM TYPE
 All
COMPETITIVE
 Yes
LANGUAGE
 Any
COUNTRY
 Any
ENTRY FEES
 None

AWARDS
 An international jury awards the Grand Prix film+arc.graz (ATS 100,000), as well as the other three main prizes that will split the remaining ATS 150,000.

● Rendezvous with Madness Film & Video Festival

Rendezvous occurs on a yearly basis and uses film as a catalyst to create an open dialogue regarding all facets of "madness". It takes place at the Queen Street Mental Health Centre where a large portion of Toronto's mental health community works and lives. Its goal is to pass on a greater understanding of mental illness through its program which screens shorts and features that touch on the fact, and mythology of mental illness.

FESTIVAL DATES
November 12-16, 1997
November 11-15 or 18-22, 1998

SUBMISSION DATES
August 29, 1997
August 29, 1998 (tbc)

ADDRESS
1001 Queen St. West
Toronto, Ontario M6J 1H4
Canada

FILM TYPE
All (feature or short format)

COMPETITIVE
No

LANGUAGE
Any (English subtitles)

COUNTRY
Any

ENTRY FEES
None

TEL: 416 583 4339
FAX: 416 583 4354
E-MAIL: rendezvous@sympatico.ca
WEB SITE: http://www3.sympatico.ca/ren-dezvous/
ENTRIES: 10 screened
ATTENDEES: 1,000+
CONTACT: **Lisa Brown**

● Sarasota French Film Festival

The goal of the Sarasota French Film Festival is to enhance the appreciation and accessibility of French film as a highly influential and artistically significant cinematic tradition. It also creates a forum for interaction among the general public, students, US film professionals and French cinema artists. A further goal is to enhance economic ties in film and other industries between France and Florida.

FESTIVAL DATES
November 12-16, 1997
November 11-15, 1998

ADDRESS
5555 N Tamiami Trail
Sarasota, FL 34243
USA

FILM TYPE
Feature, Short (primarily)

COMPETITIVE
No

LANGUAGE
French

COUNTRY
French countries

ENTRY FEES
Contact festival

TEL: 941-351 9010 ext. 4300
FAX: 941-351 5796
E-MAIL: FFFFN2ASM@aol.com
WEB SITE: http://www.sarasota-online.com/film/
ATTENDEES: 26,000
CONTACT: **Patricia Richmond**

● Verzaubert Gay and Lesbian Film Festival (Munich / Cologne)

Verzaubert showcases gay and lesbian films from around the world. It is one of the longest and most popular annual German Gay & Lesbian Film Festivals.

FESTIVAL DATES
  November 12-December 3, 1997
  November 11-December 2, 1998
SUBMISSION DATES
  June 30, 1997
  June 29, 1998
ADDRESS
  Wittelsbacher Str. 26
  c/o Rosebud Entertainment
  10707 Berlin
  Germany

FILM TYPE
  All
COMPETITIVE
  No
LANGUAGE
  Any (English or German subtitles)
COUNTRY
  Any
ENTRY FEES
  None

TEL: 49-30 861 4532
FAX: 49-30 861 4539
ENTRIES: 70
ATTENDEES: 15,000
CONTACT: **Schorsch Muller**

● Mediterranean Film Festival

This festival showcases feature and short films from the Mediterranean region, including Turkey, North Africa, Greece, and Spain.

FESTIVAL DATES
  Mid-November, 1997
  Mid-November, 1998
SUBMISSION DATES
  Mid-October, 1997
  Mid-October, 1998
ADDRESS
  Postfach 1549
  D-72005 Tubingen
  Germany

FILM TYPE
  Feature, Short
COMPETITIVE
  No
LANGUAGE
  Any
COUNTRY
  Mediterranean countries (e.g. Italy, Israel etc.)
ENTRY FEES
  None

TEL: 49-7071-32828
FAX: 49-7071-31006
ENTRIES: 20-30
ATTENDEES: 2,000
CONTACT: **Dieter Betz**

● Puerto Rico International Film Festival

Puerto Rico is one of the most exciting film events taking place in the Caribbean today. It screens approximately 100 features and has achieved a solid reputation for the quality of its film selection, and the seriousness of its organization.

FESTIVAL DATES
Mid-November, 1997
Mid-November, 1998

ADDRESS
70 Mayaguez Street, Ste B-1
San Juan, PR 918
USA

TEL:	787-763 4997/764 7044
FAX:	787-753 5367
ENTRIES:	100
ATTENDEES:	30,000
CONTACT:	**Juan Gerard**

FILM TYPE
Feature

COMPETITIVE
No

LANGUAGE
Any

COUNTRY
Any

ENTRY FEES
None

AWARDS
The Best Latin American Film, as well as, the best film at the festival.

● Turin International Film Festival

Turin's goal is to make people aware of films made by new directors and assist in getting these films distributed. Particular attention is paid to those films whose themes and plots show evidence of newly emerging kinds of sensitivity, and show attempts at innovation in film form and language. Programs also include retrospectives and special events.

FESTIVAL DATES
November 14-22, 1997
November 13-21, 1998

SUBMISSION DATES
August 31, 1997
August 31, 1998

ADDRESS
Via Monte di Pieta 1
I-Torino 10121
Italy

TEL:	39-11-562 3309
FAX:	39-11-562 9796
E-MAIL:	ficg@webcom.com
WEB SITE:	http://www.webcom.com/~ficg/
ENTRIES:	300
ATTENDEES:	45,000
CONTACT:	**Alberto Barbera**

FILM TYPE
Feature, Short

COMPETITIVE
Yes

LANGUAGE
Any

COUNTRY
Any

ENTRY FEES
None

AWARDS
The competitions are the International Short Film and Feature Film Competition with a 1st prize and two special jury prizes in each. The former awards 30 million lira for 1st and 10 million lira for the jury awards while the latter is 5 million lira for 1st and 2 million for the jury awards, respectively. The other two competitions are the Italian Space Competition(1st Prize is 10 million lire in technical services and film 2nd Prize 2 million lire) and the Turin Space Competition worth 1st Prize 5 million lire 2nd Prize 1 million lire.

● Welsh International Film Festival (Aberystyth)

The Welsh International Film Festival is non-competitive for feature and short films in Welsh and English. The festival also features retrospectives, workshops and seminars.

FESTIVAL DATES
  November 14-23, 1997
  November 13-22, 1998
SUBMISSION DATES
  August 31, 1997
  August, 1998
ADDRESS
  6g Parc Gwyddeniaeth, Cefn Llan
  Aberystwyth, Wales SY23 3AH
  UK

TEL: 44-1970-617995
FAX: 44-1970-617942
E-MAIL: wff995@aber.ac.uk
WEB-SITE: http://aber.ac.uk/~wff995/
ENTRIES: 110+
ATTENDEES: 10,000+
CONTACT: **Berwyn Rowlands**

FILM TYPE
  All
COMPETITIVE
  Yes/No
LANGUAGE
  Any
COUNTRY
  Any
ENTRY FEES
  None

AWARDS
  D.M. Davies Award for Best Short Film by Young Filmmaker from Wales (25,000 pounds).

● Oulu International Children's Film Festival

Oulu introduces the latest children's productions in feature length and animation. Sections include retrospectives, reviews of Finnish children's films, and a forum at which filmmakers can discuss issues related to the production of children's films . There are 15 features entered into the competition. In addition to the screenings, Oulu will include discussions with directors, exhibitions and seminars.

FESTIVAL DATES
  November 17-23, 1997
  November 16-22, 1998
SUBMISSION DATES
  September 16, 1997
  September 16, 1998
ADDRESS
  Toriatu 8
  90100 Oulu
  Finland

TEL: 358 8 881 1293/881 1294
FAX: 358 8 881 1290/3141 730
E-MAIL: raimo.kinisjarvi@oufilmcenter.inet.fi
WEB SITE:
  http://www.festivals.fi/ffoukaen.htm
ENTRIES: 40
ATTENDEES: 10,000
CONTACT: **Pentti Kejonen**

FILM TYPE
  Feature, Animation
COMPETITIVE
  Yes
LANGUAGE
  Any
COUNTRY
  Any
ENTRY FEES
  None

AWARDS
  Each year a jury of children awards the prize of 3000 ecus as well as the Kaleva newspaper's Starboy figurine to the director of the best film in the main programme.

● New York Expo of Short Film and Video

The New York Expo celebrates the art of the short film/video. They screen both traditional, well-crafted work and challenging, experimental and innovative productions. The Expo has provided early recognition for many major directors, including Spike Lee, Martha Coolidge and George Lucas. Award winners will be screened at the Donnell Media Center, New York City. The Expo will tour selected finalist films to a limitied number of non-profit festival venues. Finalists will also be offered a non-exclusive distribution opportunity through Drift Distribution, the Expo's sister organization.

FESTIVAL DATES
November 19-22, 1997
November, 1998
SUBMISSION DATES
July 1, 1997
July, 1998
ADDRESS
532 La Guardia Place, Suite 330
New York, NY 10012
USA

TEL:	212-873 1353
FAX:	212-724 9172
E-MAIL:	rswbc@cunyvm.cuny.edu
ENTRIES:	800 (45 screened)
ATTENDEES:	1,500
CONTACT:	**Robert Withers**

FILM TYPE
Short (60 mins. or less)
COMPETITIVE
Yes
LANGUAGE
Any (English subtitles)
COUNTRY
Any
ENTRY FEES
$35US

AWARDS
All entries selected for screening are considered Jury Award winners and receive an award certificate. In addition, there will be Gold, Silver and Bronze prizes in each category, selected by judges who are award-winning video and filmmakers, critics and writers. Blockbuster and Cyberfelds cash awards and Eastman Kodak filmstock awards will be granted to selected Jury Award winners.

● Action and Adventure Film Festival (Antwerp)

This festival focuses on the craft of the filmmaker. The program consists of 40-50 films, including the Official Section which previews 10 new films, tributes to directors,and a spotlight on masters if special effects experts.

FESTIVAL DATES
November, 1997
November, 1998
SUBMISSION DATES
Mid-September, 1997
Mid-September, 1998
ADDRESS
1104 Kortrijksesteenweg
B-9051 Ghent
Belgium

TEL:	32-9-221 8946
FAX:	32-9-221 9074
E-MAIL:	filmfestival@infoboard.be
WEB SITE:	http://www.fug.ac.be/filmfesti-val/Welcome.html
ENTRIES:	40-50
ATTENDEES:	15,000+
CONTACT:	**Jacques Dubrulle**

FILM TYPE
Feature
COMPETITIVE
No
ENTRY FEES
None

● Ohio Independent Film Festival

November

Ohio provides a unique networking and exhibition forum for independent filmmakers. It also provides a year-round Screenplay Reading Program and Fiscal Agent Sponsorship Program to independent artists. By exhibiting not only completed works but also works-in-progress as well as mixed format work (e.g., 16 mm film with soundtrack on a cassette) these forums have a more unique appeal. The festival takes place twice every year (in April & November) at the Cleveland Public Theatre. Past panel discussions have included; Film Making: Art or Commerce and Selling Your Film at the Independent Feature Film Market.

FESTIVAL DATES
November 20-23, 1997
April and November, 1998

SUBMISSION DATES
October 15, 1997
March, 1998

ADDRESS
2258 West 10th Street, Suite 5
Cleveland, OH 44113
USA

TEL:	216 781 1755
E-MAIL:	OhioIndieFilmFest@juno.com
WEB SITE:	http://www.rinestock.com/flick-fest/
ENTRIES:	50 screened
ATTENDEES:	1,000+
CONTACT:	**Annetta Marion**

FILM TYPE
All

COMPETITIVE
No

LANGUAGE
Any (English subtitled)

COUNTRY
Any

ENTRY FEES
$15 short; $20 feature

AWARDS
A cash award is given to the Best of the Fest as voted on by the audience.

● Gijón International Film Festival

Gijon's aim is to present the newest works of young cinema worldwide. The obstacle is to show the kind of films which can be made under non-conventional rules, but are still creative and independent in their form. The festival also focuses on those films dealing with the problems and concerns of youngsters. One of the goals of this festival is to feature first-time filmmakers. Other programs include retrospectives as well as "The Secret Cinema".

FESTIVAL DATES
November 21-28, 1997
November 20-27, 1998 (tbc)

SUBMISSION DATES
September 29, 1997
September 29, 1998

ADDRESS
Paseo de Begona, 24 Entresuelo, PO Box 76
33205 Gijón, Asturias
Spain

TEL:	34 8 534 3739
FAX:	34 8 535 4152
E-MAIL:	festcine@airastur.es
ENTRIES:	150 screened
ATTENDEES:	20,000
CONTACT:	**Jose Luis Cienfuegos**

FILM TYPE
Feature, Short

COMPETITIVE
Yes

LANGUAGE
Any (Spanish, French or English subtitles)

COUNTRY
Any

ENTRY FEES
None

AWARDS
The International Jury awards the "Principado De Asturias" to best feature and short film, "Special Prize of the Jury" to the best director, actress, actor, script and the "Gil Parrondo" for the best art direction. There is also a young jury made up of 50 people from age 17-26 years old. It awards the Prize of the Young Jury to the best feature and short film. Each film in the Official section receives a Certificate of Participation.

● International Thessaloniki Film Festival

Thessaloniki is the oldest major film event in Greece. It features international films including many independent productions. Different sections are: first and second time directors (International Competition), the Greek film production of the year (Greek Film Competition), and a major retrospective of a known director's work. In 1996, Peter Greenaway received this honour.

FESTIVAL DATES
November 21-30, 1997
Second half of November, 1998

SUBMISSION DATES
October 6, 1997
October 6, 1998

ADDRESS
36 Sina Street
10672 Athens
Greece

TEL: 30-1-361 0418/30-31-286678
FAX: 30-1-362 1023/30-31-285759
E-MAIL: filmfestival@compulink.gr
WEB SITE: http://www.compulink.gr/filmfestival
ENTRIES: 150+ screened
ATTENDEES: 42,000
CONTACT: **Michel Demopoulos**

FILM TYPE
Feature, Documentary

COMPETITIVE
Yes

LANGUAGE
Any

COUNTRY
Any

ENTRY FEES
None

AWARDS
The Golden and Silver Alexander are awarded to the best film(US$50,000) and special jury selection (US$30,000) in the competition. Prizes are also awarded for best director, actress, actor, screenplay, and artistic achievement.

● Latin American Film Festival of Huelva

Huelva showcases feature and short films from around the world and takes place in the Columbus House. This structure has four pavilions of which two, the Congress Palace and the Auditorium, can accommodate 800 people. Rooms are set up for seminars and meetings that can accommodate over 200 people. Cinemas that are used by Huelva are The "Gran Teatro" which is a magnificent antique building, the Emperador Cinema and the Rábida Cinema, each with three projection rooms.

FESTIVAL DATES
November 22-29, 1997
November 21-28, 1998

ADDRESS
c/o Palacio de Festivales de Huelva
Casa Colon, Plaza del Punto
21003 Huelva
Spain

TEL: 959-210 170
FAX: 959-210 173
E-MAIL: festihue@onuba.otd.es
WEB SITE: http://www.otd.es/iberoamericano/
ATTENDEES: 32,000
CONTACT: Jose Luis Ruiz

FILM TYPE
Feature, Short

COMPETITIVE
Yes

LANGUAGE
Any

COUNTRY
Any

ENTRY FEES
None

AWARDS
The "Colon De Oro" is awarded worth 3,000,000 ptas.

● Junior Dublin Film Festival

November

Junior Dublin is a non-competitive international showcase of world cinema for young people. More than thirty titles are screened for two weeks in November/December.

FESTIVAL DATES
November 23-Dec. 5, 1997
November 22-Dec. 4, 1998

SUBMISSION DATES
August , 1997
August, 1998

ADDRESS
c/o Irish Film Centre
Eustache Street
Dublin 2
Ireland

FILM TYPE
All

COMPETITIVE
No

LANGUAGE
English

COUNTRY
Any

ENTRY FEES
None

TEL:	353-1 671 4095
FAX:	353-1 677 8755
E-MAIL:	jdff@indigo.ie
ENTRIES:	100 (30 screened)
ATTENDEES:	10,000
CONTACT:	**Alan Robinson**

● International Festival of Documentary and Short Films (Bilbao)

The films screened at Bilbao are strictly that of the documentary and short film variety. Its competition is large and award-winning films are kept (with the producers permission) in the festival's archives. The prize money given to these films is split evenly between producer and filmmaker. It's theme is "Understanding between men through pictures".

FESTIVAL DATES
November 25-31, 1997 (tbc)
End of November, 1998

SUBMISSION DATES
September, 1997
September, 1998

ADDRESS
C/Colon de Larreategui
n 37-4 Apartado 579
48009 Bilbao
Spain

FILM TYPE
All

COMPETITIVE
Yes

LANGUAGE
Any (dialogue in French, English, Spanish)

COUNTRY
Any

ENTRY FEES
None

AWARDS
   The awards include, Grand Prize for The Bilbao Festival (400,000 ptas), for Spanish Films (350,000ptas), and for Basque Films (250,000 ptas). It also awards the Gold and Silver Mikeldi for animation, documentaries and fiction, worth 250,000 and 150,000 ptas., respectively.

TEL:	34-4-424 8698
FAX:	34-4-424 5624
CONTACT:	**Maria Angeles Olea**

● Golden Knight International Amateur Film & Video Festival (Malta)

This Festival allows both films and videos to be entered into its three separate classes. It takes place each year on the last Thursday, Friday, Saturday in November.

FESTIVAL DATES
  November 27-29, 1997
  November 26-28, 1998
SUBMISSION DATES
  September 15, 1997
  September 15, 1998
ADDRESS
  Malta Amateur Cine Circle, PO Box 450
  Valetta CMR 01
  Malta

TEL:	356-222345/574544
FAX:	356-225047
E-MAIL:	macc@global.net.mt
WEB SITE:	http://wwwlglobal.net.mt/~macc
ENTRIES:	95-110
ATTENDEES:	500
CONTACT:	**Alfred Stagno Navarra**

FILM TYPE
  All
COMPETITIVE
  Yes
LANGUAGE
  Any (synopsis in English)
COUNTRY
  Any
ENTRY FEES
  Ranges from $17-$56 US

AWARDS
  This festival awards prizes in three separate classes. In class A (amateur) and B (student) the prizes include, the Golden, Silver and Bronze Knight for first, second and third best entry, respectively. Class A also awards a prize to the best documentary and animation film. Class C (open class) awards a prize to best entry, and the Sultana's Cup is given out to the entry that best extols the merits of Malta.

● International Documentary Film Festival Amsterdam (IDFA)

IDFA is among the world's best known documentary film festivals. Its programs include a film and video competition, "Highlights of the Lowlands", unique archival footage and debut films. At the end of the festival, an international co-financing forum of documentaries will take place. The festival runs into the first week of December each year.

FESTIVAL DATES
  November 27-Dec 4, 1997
  November 26-Dec 3, 1998
SUBMISSION DATES
  September 1, 1997
  September 1, 1998
ADDRESS
  Kleine Gartmanplantsoen 10
  1017 RR Amsterdam
  Amsterdam
  The Netherlands

TEL:	31-20-627 3329
FAX:	31-20-627 5388
E-MAIL:	idfa@xs4all.nl
WEB SITE:	http://www.dds.nl/~damocles
ENTRIES:	150
ATTENDEES:	35,000+
CONTACT:	**Ally Derks**

FILM TYPE
  Documentary
COMPETITIVE
  Yes
LANGUAGE
  Any
COUNTRY
  Any

AWARDS
  IDFA has a film and video competition. In the former, approximately 25 film compete for the Joris Ivens Award whereas in the latter approximately15 videos compete for the Silver Wolf.

● Festival dei Popoli International Review of Social Documentary Film (Florence)

Festival dei Popoli is open to documentaries dealing with social, political and anthropological topics as well as with the world of arts.

FESTIVAL DATES
November 22-27, 1997
End of November, 1998

SUBMISSION DATES
September 1, 1997
September 1, 1998

ADDRESS
Via Castellani 8
Firenze 50122
Italy

TEL: 39-55-244 778
FAX: 39-55-213 698
E-MAIL: festpopol@data.it
ENTRIES: 700
ATTENDEES: 2,000+
CONTACT: **Mario Simondi**

FILM TYPE
Documentary

COMPETITIVE
Yes

LANGUAGE
Any

COUNTRY
Any

ENTRY FEES
None

AWARDS
Awards include Best Documentary, Best Research and Best Ethographic Film.

Brief Entries
● Boston Jewish Film Festival

ADDRESS
99 Moody
Waltham, MA 02854
USA

TEL: 617-899 3830
E-MAIL: BJFF@cyways.com
WEB SITE: http://www.bjff.cyways.com/
CONTACT: **Sara Rubin**

● Carthage International Film Festival

ADDRESS
c/o The JCC Managing Committee
P.O. Box 1029-1045
Tunis RP
Tunisia

TEL: 21-61 260323
FAX: 21-61 260323

● Duisburger Filmwoche (Duisburg)

ADDRESS
Am konig-Heinrich-Platz
D-47049 Duisburg
Germany

TEL: 49-203-283 4171/283 4187
FAX: 49-203-283 4130
CONTACT: **Werner Ruzicka**

● Festival des Trois Continents (Nantes)

ADDRESS
19a Passage Pommeraye, BP 3306
F-44033 Nantes Cedex 01
France

FESTIVAL DATES
November 25-Dec. 2, 1997
TEL: 33-2-40 69 74 14
FAX: 33-2-40 73 55 22
CONTACT: **Alain Jalladean**

● Festival Internacional de Cine e Artes Audiovisuales de Buernos Aires

ADDRESS
c/o INCCAA, Lima 139
1073 Buenos Aires
Argentina

TEL: 541-3 831698
FAX: 541-3 811776
CONTACT: **Bernardo Zupnik**

● Holland Animation Film Festival

ADDRESS
Hoogt 4
NL-3512 Utrecht
The Netherlands

FESTIVAL DATES
November, 1998
TEL: 31 30 233 1733
FAX: 31 30 233 1079
E-MAIL: haff@knoware.nl
CONTACT: **Gerben Schermer**

● International Festival of Film Schools (Munich)

ADDRESS
c/o IMF GmbH
Kaiserstrabe 39
D-80801 Munich
Germany

TEL: 49 89-38 19 04/0
FAX: 49 89-38 19 04 27

● Kidscreen (Como)

ADDRESS
Rue royale St Marie 2
B-1030 Brussels
Belgium

TEL: 32-2 219 48 96
FAX: 32-2 219 58 60
CONTACT: **Felix van Ginderhuysen**

November

● London Program Market

ADDRESS
23-24 George Street
Richmond, Surrey TW9 1HY
UK

TEL: 44-181-948 5522
FAX: 44-181-332 0495
CONTACT: **Andrew Goodsir**

● MIP-ASIA (Hong Kong)

ADDRESS
Reed Midem Organisation
179 avenue Victor Hugo
F-75116 Paris
France

TEL: 33-1-44 34 44 44
FAX: 33-1-44 34 44 00
CONTACT: **Andre Vaillant**

● Oslo International Film Festival

ADDRESS
Ebbellsgate 1
N-0183 Oslo
Norway

TEL: 47-22 20 07 66
FAX: 47-22 20 07 67
WEB SITE: http://wit.no/FilmFestival/
CONTACT: **Tommy Lerdahl**

● Sinking Creek Film and Video Festival

ADDRESS
Vanderbilt University
402 Sarratt Centre
Nashville, TN 37240
USA

TEL: 615-322-4234
FAX: 615-343-8081

● Cairo International Film Festival

The object of the festival is to spread the artistic taste, to promote better understanding among the various nations of the world community and to be a progress report on development of the international film industry.

FESTIVAL DATES
  December 1-14, 1997 (tbc)
  Beginning of December, 1998
SUBMISSION DATES
  September, 1997
  September, 1998
ADDRESS
  17 Kasr el Nil Street
  Cairo
  Egypt

TEL:	20-2-392 3562/392 3962
FAX:	20-2-393 8979
ENTRIES:	200
ATTENDEES:	2,000+
CONTACT:	**Saad Eldin Wahba**

FILM TYPE
  Feature
COMPETITIVE
  Yes
LANGUAGE
  Any (English subtitles)
COUNTRY
  Any
ENTRY FEES
  None

AWARDS
  Prizes awarded include, the best picture (Golden Pyramid), special jury prize (Silver Pyramid), best actress, actor, direction, script and artistic contribution.

● Diagonale-Festival of Austrian Films (Salzburg)

Latin American films and videos may participate in this festival's competition. Prizes are awarded in the fiction, documentary, and animation sections as well as for scripts and posters. International films are also screened at this festival, but they cannot be part of the competition.

FESTIVAL DATES
  Between December 1-15, 1997
  Between December 1-15, 1998
SUBMISSION DATES
  September 30, 1997
  September 30, 1998
ADDRESS
  Stiftgasse 6
  A-1070 Vienna
  Austria

TEL:	43-1-526 3323
FAX:	43-1-526 6801
E-MAIL:	AFILMCO@PING.AT
ENTRIES:	400
ATTENDEES:	500,000
CONTACT:	**Martin Schweighofer**

FILM TYPE
  All
COMPETITIVE
  Yes
LANGUAGE
  Spanish
COUNTRY
  Latin America (competition)
ENTRY FEES
  $30 US

AWARDS
  Coral Awards are out every year.

● PIA Film Festival (Tokyo)

PIA centres around an amateur competition called the PFF Award, which accepts entries regardless of format from the general public, both within Japan and abroad. PFF has a history of generating talented filmmakers who are now working in the forefront of Japanese film.

FESTIVAL DATES
Beginning of December, 1997
Beginning of December, 1998

SUBMISSION DATES
July, 1997
July, 1998

ADDRESS
Pia Corporation,
5-19 Koji-Machi,
Chiyoka-ku, Tokyo
Japan

TEL:	81-3-32 65 14 25
FAX:	81-3-32-65 56 59
ENTRIES:	500
ATTENDEES:	5,000
CONTACT:	**Keiko Arachi**

FILM TYPE
All

COMPETITIVE
Yes

LANGUAGE
Any

COUNTRY
Any

ENTRY FEES
None

AWARDS
The grand prize awarded at this festival is the PFF Award.

● Autrans Festival of Mountain and Adventure Films

Documentary films screened at Autrans "should contribute positively to knowledge on the one hand of the mountain world and on the other to developing and examining human resources in adventure". Feature films that take part in the competition can be of any length, but must be filmed in a mountain setting.

FESTIVAL DATES
December 3-7, 1997
First week in December, 1998

SUBMISSION DATES
September 20, 1997
September 20, 1998

ADDRESS
Festival International du Film d'Autrans
Office du Tourism
38880 Autrans
France

TEL:	33 4 76 95 30 70
FAX:	33 4 76 95 98 63
E-MAIL:	autrans@alpes-net.fr
WEB SITE:	
ENTRIES:	30-35 documentaries and 10 features screened
ATTENDEES:	10,000

FILM TYPE
Feature, Documentary, Short

COMPETITIVE
Yes

LANGUAGE
Any (summary in French or English)

COUNTRY
Any

ENTRY FEES
Contact festival

AWARDS
Documentaries compete for the "Grand Prix d'Autrans, Best enviromental film, social life, anthology or mountain culture film, adventure and exploration film, expedition documentary film and best snow, ice or mountain film. Feature films compete for best "cinema" film and best "TV" film. All award winners receive cash or mountain sports article and the film festival trophy.

● MECLA (Havana)

MECLA is a heavily attended competitive film festival that showcases Latin American films and videos. Each year the Coral Awards are presented to deserving films and videos.

FESTIVAL DATES
Beginning of December, 1997
Beginning of December, 1998

SUBMISSION DATES
End of September, 1997
End of September, 1998

ADDRESS
Calle 25, No. 1218
Entre 10 Y 12 Vedado
La Habana 10600
Cuba

TEL:	53-7-333 862/304 666
FAX:	53-7- 333 032
ENTRIES:	300
ATTENDEES:	500,000
CONTACT:	**Francisco Leon**

FILM TYPE
All

COMPETITIVE
Yes

LANGUAGE
Spanish

COUNTRY
Latin America

ENTRY FEES
None

AWARDS
This festival awards the Coral Awards.

● Noir Film Festival

Noir Film Festival focuses on the promotion and diffusion of the various mystery genres. This includes world previews, competitive and non-competitive sections, retrospectives, meetings, and seminars.

FESTIVAL DATES
December 3-9, 1997
December 2-8, 1998

SUBMISSION DATES
November 15, 1997
November 18, 1998

ADDRESS
Via Torso
I-Rome 00198
Italy

TEL:	39-6-884 8030
FAX:	39-6-884 0450
ENTRIES:	30
ATTENDEES:	2,500
CONTACT:	**Giorgio Gosetti**

FILM TYPE
All

COMPETITIVE
Yes

LANGUAGE
Any

COUNTRY
Any

ENTRY FEES
None

AWARDS
Awards for best film and actor (female & male).

● Cinemagic International Film Festival for Young People (Belfast)

December

Cinemagic focuses on the work of young people. Its target age is between 14-18 years old. Aside from the films, Cinemagic also presents educational workshops, directors talks and master classes which include well known film industry professionals.

FESTIVAL DATES
December 4-14, 1997
December, 1998

SUBMISSION DATES
August 20, 1997

ADDRESS
21 Ormeau Ave
Belfast BT2 8HD
Northern Ireland

TEL:	44-1232-311 900
FAX:	44-1232-239 918
ENTRIES:	45
ATTENDEES:	14,000
CONTACT:	**Marie Barne**

FILM TYPE
All

COMPETITIVE
Yes

LANGUAGE
Any

COUNTRY
Any

AWARDS
Cinemagic Young Jury Award worth 1,000 pounds to a chosen film.

At Festival Products, we care about your feedback. If you have any questions or comments, please contact us by mail, fax, or email.

Brief Entries

● Forum for the International Co-financing of Documentaries (Amsterdam)

ADDRESS
Skindergade 29A
1159 Copenhagen
Copenhagen
Denmark

FESTIVAL DATES
December 1-3, 1997
TEL: 45-33-13 11 22/33 11 51 52
FAX: 45-33-13 11 44
CONTACT: **Tue Steen Muller**

● International Festival of New Latin American Cinema (Havana)

ADDRESS
Calle 23, No. 1155
Entre 10 Y 12 Vedado
La Habana
Cuba

TEL: 53-7-34169/36071
FAX: 53-7-334 273/333 078
E-MAIL: sitcin@teniai.CU
CONTACT: **Alfredo Guevara**

Part 3

The Festival Circuit

Australia

by Mary Colbert

Over the past five years the Australian film industry has enjoyed unprecedented world spotlight. Jane Campion's *Sweetie* and Jocelyn Moorehouse's *Proof* heralded the way for a new kind of Oz cinema ; offbeat, idiosyncratic original visions of younger writer -directors. The Golden era truly set in with the break- out commercial success of *Strictly Ballroom, Muriel's Wedding, The Adventures of Priscilla Queen of the Desert, The Piano, Babe and Shine*. It wasn't only the cash registers that were ringing as Australian films brought home artistic gongs : the world's most prestigious critical award, the Cannes Palme D'Or (*The Piano*), Camera D'or (Shirley Barrett's *Love Serenade*), Golden Globes, Oscars (Geoffrey Rush, John Seale) and multitudes of festival accolades.

If Peter Weir, George Miller, Bruce Beresford, Gillian Armstrong , Phil Noyce, Fred Schepsisi, Paul Cox and co had put Australia on the cinematic map a decade or more ago the new breed of filmakers consolidated Australian cinema's reputation (and added cachet) on both fronts : commercial and artistic success.

Generally assumed uneasy bedfellows in Australia after years of experimentation the two forces have reached orgasm to produce a unique film environment : a diverse range of mostly low budget features (average just under $3 million, with last year's peak *Shine* at $6 million) though with the establishment of Fox Studios a few will now be increasing, a rich talent base in a cultural climate where the participation of new players is encouraged and often matched with very established producers, underpinned by a sophisticated infrastrucure of government subsidy which supports both commercial and riskier projects. Add to that the dynamism of new ideas and confidence of success : the result is an exciting mix.

The key to industry success - more precisely existence and survival - is government subsidy, supported this financial year at $115 million targeted for the film and TV industry. Despite concerns about major funding cuts by the incoming Liberal government, the industry breathed a sigh of relief when the funding levels were to be maintained with a guaranteed $48 million allocated to the Australian Film Finance Corporation(FFC) and $29.7milion to the Australian Film

Commission(AFC). Direct funding to the industry is set to remain intact.

Since its inception in 1988 the FFC alone through an investment of $600million has generated $2 billion worth of production. Developed as a replacement for the tax concessions scheme (known as 10BA) which was cut back in 1987 (and offered investors high levels of write-offs), the FFC provides equity investment in projects of Australian origin and invests in co-productions in association with producers from countries which have a formal co-production treaty or other agreements with Australia. It's a subsidy vehicle, commercial in orientation, and favours recouping on a pro rata basis with its partners. Most of the co-financing for the projects now comes form the marketplace - other players in the industry such as sales agents (especially Beyond, Southern Star), distributors, or in the case of documentaries and tele-movies, broadcasters. With the constant erosion of the funding envelope and increased success of Australian films in the global marketplace, an increasing number of projects have relied on off-shore co - investment.

Last year government stumped up 42% of the $89 million invested in 25 feature films.. With the release of the 'uncut' new budget (financial year in Australia from starts July 1), the industry breathed a sigh of relief setting sail on 36 feature projects.

Federal level funding is supplemented by strong activity especially in script development (and location services) generated by state agencies: New South Wales Film & Television Office, Victoria's Cine-media, South Australian Film Corporation, Screen West, and Film Queensland and the Pacific Film and TV Office now the hub of production activity centred around the Warner Bros Village Roadshow studios.

The studio located on Queensland 's Gold Coast(with an adjacent theme park) has become a back-lot for American TV and feature as well as Asian production, attracted by state government tax incentives, diverse locations, and ample supply of technical expertise. In June the most expensive feature to be shot in Australia, Terence Malick's $80 mill world war II epic, *Thin Red Line*, with a top Hollywood male star line up, began production in the state's far north.

Confirming Australia as the southern hemisphere's hub of film activity, is the construction of the latest state of the art Fox Studios in Sydney, capitalising on the rich local talent base. The $150 million decision by Rupert Murdoch to build the studios(and accompanying theme complex) - at time of printing under construction - was driven by a desire to capitalise on talent : consolidation of enthusiasm for local filmakers through financial commitments. The studio's investments in Bruce Beresford's *Paradise Road* and Gillian Armstrong's *Oscar and Lucinda* confirms the return of Australian major directors to higher budget home-grown projects.

At least its presence may reverse some of the talent drain, the by-product of Aussie success : with directors Geoffrey Wright (*Romper Stomper*), PJ Hogan and wife Jocelyn Moorehouse (*Proof*), joining Phil Noyce, Baz Luhrmann, Emma Kate Croghan (*Love and Other Catastrophes*), Scott Hicks lured by Hollywood projects. Yet the anticipated talent drain has not caused a major gap with new talents quickly filling up the ranks and first or seond time (writer)directors attrracting major international actors like Judy Davis (*Children of the Revolution*) or *Secrets and Lies* Brenda Belthyn (James Bogle's *In the Winter Dark*)to their projects.

Much of the inspiration a major source of generating talent has been the government financed national film education arm , AFTVRS (Australian Film,TV and Radio School), in Sydney 's North Ryde. Ex - students read like a who's who of Australian talent : Phil Noyce, Gillian Armstrong, Rolf de Heer, Jane Campion, P.J.Hogan, Jocelyn Morehouse, Peter Duncan (*Children of the Revolution*), Monica Pellizzari (*Fistful of Flies*), Shirley Barrett and a host of others. Its perfomance drama equivalent, NIDA(National Institute of Dramatic Art) has spawned Baz Luhrmann, actors Judy Davies, Mel Gibson, Jacqueline Mc Kenzie, Cate Blanchett - just to name a few.

Much of the industry's energy and enthusiasm has spilled over into the festival circuit. Over the past few years there has been a stronger symbiosis between Australian film and the main festival events. Local audiences' increased appetite for Oz cinema has prompted all major international festivals - Sydney, Melbourne and Brisbane - to program Australian features in prominent slots of their schedule -wherever possible as closing or opening nights, as galas or - ideally - world premieres. In 1997 for instance, country western flavoured *Doing Time With Patsy Cline* opened the Sydney venue, closed Brisbane and strummed mid-way through Melbourne's programme. Last year *Shine* followed its Sundance Cinderella outing witha Sydney Film festival premiere.

Film buffs of the local product can now view the entire year's crop of films by participating in the Australian Film Festival, which also includes forums and seminars on various aspects of moviemaking: craft and thematic matters conducted by leading industry figures. For a small fee anyone is eligible to join as a member of the AFI, Australian Film Institute.

The buoyant climate, proliferation and constant search for new talent, is reflected by the resurgence of a strong short film culture. Not only is the evident throughout the film school institutions but at the Sydney's Tropicana (Tropfest) festival for instance, the brainchild of actor/director John Polson (*The Sum of Us, The Boys*) which stipulates a annual theme (in 97 a pickle), has been supported by local industry who figure prominently on the jury : Jan Chapman, Jane Campion, George Miller, Gillian Armstrong, Brian Brown , Geoffrey Rush. Flickerfest and Melbourne International Festivals accept international as well as Australian entries while the Dendy Awards - for local entrants only - screen finalists work and present awards at the outset of the Sydney Film Festival. Most of the major international festivals take place in winter but desperate buffs can even enjoy short films in their floats at the Coogee swimming pool and baths.

Right now Australia's talent pool is immense. For filmakers the place is scorching hot.

Mary Colbert is a contributing editor for Vogue and the Hollywood Reporter.

(Note : All figures in Australian dollars)

The German Film Industry
by Petra Hobel and Josef Wutz

Show business is booming in Germany: Ticket sales at movie theatres hit a record high last year, German films recently recorded their strongest quarter in four decades, and multiplexes are being built at dizzying speed. Above all, in the first quarter of 1997 the market share of German films was reported with astonishing 37%, an astronomically high figure in comparison to previous years. The German film business, it seems, has rediscovered its self-confidence. Yet, competition is intense in the German entertainment market which, together with Japan, is among the largest in the world.

While German filmmakers are producing spectacularly successful mainstream titles, independent distributors are in fact struggling to capitalize on the success of local fare: German films carved out a local box-office cut of over 16% (up 72% on 1995) but German independent distributor's market share fell 0.3% to 29.1%. It's the US Majors that are handling most German product. Increasingly aggressive, they are acquiring and also co-producing German films. Involvement now often starts at the production stage with guarantees. Out of the six German films that sold over a million admissions last year three where distributed by Majors, which are favored over German distributors for their larger publicity and advertising budgets. Local distributors fear that the average marketing costs rose 40% over the last year.

German films have been received overwhelmingly positive in the past months. Weighed down for decades by bloated arthouse productions the German film industry was left commercially dead. This changed when crowd-pleasing German comedies started to stir up local audiences' interest in home-grown fare again. Last year admissions for local titles rocketed from 11 million in 1995 to 20.8 million.

This German films' current box-office success is due to the new filmmakers' apparent adoption of a commercial imperative. The Majors, weather exploiting or fueling it, have struck a string of financing deals with local productions over the last months. Warner Bros., as well as BVI and PolyGram Filmed Entertainment have moved into financing and co-producing German films. Therefore fiscally leashed state governments, hoping to attract the "industry of the future" to their regions, are freeing up as much funding as possible for film and other media subsidies. The regional film boards weighed in with a combined budget of up to $119 million last year. They, too, are adopting more commercially-oriented approaches to refinance their investments and are increasingly seeking private sector financing.

Romantic comedies like *Der bewegte Mann (Maybe...Maybe Not)* or *Das Superweib(The Super Wife)* helped propel German films out of the arthouses and into the multiplexes. However, filmmakers are now looking beyond the popular comedy formula and are aiming for success with native drama, like Thomas Jahn's *Knocking on Heaven's Door*, for example, a metaphysical road movie about two fatally ill young men or *Jenseits der Stille (Beyond Silence)*, by Caroline Link, the story of the daughter of deaf parents who becomes a musician. Another example is Katja von Granier's *Bandits*, a music film about four females escaped conflicts who start a cult band. However, most German distributors still have a slate of romantic comedies on offer for the coming season.

Despite their recent boom in Germany, German pictures still have trouble crossing the border. Especially the ever so popular romantic comedies do not travel well. For decades it has almost been impossible to sell a German-language film to audiences abroad. Working on the safe ground of light entertainment the emerging generation of young filmmakers in their attempt to make movies without sacrificing commercial viability, yet has to develop a broader spectrum of movie entertainment, a wider range of genre, and more complex stories to target international markets successfully. Developing international co-production links is also an important issue here.

Gradually, German stars need to become known abroad again. The success of German films has brought fresh faces and somewhat-known actors alike into the national spotlight, following in the footsteps of first-generationers, like Til Schweiger, who made the German industry go boom. He has appeared in *Knocking on Heaven's Door* in 1997, in *Männerpension*, 1996's second highest grossing German film and in *Der bewegte Mann*, the most successful film in both 1994 and 1995.

Schwaiger, who recently signed up to star opposite Mira Sorvino in the US action film *The Replacement Killers* (Columbia Pictures/WGG), is headed for America now.

With revenues of US $ 764 million (1.3 billion marks) German box offices sold 132.9 million tickets in 1996 which is 1.62 per capita cinema visits a year. While these figures set a new record, they were just a touch above 1994's 132.7 million admissions.

The one problem that arose for exhibitors is that currently there is not enough screens for the up to 6,500 prints crowding onto Germany's 4000 screens each week. Many small to mid-sized films are left without an attractive long-term time slot. Independence Day on the other hand opened with 800 prints whereas a couple of years ago the maximum was set around 250. Therefore local cinema operators facing US competition have responded with an overheated multiplex building boom. Local exhibitors now have 224 multiplex screens against the US's 77. 119 new ones opened in 1996. In total, 321 new screens opened that year making the number of screens 4070 (1995 saw only 106 new screens). With this boom of multiplex theatres, small theatres and art-house operators fear to be shifted out of the market. Traditional art-houses, loyally playing small pictures, are indeed disappearing slowly.

Film festivals now have to offer a niche for smaller productions and independent fare - something oversized A-festivals like Cannes and Berlin can no longer provide. In their crazed atmosphere smaller films often fail to get noted. Medium-sized festivals, like Hamburg or Munich (Germany's only two festivals without competition acknowledged by F.I.A.P.F.), as well as the events in Mannheim or Hof have began to fill this gap by offering a platform for independent films, a lively local cinema scene, and a meeting place for independent producers and distributors, filmmakers and other industry professionals.

Filmfest Hamburg is supported by the media-friendly attitude of the local government and backed by a vivid local film, television and media industry. Warner moved their German headquarters from Munich to Hamburg two years ago and Polygram Filmed

Entertainment is following this year. With the country's highest concentration of press and publishing houses Hamburg is indeed Germany's media capital.

After all, it is a combination of commerce and culture, independent fare and major productions, stars, established filmmakers and new talent alike, that gives a festival its special flair. With perhaps 95% of theatres showing major commercial fare an international film festival like Filmfest Hamburg offers a refreshing look on a variety of films, styles, genres and national cinemas. Many of the 100 films shown every year do not have distribution, yet, and might otherwise never come to a screen.

Petra Hobel is the director of Public Relations for Filmfest Hamburg and Josef Wutz is its director. Before he took over the directorship of the festival he worked as an independent theatrical distributor, e.g. for Arsenal, and headed Filmstiftung Nordrhein-Westfalen's distribution and exhibition fund for three years.

The Norwegian Film Industry

by Tor Fosse

A new era of Norwegian film production started with the inauguration of the Labour Party Minister of Culture Åse Kleveland in 1991. Her scheme was to raise the funds for film production to a far higher level than what had been granted from the former conservative government. Until then, Norsk Film AS had been the governmental company body in charge of film production. In addition, several private production enterprises contributed to an average of some ten Norwegian films at a total being produced each year. The governmental support for these private companies was that of a bonus system, contributing a 55% pay off bonus of the gross ticket revenue of each film (for children's films 100 %). The administrative body in charge of this support was, and still is, the Norwegian Film Institute.

A boom in Norwegian film production

The new policy for greater support of Norwegian film production ultimately resulted in the emergence of the Norwegian Film Institute's production support by the Commissioning Editor, who in 1996 supported private productions at a level of NOK 38.4 millions (US$ 5.3 mill). The Institute's ticket bonus arrangement was maintained as before and constituted in 1996 NOK 30 millions (US$ 4.6 mill). In addition, the Audio Visual Fund was established also for direct support to private enterprises' productions being approved before hand, based on the scripts, both for theatrical release and TV. This fund had a budget of NOK 50 millions (US$ 7.7 mill) in 1996. The governmental production company Norsk Film AS was also maintained. In 1996 the company's budget consisted of NOK 28.8 million (US$ 4.4 mill).

As a result of this policy, the Norwegian film production is currently experiencing progress, resulting in as many as almost twenty film productions annually. At the 50th Cannes festival Pål Sletaune's *Junk Mail* and Erik Skjoldbjærg's *Insomnia* were both to be found in the Critic's Week program section. Junk Mail has been sold to more than 30 countries and territories, which is very rare for a Norwegian film. Both these films have done fairly well at national box office. The director Bent Hamer, who was in the Director's Fortnight in Cannes 1996 with his film *Eggs* was also quite successful. Common denominator for all three films is the contemporary approach thematically, by three first film directors, contrary to for instance Liv Ullmann's *Kristin Lavransdatter*, which was based on the novel set to medieval Norway, by Sigrid Undset. Both *Eggs* and *Junk Mail* are furthermore highly original and unique stories, not copying other films or genres, whereas *Insomnia* is a kind of cop thriller set above the Arctic Circle in the land of the midnight sun, which can seem exotic to foreign viewers. Another film worth notice is of course *The Other Side of Sunday* by Berit Nesheim, who was nominated Best Foreign Film at the Academy Award 1997. Another female director, Vibeke Idsøe, experienced that her script and directing debut *Hunting the Kidney Stone*, has been bought for re-make in Hollywood. The Swedish veteran director Jan Troell's Hamsun, co-produced with Norway, was an artistic success, with an outstanding performance by Swedish actor Max von Sydow. Other films worth mentioning are *Zero Kelvin* by Hans Petter Moland, very busy at the festival circuit around the world, *Mendel* by Alexander Røsler, a film which premiered at the Berlinale's Panorama 1997 and the children's film *Maja Stoneface* by Lars Berg. Norsk Film AS also produced the five-stories-in-one Breath by the five established directors Eva Dahr, Oddvar Einarson, Mona Hoel, Marius Holst and Eva Isaksen. Both Breath and the lap director Paul-Anders Simma's Minister of State premiered at the 7th Tromsø International Film Festival 1997.

Film festivals

At the Norwegian Film Festival in Haugesund, August 1997, five new Norwegian films will be released. Among these, Knut Erik Jensen's *Burnt by the Frost* is to be met by high expectations after his last film *Stella Polaris*. *The Successor* by Tor M. Tørstad is the opening film at this festival, which celebrates its 25th anniversary this year. The Haugesund festival is the meeting place for the Norwegian Film and Cinema Industry celebrating itself with the Amanda Awards and other festivities. This festival is basically screening films which already have been imported for theatrical distribution.

The Tromsø International Film Festival, in January, aims to present films that have not been imported theatrically, and in this way enhance the possibilities of import and distribution. In its seventh year 1997, this is one of the northern most film festival's in the world and was quite successful in becoming a meeting place for both the industry, the media and the audience at the same time. It has established itself as the biggest audience film festival in Norway, set in the Winter Wonderland of the Norwegian Arctic. Tromsø International Film Festival presents films from all over the world, basically non-US films and a substantial part consists of art house films.

Other festivals are The Oslo Animation Film Festival in April, The Gay & Lesbian Film Festival in Oslo, The Norwegian Short Film Festival in Grimstad, both in June, The Films from the South Festival in September - basically screening films from Latin-America, Africa and Asia - and Oslo International Film Festival in November.

A unique cinema and distribution structure

The Norwegian Cinema system is quite different from that of most other countries. From the early age of film and cinema history, the Norwegians developed a structure of municipally owned cinemas on one side and private import and distribution companies on the other. The publicly owned cinemas (rented) the films from the distributors, and 2/3 of the gross ticket revenue still goes to the cinemas. The block-busters, however, give the distributors a higher percentage. As the video market exploded in the 80's, the admission figures have been reduced as in other countries, but still Norwegian cinemas hold higher admission figures per capita than most countries. This is both due to fairly reasonable ticket prizes and the emphasis on cinema comfort in multiplex cinemas. A 2.5 % (tax) of each cinema ticket sold and of each video cassette hired, goes to the Norwegian Film and Cinema Foundation, aka the Federation of Municipal Cinemas. The institution gets about NOK 25 million per year from this arrangement. The fund re-invest much of this in different issues such as grants to distributors for import of extra prints, both for blockbusters (aiming prints to go to smaller cinemas at the same time as the release at the bigger cinemas), as well as grants being given to distributors who import certain art house films. The Norwegian cinema industry is thus quite powerful and the measurements often successful.

Tor Fosse is Head of Programming at the Tromsø International Film Festival. As the former manager of Arthaus, a distribution foundation in Oslo, he also worked at the acquisition department of Norwegian television NRK. In the 80'ies, he ran the Bergen Film Society, which still is the leading film society in Norway.

Gay & Lesbian Film Festivals
by Michael Lumpkin

At a time when it seems film festivals are turning up in every corner of the globe, no other type of film festival has seen the growth that lesbian and gay festivals have seen over the past two decades.

Currently there are no less than 85 lesbian and gay film festivals around the world. Some of these queer film events may stretch the definition of a "film festival", but whether organized screenings of rented tapes from the local video store or the massive, multi-day screenings attended by tens of thousands in major metropolitan cities, lesbian and gay film festivals are very popular events giving a community the opportunity to see their lives openly and honestly played out on the big screen.

Lesbian and gay film festivals have for the most part grown out of the modern homosexual rights movement which has created a very distinct and identifiable culture. Most, if not all, cities of any size now have lesbian and gay identified neighborhoods with their own political and social organizations, community centers, publications and business districts, making it relatively easy to reach a targeted audience of lesbians and gay men.

The world's first (and currently the largest) lesbian and gay film festival is the annual event produced in San Francisco California by Frameline, a lesbian and gay media arts organization. The 1997 edition held in June attracted nearly 75,000 attendees over 10 days, just 2,000 short of the 15-day San Francisco International Film Festival held two months earlier.

Sister festivals in Los Angeles and New York City along with the San Francisco event (held within 6 weeks of each other) form the big three for the U.S., the venues where most independent lesbian and gay features are introduced to lesbian and gay audiences on a national level.

Though a large percentage of the programming is the same each year, each of these three major U.S. festivals reflects its own community by programming works by local artists and putting together programming which reflects local interests. These festivals also possess unique characteristics specific to their local communities.

Outfest, the Los Angeles Gay and Lesbian Film Festival, located in the entertainment capitol of the world, is influenced by and receives a tremendous amount of support from the film industry. Filmmakers bring their films to Outfest with hopes of persuading influential industry professionals to attend their screenings. Many industry professionals also participate in Outfest by serving on the Festival's governing board, contributing to panel discussions and providing the financial support of their companies via the Festival's corporate sponsorship program.

Culminating with San Francisco's Lesbian/Gay Pride Celebration, the San Francisco International Lesbian & Gay Film Festival attracts tourists from across the U.S. and around the world who come to the City for participate in the celebration and to attend the ten-day film festival. Among these out of town visitors are lesbian and gay industry professionals who come to San Francisco at this time of the year for both business and pleasure. The San Francisco festival is very much a community event and is probably best known for its vocal and enthusiastic audiences.

New York is unique in that it hosts two major lesbian and gay film festivals, the New Festival: New York Festival of Lesbian and Gay Film and MIX, the New York Lesbian & Gay Experimental Film/Video Festival which began as a response to the lack of support for experimental work at the long established New Festival.

Lesbian and gay film festivals have been started in a variety of ways. The origins of the top three U.S. fests demonstrate the variety of ways that lesbian and gay film festivals are born.

The Los Angeles Festival grew out of an academic conference held at UCLA in the early 1980s, and quickly moved out of its university setting when it became clear that the event could attract a general mainstream audience . The San Francisco Festival began when gay filmmakers decided to come together and screen their own works for friends and each other at a gay community center, and the New York Festival was born out of the dreams and hard work of one dedicated individual.

Festivals in the U.S. have had a mixed relationship with the film industry. It is safe to say that a large portion of the programming at most lesbian and gay festivals has little commercial potential outside of a small, local, lesbian and gay market. But as lesbian and gay films become more commercially viable and distributors and exhibitors become more savvy at marketing to lesbian and gay film-goers, these festivals have found themselves successfully competing for lesbian and gay films and being taken more seriously as a viable launching point for the latest lesbian or gay feature.

Outside of the U.S., there are lesbian and gay film festivals in almost every western European country with festival also in Budapest, St. Petersburg, and Riga, Latvia. Other lesbian and gay festivals can now be found in Hong Kong, Sydney, Jerusalem, Tokyo, Sao Paulo and South Africa.

Michael Lumpkin is the festival director of the San Francisco Gay & Lesbian Film Festival, the oldest and largest event of its kind in the world.

Part 4

Festivals Firsthand

A Daily Account of the Hudson Valley Film and Video Festival

by Shael Stolberg

Once I got off the train at the Rhinecliff stop I was greeted by Nancy Couzean, a member of the Board of Directors of the Hudson Valley Film and Video Festival. As it happens, it was at her home that I spent the duration of my stay. Her friendly and helpful demeanor was matched by every member of the festival staff, and more importantly, the festival itself. As a visiting New York City actor mentioned after a film screening, "the feeling is more like the theatre". When asked to elaborate on this point he said "the sense of community and cama-raderie that exists in the theatre is what I have experienced today".

The first event of the festival was the Screenwriters Panel. Each member of this panel had direct experience with the creation and produc-tion of a motion picture from the screenwriting process on though its production and finally its release. The panel consisted of Geraldine Creed, Ron Nyswaner, Adrienne Shelly, Zachary Scott and Donald Westlake. It was moder-ated by John Pierson who is well known in the independent film community. After John had led the discussion the floor was then open for questions from the interested audience.

Following the Question and Answer period ("Q&A"), the audience was joined by the panel on the terrace of the Mills Mansion, a beautiful old style mansion, where the panel discus-sion was held. During this reception, both food and drink were avail-able and there was an opportunity to talk to any of the panel members on a one-to-one basis.

Once the reception was over, an eclectic group of people who wanted to continue the evening was treated to a spontaneous journey to a bar in Rhinecliff where the night continued. This group included produc-ers, filmmakers, writers, actors and people who just went to see the

film panel and got more than they expected. Aside from some engaging conversions, a few potential projects were discussed.

On Saturday, aptly named "Independents Day", the festival started its first full day of programming with six feature films and two receptions all held at Upstate Films . This particular theatre has been a refuge for independent films for the last 25 years. The films ranged in style from a heart-warming Irish multi-generational coming of age film (*The Sun, The Moon & The Stars*) to (as the the promotional material states) "a surreal, satirical journey through New York's East Village youth culture" (*The Electric Urn*). These two films acted as bookends for the entire day's screenings. The program also included a film about an over-stressed, self absorbed man's revelations toward life brought on by his "chance" meeting with a fascinating woman (*The Irreversible Year*); a humourous look into the life of a congenial meat shop owner who just happens to be a very bad gambler (*The Deli*); an actress' exploration of her own identity brought on when she is offered an interested movie role (*Naked Acts*) and the romance and adventure of two young people, one with Tourette's Syndrome and the other with a history of physical abuse (*Niagara, Niagara*). This latter film was shot in the Hudson Valley and was produced by *The Shooting Gallery* whose previous

Steven Olivieri, David Tuttle

film Slingblade, won an Academy Award. All these films had one very important element in common: quality. Denise Kasell, the executive director, must be commended for the slate of films she was able to screen.

Before the first film had screened, a breakfast was sponsored by the New York City entertainment law firm Rudolph & Beer, for the valiant filmgoers up at nine in the morning. A second reception was held after the *Niagara, Niagara* screening and was sponsored by the Directors Guild of America. This reception gave the audience a chance to meet with the people involved in the film (including the producer, director,

and main female lead) as well as a chance for the filmmakers to receive feedback from an enthusiastic audience for the first time. A few months later, it was announced that *Niagara, Niagara* was to be included in the very prestigious film competition of the Venice Film Festival.

Samdar Levy, Ester Gen, Steven Olivieri

Once the planned schedule was completed an intrepid few were taken to Pongo a café/bar in the village of Tivoli where one could roll dice for a free drink. We also were treated to an improvised performance of a soul classic by Ester Gen, a resident of the Hudson Valley, who had caught the day's final screening of the *Electric Urn*.

On the last day of the weekend sponsored by the New York Times, the festival program ("Short Sunday") consisted of three sections showcasing short films. The first screened shorts by children from the ages of 6-18. These films/videos were part of the Children's Media Project which offers workshops to young people who are interested in filmmaking. After each screening, the filmmaker received feedback on his/her work by film industry professionals like Fisher Stevens (actor/filmmaker) and Amy Kravitz (Animation Chair, Rhode Island School of Design). The films ranged from animation/claymation to experimental and narrative. Once all the films were screened, the filmmakers participated in a Q&A with the audience. The second part included shorts by college students. This program showed that an extremely important part of filmmaking are the basics learned in school or at the beginning of one's career.

The third part of "Short Sunday" was scheduled for the evening and included twelve professional shorts compiled by Meira Blaustein and hosted by Roy Frumkes. The mandate of this particular program was to show "provocative short films by emerging filmmakers ". The slate of films compiled for this program acheived this goal admirably. A short synopsis of a few of the short films will justify this viewpoint. *Luna and the Donkey* portrayed a town's mistaken impression that a woman was impregnated by a donkey. The plotline of the short film's *Sullivan's Last Call* and the *Seven Virtures* also lived up to the programs agenda. The former is a black & white film that deals with the idea of celibacy in a sexy manner and the latter portrays a post-modern version of the seven virtues with seven short vignettes, each vignette representing a virtue. As in the selections on "Independent's Day", the films were of high quality. Many of the short films chosen had been screened at other festivals and won awards. At the end of the program the filmmakers were available for a formal Q&A immediately following the screenings as well as an informal one during a reception which the audience attended.

During the next three days the festival shifted gears and presented seven screenplay readings. One the first day the screenplay readings consisted of *Blue Moon* (a generational love story of unrequited love), *Chocolate Waltz* (a young girl's coming of age story) and *Salute Love* (a romantic comedy about a man accused of being the world's greatest lover by an aging starlet). On his day off from performing the *Gin Game* on Broadway, Charles Durning read for one of the main characters in Ken Topolsky's *Blue Moon* and Dan Lauria's *Salute Love*. Dan Lauria himself read a main role in Rebecca Chianese's *Chocolate Waltz*. All three screenplays were performed admirably with very little rehearsal time for the actors. The audience seemed to enjoy the performances and the appearance of some name actors (Dennis Farina, Chris Noth, and Joanna Kerns) who took part in the reading.

On the second day the screenplay readings included *Last Dance at the Paradise Hotel* (about a gay man trying to learn to live again after the death of his companion and mother), *Pretty Bert* (an interracial love story set in the end of the 19th century in Jamaica) and *Running Wild* (a reporter's adventure with the Dillinger gang). In *Pretty Bert*, the main character is extremely convincing and at the end of the reading is given a good deal of applause. Taking the performance into effect it was not surprising that she was also the writer of the piece (as was found out later, the screenplay *Pretty Bert* was accepted into the Equinoxe film workshop mentioned below). *Running Wild*, the third and final screenplay for the evening was written by Pulitzer prize winning playwright Frank Gilroy. Even though this screenplay has a lot of location and action sequences, it worked very well in the reading. This is primarily due to the excellent cast and the writers admission that he "prepared the screenplay" for the reading.

Frank Gilroy

The last screenplay of the reading series was called *Traveling Light* (about a twentysomething's relationship with a travelling theatre company). With this screenplay the writer, Aileen Ritchie, took part in the Equinoxe program which sent her to France for a week long workshop with well respected industry professionals. The Equinoxe program is under the presidency of Jeanne Moreau, and enlists experienced members of the film community to help the writers with their work. The audience of this particular reading was lucky enough to see the result. Aside from the reading being very well performed, the storyline and structure were well written and should make a very enjoyable film.

The next event scheduled by the festival was a documentary screening of *The Political Education of Maggie Lauterer*. After the screening, an accompanying panel discussion on the role of media in politics was scheduled. This panel consisted of well-known award winning documentary filmmakers and political consultants. This event was very well attended, and the audience was presented with a few new ways of looking at the connection between politics and the media.

By far, the most unique program of this film festival was the "Scored Shorts" segment. This program combined live orchestra music with six different short films. Randall Craig Fleisher the director of the Hudson Valley Philharmonic, did an excellent job of creating a musical score for six different films. To give you an idea of how diverse the films were one just has to read a few of the titles: *Why I Hate Italians, Black Boots* and *Once Upon a Time for the Children*. The first is a comedy, the second an experimental dance film, and the third a poinant documentary. Tamela Sloan, the director of *Once Upon a Time for the Children*, was so impressed with the score written for her film that she approached Randall and asked if she could use the music for the film. At the end of the screenings a Q&A was scheduled with both the orchestra and filmmakers to enlighten everyone on the process of collaboration between the two art forms.

The motto of the Hudson Valley Festival is "celebrating the screenwriter" and its final event did just that. A gala tribute was held in Walter Bernstein's honour for his contributions to screenwriting for more than three decades. His work includes such acclaimed films as *Fail Safe, The Molly McGuires, Semi-Tough and The Front*. The first part of the tribute featured surprise guests praising Mr. Bernstein's contribution to screenwriting. His integrity and kindness to new screenwriters, actors and the film industry were also spoken of in the most positive way. Once the tribute was completed, everyone went to enjoy a party held in his honour. During this time, his movies were being screened in the theatre to be appreciated by all.

On the whole, the Hudson Valley Film and Video Festival was an enjoyable experience. For a new festival (it is only three years old) there were some interesting programs and it stayed true to its mandate of "celebrating the screenwriter". The proximity to New York City encourages people to visit and perhaps view some new talent or just enjoy the surroundings and festival events. It is primarily sponsored by the Hudson Valley Film Office which has a mandate to bring filmmaking to the Hudson Valley. So far, it is on the right track.

A Festival Experience

by Roy Frumkes

Film Festivals aren't just for films. Screenplays, like films, can have a life on the Film Festival circuit, earning recognition for the writers and generating much-needed revenue. My partner, Rocco Simonelli, and I, have entered scripts in the Houston International Film Festival, and here's our tale.

I had been entering two films (*Document of the Dead, Burt's Bikers*) in festivals, mainly in the hopes of pumping up video sales with the validation of being an award-winner. And I had won several honors, the cumulative effect on sales of which was ultimately hard to determine. Certainly, at the very least, it intrigued distributors enough to screen the films. But with our screenplay, *Dust*, it was another story entirely.

Rocco and I were very happy with the script, but our manager didn't share our enthusiasm. You would think a manager would relentlessly push whatever script you gave him. After all, he stands to share in the profits. And after all, it's Hollywood... Whoever imagined that personal taste would get in the way of "The Deal"? But he didn't much care for the script, and refused to represent it. We were baffled.

One day Rocco informed me that he had entered *Dust* in the Houston World Fest. I frankly didn't see how that would increase our chances of getting it sold, but the festival had been good to me in the past, and I thought it might be again. Also, I have friends in Houston, and the food is good. Why should those things enter into this essay? Because festivals are money-making entreprises, some morethan others, and they want you to attend to spend more money on them. They give a number of awards in each category, and there are a great many categories, and they let you know in advance that you've won (though not which level award you've won - bronze, silver, gold, special, etc -- that information they withhold in the hopes of luring you onto the premises.)

Down we went. We had a nice time, attended several of the films being shown (having had to purchase a festival pass to do so) and attended the Awards Banquet (having had to purchase a Banquet ticket each to do so) ...you get the picture. There were noted filmmakers present, seminars given, parties thrown, etc. All the standard Festival hoopla. We won the Certificate of Merit, and were escorted up to receive our award by a beautiful model, who then had her picture taken with us (the resulting 8X10 of which could be purchased for a nominal sum), and we met some fellow filmmakers/screenwriters. And we schmoozed with J. Hunter Todd, the Festival's colorful organizer, who apprenticed under the king of '60's epic films - Samuel Bronston.

Cut to New York. We're back home, having enjoyed the experience but weighing the relative merits of spending a grand or so for the 8 honor. Just how would the benefits make themselves apparent, except as a salve to our wounded egos for not having had the script adequately represented by our manager? Well, here's the surprise twist - the Act Three of our little story, and you can do with it as you will. In the quest for even-handedness, I've presented it all as closely as possible to the way it happened - any cynical overtones you can write off to creative license or writer's POV.

One of the little percs of winning in one of the screenplay categories is that the festival management sends your script to agents to look at. Lo and behold, we were called by an agent, who responded positively to the script and wanted to represent it. Our manager had no problem with this - how could he, after having rejected it himself - and to everyone's amazement, it was instantly optioned by Charlie Matthau's company. When that option ran out two years later, it was instantly optioned again, by Gary Shusset's company, and after that, again...

Dust has never been produced, but we did moderately well off the option money, which is a genuine source of revenue for screenwriters in this country. It paid for our festival expenses several times over, got us lots of exposure, and still does now that it's back in our script repertory. Our manager never did confess to a misjudgment in regards to the material, though he was unabashedly supportive and happy for us as the options wondrously appeared (and well he should have been - he collected his percentage whether he represented the script or not.) And these other agents, who did so remarkably well for us with *Dust*, have kept in touch, though we have not worked together again since.

Mind you, we have been lucky outside of the festival circuit. Most recently, our screenplay *The Substitute* made it to the screen (in something less satisfying than the form we submitted, but hey, one can't argue too vociferously with six figures) and its performance, particularly on home video, spawned a franchise from which we profit whether or not we contribute further to each installment.

I put all this to you as something to consider in an industry fraught with duplicity and false hope on every possible level, yet one in which miracles do happen, every single day. The fees for submitting a screenplay are higher than those for submitting films, and this makes sense, since one or more judges has to invest a substantial amount of time in reading and critiquing a screenplay. Still it's daunting for the independent, coughing up perhaps as much as two hundred dollars in the knowledge that even if the script garners some kind of honor, it may only translate into two lines on a resume. Another decoration, an increment more cache perhaps, but hard to measure against the outlay from one's meager bank account.

The Festival circuit, if one comes out with a prize, can at the very least be rewarding on some ego level necessary to sustain the struggling artist while he or she does battle with the dark forces of the film universe. At its best it can lead to the elusive Deal. There are mercenary motives behind all festivals, some more blatant than others. But aren't mercenary goals behind everything we do as well, to some degree? Rocco and I got lucky ego wise and Deal-wise, and I don't think we were a major exception to the rule. So consider Festivals for what they are. Let them use you, and be prepared to use them, if that route seems appropriate to your purposes.

Roy Frumkes is the Managing Editor and co-owner of the prestigious Films In Review magazine and co-author of many screenplays including The Substitute and Dust. When The Substitute was released it reached the number two spot on Variety's top 50 grossing films of the week. He has also directed/ produced the D.W. Griffith Awards and taught courses on film production and screenwriting as well as lectured at the School of Visual Arts in New York, Harvard University, Cornell Medical Centre and other respected institutions.

Points on how to make "points" at a Film Festival

by Scott Felixson

You finally have a finished film. Now you want the world to see it, you want a distributor, you want a three-picture deal and, sure, while we're at it, you want to make your (parent's) money back. Where's a good place to start? Hey, film festivals. But you're not alone. Every other kid with a strip of celluloid is there wanting the same things you do. So how can you rise above your festival-attending peers to be a filmmaker without peer? First, make a darn good film -- you'll be half-way there. Then, heed the following advice.

When attending a festival be prepared to switch gears. You're no longer in filmmaking. You're in marketing. Some festivals attract industry reps and others only the film going public. Both can be very worthwhile venues for your film. Just find out which one you're attending before knocking yourself out preparing time consuming, expensive promotions and press kits useful only to the industry.

Even though a festival can feel like an island unto itself, it is probably of much interest in its host community. Notify the local print and radio media about your film. Do this as soon as you arrive in town or, even better, contact them about two weeks in advance and then again the day before your screening. You may be one of the only filmmakers at the festival making this effort. Just a brief press release stating the most basic information (don't forget a phone number) can work to your advantage, getting you anything from a mention in a piece about the festival to a feature article (with photos!) exclusively about your film. At my first festival as a filmmaker, the local radio station's movie reviewer came to my screening and loved my film. The next day he generously talked up my film on his show, even though he usually only reviewed Hollywood features. I was then able to quote him in all my future publicity. From then on, I've always contacted radio stations when attending a festival as a filmmaker. An important item to note is European festivals almost never have an entry fee, but almost all the American ones do. Call them up, tell them you'd love to enter your film in their festival then remind them you're just a poor film-maker. More often than not, I've had the fee reduced or eliminated altogether. Try this, it works. Back up plan: offer to pay the fee only if your film gets accepted.

When approaching (or approached by) a distribution executive at a festival, remain calm. You may need them but that doesn't mean they don't need you. Remember, you're the one in possession of the product. Retain control of what little power you actually have in the situation. Newer filmmakers often get nervous and speak over-enthusiastically, making themselves breathless and flustering potential buyers. I think no flyer could ever persuade a distributor to walk into your screening as effectively as a filmmaker possessing a composed, "in his element" demeanor. Most importantly, don't act desperate. Don't share your amusing, yet tragic stories of production hell. Don't admit your mother footed the bill (from now on, refer to her as an "outside investor"…especially at Thanksgiving). Be, or at least act, professional. And please, for the love of Scorsese, when asked what your film is about, be concise! It's unfair to reduce your two-hour, four-years in the making story to a two sentence description (called a "log line"). Do it anyway. Mention the genre (i.e. "a black comedy about…") then stick to describing the major story conflict. When a distributor's eyes glaze over, there's no getting him back. As my old theatre director used to tell me, "Less is more." Now remember, this is your film so don't expect a distributor to love it with the same passion you have. It may be your baby, but the distributor is hoping its his sugar daddy. It may be art to you but it's business to them. Don't be offended and don't take it personally.

This next one's not easy but is really worthwhile. Rather than racing over to a distributor who's in mid-conversation, thrusting out a flyer and breathlessly inviting her to your screening, try instead to casually strike up a dialogue first about something, anything, other than your film. You will make a better, more effective, impression. In my work acquiring films at festivals, I've always been MUCH more likely to attend the screening of someone I've actually conversed with than someone who merely placed a flyer in my hands. I know this one might really be a tough one but please try extra hard to resist saying the phrase, "Yep. It's a crazy business", as if you've seen it all. From newcomers it sounds pathetic. From the experienced, it sounds merely egotistical. Mind you, I still struggle with this one myself, after all, it is a crazy business.

Even though you may think your film is the definitive film to see, please DO NOT tape up your flyers over those of other films. It's disrespectful, petty and inevitably creates a vicious cycle of one-upmanship. I attended the IFFM (Independent Film Festival Market) in New York one year prepared with thousands of flyers, planning to tape most of them to the walls. Unfortunately, thousands of filmmakers had beaten me to all the available wall space. So I had to find some other way to stand out. I ran to the nearest art supply shop and bought an easel, a large cardboard and some colored paper (to cover the cardboard). I then glued onto it my flyer, a press release and two promotional photos. I set up the easel in the theater lobby. This simple setup attracted crowds. People even took time to read the release. The moral: You're in the creative arts. Be creative. Save the gorilla suits and other corny promotions for the public release of your film. Industry professionals will not be impressed. If you choose to do a promotion, make it simple and tasteful (fun is good, too) and don't spend a fortune on it. The more your promotion ties in to your film the better. When I was taking my short film "HeliumHead" to festivals, I would rent a helium tank, inflate balloons pre-printed with the title and slogan of my film, which I then tied to the backs of all the chairs in the lobby. Floating a few feet above peoples heads, the balloons were omnipresent yet unobtrusive. Even other filmmakers complimented me on a dignified promotion. I created awareness for my film in a way appreciated both by the industry and the attending public, many of whom took the balloons home.

Some of the better festival promotions I've seen involved waiters with trays of hors d'ouevres (people ALWAYS love food) for a documentary on catering and another filmmaker who projected a slide with his film's title and screening time on a wall outside the theater (this one works best after dark). If you can produce a slick press kit and poster without spending lots of money, do it. Otherwise, a simple, attractive information packet is all that is really necessary. Spend a few extra dollars to laminate your posters. They'll keep better in transit and storage between festivals, but more importantly, the layer of gloss has the marvelous effect of enhancing the poster's quality, making it, and your film, appear more professional.

I'm not sure if getting press directly benefits your film and your pocketbook. My film, "HeliumHead", has been featured in numerous articles in newspapers and trade papers across the country. Not one ever led to a deal of any kind. Still, getting press is a wonderful and well-deserved ego boost and also makes a nice addition to your press kit. It at least shows that your film is considered worthy of public attention. Enjoy the attention but don't let it go to your head or you'll soon be as interesting as yesterday's news. After all, getting press has little to do with the actual quality of your film (e.g. "Independence Day").

The most important piece of advice is to have an honest, unbiased assessment of your film's potential before holding out for theatrical distribution. Appreciate that its the rare low-budget indie that's worthy of theatrical release. Be realistic about your film's appeal. If you can honestly accept that you're first film may not be of theatrical quality (chances are it isn't if its shot in 16mm, Super 8 or video and especially if its about a group of friends and its set on a college campus), then be open to direct-to-video and cable exhibition. It's unlikely that a distributor will advance you money to finalize a release print. It's not a knock against your project, it's just not in their best interest Getting your first film into video stores or onto television is excellent evidence of your ability to produce marketable films. This should make getting both financing and distribution easier for your next project. Take the time to build a career. While, of course, it can happen, its better not to expect success on your first try.

Scott Felixson has attended festivals as both filmmaker and distributor. His comedy, "HeliumHead", starring celebrity Dick Cavett, won awards at festivals. He has served as VP of Acquisitions for two New York-based distributors. Felixson is currently President of Lighter Than Air Film Marketing and Consulting, which helps filmmakers promote their work. He can be reached at 212-726-0443 or LighterThanAir@juno.com for a free half hour consultation.

Festival Comments

Comments

● **Cannes Film Festival** – If you ever work at the Cannes Film Festival, make sure there is someone at home to video tape the festival highlights because you'll never see what's going on out there. Another bit of advice;beware of overbooked screenings. If you're working in office attire and run back to your hotel room thinking you have time to change and make it up the red carpet before show time, think again. There are always more tickets issued then there are seats, so even if you arrive all dressed up, you can find yourself amongst a large group of angry disappointed ticket holders. One way to shorten the dress up time; invest in areally nice raincoat. Since the festival weather is notoriously rainy, you can cover up your day wear and get on line earlier. If the weather permits slip on a pair of evening shoes. Men still need to have a white collar and black bow tie showing.
Linda Thomases Lafourcade, Equinoxe

● **Chicago International Film Festival** – I wish more festivals would elicit advice from the filmmakers as to how to make things a little easier for travelling filmmakers. They let us know a lot of info ahead of time and then picked us up from the airport and took us to a special fimmaker's welcoming office set up in a local hotel. There we received a folder and packet with the catalog, screening schedules, itinerary and miscellaneous stuff that really did make us feel welcome. We were encouraged to put out our press materials and, at the theatre, rpp, was found for our poster to be displayed. There were always lots of very helpful, cheerful assistants, interns and clean cars around to answer questions and take us places. After our short film block screening, which was very well-attended, we were invited to a local pub for a fun, cosy Q&A with audience members and our fellow filmmakers. The next evening, we were all taken out to a fancy dancy restaurant for a wonderful dinner and lots of film talk
Fran Rizzo, Sullivan's Last Call

● **Cinequest International Film Festival** – this one is run entirely by college students; a really likable bunch. They've done a good job of getting corporate sponsorship so were able to offer me four complimentary nights in a hotel room with a private Jacuzzi. They selected "HeliumHead" as a closing night film, then proceeded to remove half my audience at the last minute by scheduling a re-screening of a well-liked film for the same time slot. Those kids! God love 'em. The real downside is there is nothing to do in San Jose and practically no nightlife. The closing night gala was over by ten. Bring a good, thick book.
Scott Felixson, HeliumHead

● **Clermont-Ferrand Short Film Festival** – One of the best festivals for short films. Gets LOTS of international attention. The festival director, is a real gentleman. Three years later, he still remembered my film and was still recommending it for special screenings.
Scott Felixson, HeliumHead

● **Filmfest Munchen** – Amazing theaters, constant all night parties, great city, not overly organized as you might suspect the Germans of doing. Sundance was definetely about movies and competition, Munich, noncompetitive, is more about having a good time and meeting other directors. At larger festivals like Sundance, films bring an entourage that stays together, but here only the directors came, so it's a great opportunity to hang out with other filmmakers.
John Schultz, Bandwagon

● **Flanders International Film Festival** – Cool pub/theater combo, and organized to the minute. The Belgiums gave you a daily schedule with items like "Depart for luncheon, 12:22 pm". I was out of competition here, so it was relaxed and full of sight seeing. Good beer here.
John Schultz, Bandwagon

● **Florida Film Festival** – My favorite theatre I've encountered is this fest's Enzian. The audiences are responsive and ask good questions in the Q & A. MEN LIE got distribution from this fest after winning the audience award for Best Feature, and the closing night party at Universal Studios Orlando was a blast. IN both '94 and '97 they honored guests like Dennis Hopper and Haskell Wexler and they were on hand for screenings and questions.

John Gallager, Men Lie and The Deli

● **Florida Film Festival** – My first festival as a filmmaker and still my most upsetting. They forgot to pick me up at the airport, stranding me for two hours. When I later complained to one of the coordinators, she shot back nastily "Well you're here NOW, aren't you?" Though they kindly put me up in a hotel, they had promised free transportation from the hotel to the festival and around town. They didn't; so I had to rent a car. The festival is run by a wealthy couple who also own the charming theater in which the festival is held. The gentleman was very generous, taking some of us filmmakers on a nighttime cruise on his boat

Scott Felixson, HeliumHead

● **Fort Lauderdale International Film Festival** – Also shows lots of films plus retrospectives. I met a lot of great people here, and the festival has receptions and parties every night. Press coberage was pretty good, venues excellent, and the whole festival run beautifully.

John Gallager, Men Lie and The Deli

● **Giffoni Children's Film Festival** – Southern Italy, along the Amalfi coast. Beautiful, so who cares about movies by this point. The "organization", like time down there, is fluid at best, so go with the flow. We never knew what was going to happen in the next 15 minutes, but thanks to friendly hosts, we knew whatever it was it was going to be enjoyable. Pompeii, the Coast, what ever. I missed a screening but it didn't matter - again, a youth oriented festival with enthusiastic "let out of school" audiences.

John Schultz, Bandwagon

● **Gijón International Film Festival** – Young, vibrant and hip. Not good for asthma sufferers or anyone who likes to get up before 5pm. A few technical hitches common to most of these european festivals held on coastal towns projecting films in rundown cinemas but a fun and fullfiling time can be had if you don't mind the rain. The festival makes sure you're well fed but now much else. You're pretty much on your own so if you're not fluent in Spanish a Berlitz guide would be useful.

Monica Pellizzari, Fistful of Flies

● **Hudson Valley Film and Video Festival** – Small, intimate festival, extremely well-organized in everything from press to screening (at a great theatre, Upstate Films) to parties. Especially recommended for the screenplay readings which in '97 included actors Dennis Farina, Charles Durning and Chris Noth. Deserves praise for honoring the screenwriter, and also for their annual tribute to a great screenwriter; this year it was Walter Bernstein.

John Gallager, Men Lie and The Deli

● **Hot Docs! Documentary Film Festival** is the only film and video festival that we've ever attended that brings filmmakers together for one purpose-to truly appreciate each other's efforts and dedication to their profession. Filmmakers generally have time only to get to know their subjects well. At "Hot Docs" Sandra and I met many very talented Canadian producer/directors and got to see their work. In three days we saw 15 films and wish we had come for the entire week...

Schedule permitting, next year whether or not we have a production entered, we plan to attend "Hot Docs".
Sandra and Joseph Consentino, Muhammad Ali: The Whole Story

● **Jerusalem Film Festival** – With a strong contingent of Jewish themed films, as well as all completed Israeli features and the top Israeli shorts, documentaries and TV dramas, the Jerusalem Film Festival is a strong middle range film festival. The most recent festival showcased some 165 films from nearly forty countries, as well as such acclaimed international guests as actor Bob Hoskins (Mona Lisa) and directors Alan Rudolph (Afterglow) and Francesco Rosi (The Truce), adding up to a significant filmic event.
Shlomo Schwartzberg (Director of Programming, Toronto Jewish Film Festival)

● **Karlovy Vary International Film Festival** – A spectacular festival in an incredible setting in a spa resort. This fest really rolls out the carpet for filmmakers with extensive press coverage and sumptuous accommadations. Incredible parties and many extraordinary directors, producers and actors in attendance. Awesome film festival.
John Gallager, Men Lie

● **Laon International Film Festival for Young People** – And small French festival way out in the country, in the 13th century medievil village of upper Laon, with one of the best groups of films I've seen yet. It helps to speak French here (I speak enough that I survived on kindergarten level conversations for four days). In the Champagne region, so the drink flows like water. The jury was made up of eighteen 13-15 year olds from around Europe and French colonies, and the filmmakers get to have a long Q&A session with this jury. I was most proud to win their prize
John Schultz, Bandwagon

International Film Festival Guide

- **Midnight Sun Film Festival** – "My film Portland made in Denmark, was screened at the Midnight Sun Film Festival in Finland and was seen by John Anderson of Newsday from New York. He liked the film and gave a very positive review in Newsday. Karen Cooper of Film Forum, read the review and called up John for more information. Because of this Portland received a 14 day commercial opening in New York City's Film Forum."
  Niels Arden Oplev, Portland

- **Montreal World Film Festival** – I probably saw more films at this festival than any one I've been to. Great selection of movies, excellent networking opportunities. Not much in the way of poarties but hey, it's Montreal, and people make their own. It's a major test so there's superior press coverage.
  John Gallager, Men Lie

- **Nantucket Film Festival** – Like Hudson Valley, celebrates the screenwriter and does readings. The setting on Nantucket Island is idyllic, everything's in walking distance, the parties were awesome and also like Hudson Valley filmmakers can make lots of contacts. Press coverage also quite good, including Boston papers.
  John Gallager, The Deli

- **New York/Avignon Film Festival** in NYC and it's sister fest the Avignon Film Fest in France, I certainly found to be worth the trip (or should I say trips) Both of these fests were designed with the filmmakers and "connecting" in mind. The programs were less "high brow" than the SFIFF but certainly entertaining. They understand we need the support and input of our peers to be able to take the next step. Here both feature filmmakers as well as short filmmakers are given the opportunity to introduce their films and then host a Q&A

session afterwards. What makes these fests great is not the screenings but the breakfasts, lunches, cocktail hours, and parties that seem endless. It's all completely informal and unpretentious. No assigned seating but fear not: if you know no one they'll introduce you and strike up the conversation to put you at ease. The founder, Jerry Rudes and his staff, were helpful and personable from the first telephone conversation right up to the return of my print. No other festival comes close to the atmosphere they create with the Avignon fests!   A note for 16mm filmmakers: the screening rooms in France are not 16mm friendly. The projector, although top quality, doesn't have a place in the projector booth so must live in the back of the theatre. Because of this, the projected image is less than half the size of a normal 35mm projection. Talk about an inferiority complex!

Myke Zykoff, Seven Virtues

● **New York Exposition of Short Film** – Touting themselves as the "oldest and therefore most prestigious" film (short) festival, they seem too caught up in their own politics. I don't know about other filmmakers present, but I felt completely overlooked. Now, the Carolina festivals, though small were certainly the most hospitable to deal with. Very accomodating-a direct contrast to the New York Exposition of Short Film .

Rick Onorato (The Method)

● **Rio Cine Festival** – The festival (also noncompetitive) is based in a grand old hotel, with cocktail hour on the massive deck over looking the ocean every night. The Brazilians are kind hosts. Unfortunately, the films are projected with "simulataneous translation", which means your movie runs with out subtitles, and the audience wears Walkman style headphones that are hooked up to ONE person reading a transcript of all the dialogue, trying to keep up with the movie. Needless to say, the translator falls way behind, and in an ensemble comedy like

BANDWAGON, it's disastrous. But being a guest in Rio is so priv-iledged, once again the experience you get attending outweighs the import of the little movie you made last year.

John Schultz, Bandwagon

● **St.John's Women's Film and Video Festival** – was the greatest! It was the first one we were invited to and, unfortunately, we weren't able to attend, but within the month we received a packet which con-tained the festival catalog, a personal note telling us how well our film was received, as well as, a stack of press reprints in which Sullivan's Last Call was mentioned or reviewed, quite favorably. Needless to say, those press clippings became very important to our subsequent mar-keting campaign...and we especially loved the quality of the copywrit-ing done by the festival itself in the catalog..."You'll feel like having a cigarette afterwards--it's that sexy" has made its way into much of our materials

Fran Rizzo, Sullivan's Last Call

● **The San Francisco International Film Festival** is the most intelli-gent festival I've attended to date. Every screening I sat in on was worthy of the time (and I sat in on over 30 in the week and a half). Not everything was to my taste but all had a definitive voice behind it. Many festivals seem to sprinkle an awful lot of crap into their pro-grams making your time "hit or miss." Not this one. Sadly though this didn't seem to be a good place for meeting other filmmakers unless you really wanted to. They have lunches all week long for small groups of us and fest organizers, but your "connect" abilty depends on who you sit next to. There's also a filmmaker's lounge. This is where you can put up a poster or drop off a stack of promo cards. Everyone goes there to register and get their credentials. Here they also have snacks and drinks for all involved with the fest. It's a place to go and hang out between screenings if you've got nowhere else to be (which is definatley not the case in SF). All said, if you're a film lover, I highly recommend you get to this one.

Myke Zykoff, Seven Virtues

● **Sinking Creek Film Festival** – I didn't get to attend this one but it will always be a favorite. Shortly after sending in my entry, the festival's director called me personally to say she and her selection assistants had just watched "HeliumHead" and enjoyed it enormously. While "HeliumHead" didn't go on to win an award there, I will forever have a fondness for Sinking Creek thanks to their refreshing personal touch

Scott Felixson, HeliumHead

● **South by Southwest Film Festival and Conference (SXSW).** – Great, receptive audiences at this increasingly important fest for indies seeking distribution. Excellent seminars included panelists Quentin Tarantino and Kevin Smith with Austinites Rick Linklater, Robert Rodriguez and Mike Judge. Screening venues were generally excellent although our print was pretty roughly handled (someone lopped off a piece of a scene on one of the reels). Great party town with tremendous music (the film fest overlaps with the SXSW Music Fest), decent press coverage. Only negative is that the festival doesn't pay travel or accomodations for participating filmmakers.

John Gallager, The Deli

● **South by Southwest Film Festival and Conference (SXSW).** A great atmosphere all around. Being in Austin, there's not much to do other than the festival so you see lots of filmgoers all day long. The lines are long waiting to get into a screening but this is a great place to meet people and talk about films. If you're not much of a talker it's a great place to fine tune your eavsdropping skill; it seems the best way to get honest reviews about the films being screened. Like with most fests, unless you've got good word on a film, your time spent on a screening here may prove a complete waste of time.   However; as a presenting filmmaker I found SXSW to have the most enthusiastic of audiences. One of the strong aspects of this fest is the lineup of seminars and conferences throughout opening weekend. They had a fair number of "celebrity" directors and producers on the panels who answered each question with the attitude of "no question is too dumb to ask." The crowds ranged from several hundred down to an intimate one on one (if you sign up quick enough). Overall, a festival worth the trip.

Myke Zykoff, Seven Virtues

● **Stockholm International Film Festival** – Dennis Hopper once said after attending a recent edition of the festival that he wishes life was like the Stockholm Film Festival. Why? I think it might be because we all seek to to be taken care of in life and this festival just does that. Plus, they chose the grooviest films and the restaurants to take to you to dinner each night. And if your lucky enough to win a gong their trophy is a spectacular solid silver ten inch horse that makes other festival trophies pale in comparison. Viva Stockholm. A festival to change your life, if you let it...

Monica Pellizzari ,Fistful of Flies

● **Sundance Film Festival** – Everyone likes to complain that it's "too much", but for the filmmakers, it's a chance to present your work to large audiences several times in a ten day period, so if anybody should enjoy the festival, the filmmakers should (except when the projection sound facilities are inadequate - my film was eaten and projected partially silent before finally finding the good projection machines, but I understand the Festival has built a brand new theater...). As far as organization, it is by far the best - hundreds of films, thousands of people, yet they keep the chaos contained and on schedule. Just keep in mind that what ever happens up there bears little resemblance to actual reality once you step back off the mountain.

John Schultz, Bandwagon

● **Sundance Film Festival** – Like Vegas, this one needs to be seen at least once before you die. Can definitely feel intimidating. Serious parties nightly (and if you make the right connections, you'll learn the location of the post-party party). My first year attending, I made friends with a female volunteer who ensured I got into all the requisite screenings and parties and had a great time. The following year, no longer on speaking terms with the volunteer, I felt like an unwelcome outsider. Which pretty much sums up Sundance: Fickle, unsympathetic and occasionally condescending. A snow-covered hell. Do everything you can to get into this festival.

Scott Felixson, HeliumHead

● **Sundance Film Festival** – The oft heard comment whilst travelling aboard one of the free shuttle buses to one of the many sprawled out locales is "who was the bright person who came up with the idea of having a film fesitval at the coldest time of year, in the remotest part of America and choose to compete with the ski season to boot! Whoever it was they can now pat themselves on the back for holding one of the most important and prestigious festivals around. If you like stars, silicone and snow then this is certainly for you. If you're American then you'll get more out of it than us aliens. The festival might be more exciting for us internationals when they decide we can compete with the local product.

Monica Pellizzari ,Fistful of Flies

● **Tokyo International Film Festival** – First Class festival all the way. (Actually, on the way there it's Business Class, but all other Festivals use Economy, so even that flight was a thrill). This was one of the best experiences of my life - intelligent audiences and journalists, tireless hosts, jaw dropping pageantry, delicious food, generally very good movies, commradery among the filmmakers, and large cash prizes for the Young Cinema Competition (Bandwagon won the Bronze medal). Possibly the best mixture of organization, hospitality, cross cultural sharing, and funny occurances like putting directors on a bizarre TV game show...
  John Schultz, Bandwagon

● **Toronto International Film Festival** – There's a lot of heat around the Toronto Film Festival, and the city really comes alive during it. What I especially like is the audience in Toronto. The Festival has a policy of limiting industry seating, so what you get is an audience that is not self-important or jaded, but one that appreciates unusual films, is smart, honest and responsive.
  Tim McCann, Desolation Angels

● **Venice Film Festival** – Very Italian.A papparazzi fest, a circus. The venetians complain thatit would be less chaotic if they were allowed to run it instead of those dreaded southerners from Rome. Well, until that happens, just like the cessation of the North and South of Italy(never!) it will help you speal the language and/or have a relative who works for the festival. ALternatively, a big briefcase of goodies, gifts or gratuities otherwise known as bribes will help get you to jump queues to get answers to the most basic of questions. Despite these unwritten rules you can usually get in to see most of the films, parties require different negotiating techniques(not printable) and the food is quite good if you're willing to bicycle your way around the isle. Take an umbrella

as the weather is somewhat temperamental as I dare I say it like this
festival and just like us Italians(check my surname, by the way I'm a
Northener!).

Monica Pellizzari, Fistful of Flies

● **Worldfest- Houston and Charleston** – They show lots of films and
gave a great award ceremony. Good local press coverage. Only bum-
mer is their entry fee which is astronomical. . I preferred Charleston
because of the quaint setting and more intimate ambience. They also
have a great venue, the Sottlle Theatre.

John Gallager, Men Lie

● **Oldenburg International Film Festival**– A tremendous festival that
has grown into a great place to get German distribution for your film.
Brilliantly organized, very good press coverage, tributes to veteran
directors and actors, retrospectives, a centralized gathering spot for
filmmakers. Highly recommended.

John Gallager, Men Lie and *The Deli*

Festival References and Industry Contacts

Canadian Producers and Distributors

● **Alberta Releasing**
PO Box 1787, Station M
Calgary, Alberta T2P 2L8
tel: (403) 293 3398
fax: (403) 293 3378
CompuServe: 72520, 240
Lars P. Lehmann

● **Allegro Films Distribution Inc.**
2187 Lariviere St., Ste. 402
Montreal, Quebec H2K 1P5
tel: (514) 529 0320
fax: (514) 529 0328
Franco Battista

● **Alliance Communication Corp.**
121 Bloor St. East, 14th Floor
Toronto, Ontario M4W 3M5
tel: (416) 967 1174
fax: (416) 960 0971
Robert Lantos

● **Coscient-Astral Communications**
33 Yonge St., Ste. 1020
Toronto, Ontario M5E 1S9
tel: (416) 956 2000
fax: (416) 956 2020
Dan Lyon

● **Astral Distribution Group**
2100, rue Sainte-Catherine Ouest,
Bureau 90
Montreal, Quebec H3H 2T3
tel: (514) 939 5000
fax: (514) 939 1515
Stephen Greenberg

● **Atlantic Independent Media**
1541 Barrington St., Ste. 305
Halifax, Nova Scotia B3J 2Z1
tel: (902) 422 5929
fax: (902) 492 2678
ac276@ccn.dal.ca
Richard LeBlanc, Managing Director

● **Atlantis Releasing Inc.**
65 Heward Ave.
Toronto, Ontario M4M 2T5
tel: (416) 462 0246
fax: (416) 462 0254
Ted Riley, President

● **BoffoBizz Inc.**
Box 30174, 1323N
6455 Macleod Trail S
Calgary, Alberta T2H 2V9
tel: (403) 242 2866

● **Bootleg Films**
188 Spadina Ave., Ste. 705
Toronto, Ontario M5T 3A4
tel: (416) 703 3456

● **Canadian Filmmakers Distribution Centre**
37 Hanna Ave., Ste. 220
Toronto, Ontario M6K 1W8
tel: (416) 593 1808
fax: (416) 593 8661
Alan McNairn, Director

● **Canamedia**
125 Dupont St.
Toronto, Ontario M5R 1V4
tel: (416) 324 9190
fax: (416) 972 6261
Les Harris, President

● **Canbium Releasing Inc.**
18 Dupont St.
Toronto, Ontario M5R 1V2
tel: (416) 964 8750
fax: (416) 964 1980
Rita Carbone Fleury, Senior Vice-
President

● **Catalyst Group of Companies**
495 Wellington St. West, Ste. 212
Toronto, Ontario M5V 1G1
tel: (416) 591 6767
fax: (416) 591 6764
Charles Falzon, President

● **CFP Distribution (Cinepix Film Properties Inc.)**
2 Bloor St. West, Ste. 1901
Toronto, Ontario M4W 3E2
tel: (416) 944 0104
fax: (416) 944 2212
Jeff Sackman, Executive Vice-President

● **The Cinar Group**
1207, rue St. Andre
Montreal, Quebec H2L 3S8
tel: (514) 843 7070
fax: (514) 843 7080
Micheline Charest

● **Cinema Libre**
4067 Saint Laurent Blvd., Ste. 403
Montreal, Quebec H2W 1Y7
tel: (514) 849 7888
fax: (514) 849 1231

● **Cineplex Odeon Films Canada**
1303 Yonge St.
Toronto, Ontario M4T 2Y9
tel: (416) 323 6600
fax: (416) 323 6711
Bryan Gliserman, Senior Vice-President

● **Devine Entertainment Corporation**
2 Berkeley St., Ste. 504
Toronto, Ontario M5A 2W3
tel: (416) 364 2282

● **Ewola Cinema**
333 Kensington Ave.
Montreal, Quebec H3Z 2H2
tel: (514) 937 5285
fax: (514) 937 8100

● **Films Transit International Inc.**
402 East Notre Dame St.
Montreal, Quebec H2Y 1C8
tel: (514) 844 3358
fax: (514) 7298
Jan Rofekamp, President and CEO

● **Great North Releasing**
11523-100 Ave.
Edmonton, Alberta T5K 0J8
tel: (403) 482 2022
fax: (403) 3036
Andy Thomson, President

● **Groupe Intervention Video (GIV)**
5505 Saint Laurent Blvd., Ste. 4203
Montreal, Quebec H2T 1S6
tel: (514) 271 5506
fax: (514) 271 6980

● **John Aaron Productions, Inc.**
3551 Pembina Highway
Winnepeg, Manitoba R3V 1A5
tel: (204) 261 8822

● **Kaleidoscope Entertainment Inc.**
23 Lesmill Rd., Ste. 300
Toronto, Ontario M3B 3P6
tel: (416) 443 9200
fax: (416) 443 8685
Randy Zalken, President

● **Keyah Productions Inc.**
4228A 4th Ave.
Whitehorse, Yukon Y1A 1K1
tel: 1 403 668 2420
fax: 1 403 668 6612
Andrew Best

● **King Motion Picture Corporation**
Canada Trust Tower
10104-103rd Ave., Ste.1702
Edmonton, Alberta T5J 0H8
tel: (403) 424 2950
fax: (403) 963 7043
Douglas Hutton

● **Lacewood Productions**
Head Office
400 Maclean St.
Ottawa, ON K2P 0M8
tel: 613 238 4455
fax: 613 238 5361

● **MaloFilm Communications Inc.**
3575, boul. St. Laurent, bur. 650
Montreal, Quebec H2X 2T7
tel: (514) 844 4555
fax: (514) 844 1471
Yves Dion, President of MaloFilm
Distribution Inc.

Mongrel Media
PO Box 68547
360A Bloor Street West
Toronto, Ontario M5S 3J2
tel: (416) 516 9775
fax: (416) 588 6300

Moving Images Distribution
402 West Pender St., Ste. 606
Vancouver, British Columbia V6B 1T6
tel: (604) 684 3014
fax: (604) 684 7165

National Film Board of Canada
Ontario Centre
150 John Street
Toronto, Ontario M5V 3C3
tel: (416) 973 9606
fax: (416) 973 9640

Nelvana
32 Atlantic Ave.
Toronto, Ontario M6K 1X8
tel: 1 416 588 5571
fax: 1 416 588 5588

Norstar Entertainment Inc.
86 Bloor St. West, 4th Floor
Toronto, Ontario M5S 1M5
tel: (416) 961 6278
fax: (416) 961 5608
Andy Myers, Vice-President of
Theatrical Distribution

Paragon International
119 Spadina Ave., Ste. 900
Toronto, Ontario M5V 2L1
tel: (416) 595 6300
fax: (416) 977 0489
Kirstine Layfield, Senior Vice-President

Paramount Pictures Canada
164 Bloor St. West, 6th Floor
Toronto, Ontario M5S 1M4
tel: (416) 969 9901
fax: (416) 922 0287
Greg Ferris

Red Ochre Productions
31 Queen's Rd.
St. John's, Newfoundland A1C 2A4
tel: (709) 739 1711
fax: (709) 739 0868
Ken Pittman

Salter Films International Limited
2507 Brunswick St.
Halifax, Nova Scotia B3K 2Z5
tel: (902) 420 1577
fax: (902) 425 8260
Benedict O'Halloran, President

Telegenic Programs Inc.
20 Holly St., Ste. 300
Toronto, Ontario M4S 3B1
tel: (416) 484 8000
fax: (416) 484 8001
telegenic@eworld.com
H. Lawrence Fein, President and CEO

Universal Films Canada
2450 Victoria Park Ave.
Willowdale, Ontario M2J 4A2
tel: (416) 491 3000
fax: (416) 491 2857
Eugene Amodeo

V Tape
401 Richmond St., Ste. 452
Toronto, Ontario M5V 3A8
tel: (416) 351 1317
fax: (416) 351 1509
video@astral.magic.ca

Video Pool
300-100 Arthur Street
Winnipeg, Manitoba R3B 1H3
tel: (204) 949 9134
fax: (204) 942 1555

Videographe Inc.
4550 rue Garnier
Montreal, Quebec H2J 3S7
tel: (514) 521 2116
fax: (514) 1676

● **Western Moving Picture Company Inc.**
2227 Victoria Drive
Vancouver, British Columbia V5N 4K7
tel: (604) 255 9373
fax: (604) 251 3041

● **Winnipeg Film Group**
304-100 Arthur St.
Winnipeg, Manitoba R3B 1H3
tel: (204) 942 6795
fax: (204) 942 6799
Terry Coles

Canadian Funding Agencies: Public

● Alberta Motion Picture Industries Association (AMPIA)

AMPIA offers a mentorship program to its members who met the eligibility requirements These include a letter of intent from a production company on what the trainee will be responsible for, the period of training as well as any money received by the trainee (aside from that given by the program).

ADDRESS
Midland Walwyn Tower
Edmonton Tower, Suite 606
Edmonton, AL
T5J 2Z2

TEL: 403 944 0707
FAX: 403 426 3057

● British Columbia Film

B.C. Film has various programs available for B.C. residents. These are included in the areas of production, distribution and multimedia.

ADDRESS
2225 West Broadway,
Vancouver, British Columbia V6K 2E4

TEL: 604 736 7997
FAX: 604 736 7290
E-MAIL: bcf@bcfilm.bc.ca

● Manitoba Film and Sound Development Corp.

Access to this fund is restricted to Manitoba companies. They focus their support in development, production and marketing.

ADDRESS
333-93 Lombard Ave.,
Winnipeg Manitoba R3B 3B1

TEL: 204 947 2040
FAX: 204 956 5261

● National Film Board of Canada (NFB)

The mandate of the NFB is to help promote the Canadian film industry by funding its various facets. Their programs centre primarily on the production and distribution of distinctly Canadian films.

ADDRESS
PO Box 6100,
Station Centre-Ville,
Monteal, Quebec H3C 3H5

TEL: 514 283 9285
FAX: 514 283 7914
E-MAIL: http://www.nfb.ca

● Nova Scotia Film Development Corporation (NSFDC)

Only Nova Scotia residents can take advantage of the NSFDC's programs. They focus on development loans, grants, equity investment, special projects and a tax credit program. Another branch of this corporation is the Office of the Film Commissioner which promotes Nova Scotia as a sight for all types of film and video production.

ADDRESS
1724 Granville St.,
Halifax, Nova Scotia B3J 1X5

TEL: 902 424 7177
FAX: 902 424 0617
CONTACT: **John Wesley Chisholm**

● Ontario Arts Council (OAC)

To access funds from the OAC one must be an Ontario resident and working in the film, photography and video field.

ADDRESS
Film, Photography and Video,
151 Bloor St. West,
Toronto, Ontario M5S 1T6

TEL: 416 969 7450

● Ontario Film Development Corporation (OFDC)

The OFDC assists Ontario independent filmmakers, producers and screen-writers with financing as well as the development of certain projects.

ADDRESS
175 Bloor St. East,
North Tower, Suite 300,
Toronto, Ontario M4W 3R8

TEL: 416 314 6858
FAX: 416 314 6876

● SaskFilm (and Video Development Corporation)

SaskFilm's motives are to help promote film industry growth in their province. Therefore only Saskatchewan residents can take advantage of their programs. SaskFilm programs are either in the form of a loan or equity investment.

ADDRESS
2445 13th Ave., Suite 340
Regina, Saskatchewan S4P 0W1

TEL: 306 347 3456
FAX: 306 359 7768

● Societe De Developpement Des Entreprises Culturelles (SODEC)

The majority of this companies resources is used for programs created in French by Quebec residents. The funds are available for distribution, production and marketing.

ADDRESS
1755 Rene Levesque blvd., Suite 200
Montreal, Quebec H2K 4P6

TEL: 514 873 7768
FAX: 514 873 4388

● Telefilm Canada

Telefilm has a variety of different programs for all areas of the film and television industry. These include the Canadian Broadcast Program Development Fund, Feature Film Fund, Feature Film Distribution Fund, Production Revenue Sharing Program, Canadian Film and Video Festivals Grants Fund and many others. If you want specific information on any of their programs the address given is their head office.

ADDRESS
Tour de la Banque Nationale,
600 de la Gauchetiere St. West, 14th Floor,
Montreal, Quebec H3B 4L8

TEL: 514 283 6363
FAX: 514 283 8212

Canadian Funding Agencies: Private

● BBS Mid-Canada Television Funds

The Development and Showcase Fund make available $100,000 and $300,000 dollars, respectively in broadcast area of Sudbury, North Bay, Timmins and Sault Saint Marie.

ADDRESS	TEL:	(613) 224-1313
P.O. Box 5813,	FAX:	(613) 224-7998
Merivale Depot,	CONTACT:	**Keith Campell, Administrator**
Nepean, Ontario K2C 3G6		

● BBS Ontario Incorporated CJOH-TV Development Fund

They make available $5,000 in interest-free loan to independents in their Ottawa broadcast area.

ADDRESS	TEL:	(613) 224-1313
P.O. Box 5813,	FAX:	(613) 224-7998
Merivale Depot,	CONTACT:	**Keith Campbell, Administrator**
Nepean, Ontario K2C 3G6		

● BBS Saskatchewan Inc. Program Development Fund

Loans are available for projects that intend to be broadcasted on the Canadian television system and are repayable once the project goes into production. The budget is $50,000 a year.

ADDRESS	TEL:	(306) 665 8600
216 1st Ave. North,	FAX:	(306) 665 0450
Saskatoon, Saskatchewan S7K 3W3	CONTACT:	**Annette Meckelborg**

● Canada Television and Cable Production Fund

Only Canadian independent producers or production companies can apply for assisstance from this fund. Its goal is to help increase the amount of quality Canadian television programming.

ADDRESS	TEL:	(416) 975 4941
45 Charles St. East, Ste. 802	FAX:	(416) 975 2680
Toronto, Ontario M4Y 1S2	CONTACT:	**Beverley Bettens**

● Canadian Independent Film and Video Fund

This fund provides support with development and production financing for videos, films and multimedia projects.

ADDRESS 666 Kirkwood Ave., Ste. 203 Ottawa, Ontario K1Z 5X9	**TEL:** **FAX:** **CONTACT:**	(613) 729-1900 (613) 729-4610 **Robin Jackson**

● Canwest Global System

This fund will allocate money only to Canadian producers who's product is expressly Canadian, and to be broadcast on the Canwest Global System. The fund's budget is more then $9 million a year.

ADDRESS The Global Communications Development Fund, 81 Barber Greene Rd., Don Mills, Ontario M3C 2A2	**TEL:** **FAX:** **CONTACT:**	(416) 446 5311 (416) 446 5398 **Nancy Anderson**

● COGECO Program Development Fund

The goal of this fund is to promote the creation of new dramatic television series by Canadian television. To take advantage of this fund applicants must have production experience (preferable at least 2 years) and writers must be Canadian.

ADDRESS 2 Carlton Street Suite 1709 Toronto, ON M5B 1J3	**TEL:** **FAX:** **CONTACT:**	416 977 8966 416 977 0694 **Andra Sheffer**

● Rogers Documentary Fund

The creation of this fund occured to help Canadian documentary productions. Its mandate is to finance two documentaries a year (one each in French and English) starting in 1996 for four years. Each productions will be able to receive a maximum of $350,000.

ADDRESS 40 King St. West, Ste. 6400, PO Box 1007, Scotia Plaza , Toronto, Ontario M5H 3Y2	**TEL:** **FAX:** **CONTACT:**	416 864 2325 416 864 2385 **Robin Mirsky, Executive Director**

● Rogers Telefund

This fund provides finacing to Canadian producers. The interest charged is lower then at any financial establishment, to help these aforementioned Canadian producers.

ADDRESS		
40 King St. West, Ste 6400,	TEL:	(416) 864-2325
P.O. Box 1007, Scotia Plaza,	FAX:	(416) 864-2385
Toronto, Ontario M5H 3Y2	CONTACT:	**Robin Mirsky, Executive Director**

● The Foundation to Underwrite New Drama (FUND)

FUND is broken up into three parts and they are: a Script Development, Senior Projects and an Equity Investment Programme. Scrip Development is broken up into four sections which will loans up to $50,000 dollars in specific increments. Senior Projects can loan up to $50,000 for script refinement, marketing and financing. Equity Investment has a $2 million and loans money on an individual project basis to established Canadian production companies.

ADDRESS		
BCE Place,	TEL:	(416) 956-5431
P.O. Box 787,	FAX:	(416) 956-2087
Toronto, Ontario M5J 2T3		

Canadian Film Schools and Training Programs

● **Academy of Canadian Cinema and Television**
158 Pearl Street,
Toronto, Ontario M5H 1L3
tel: (416) 591-2040
fax: (416) 591-2157
Kelly Lettner, Communications Manager

● **Canadian Film Centre**
Windfields,
2489 Bayview Avenue
North York, Ontario M2L 1A8
tel: (416) 445-1446
fax: (416) 445-9481

● **Canadian Screen Training Centre**
61A York Street,
Ottawa, Ontario K1N 5T2
tel: (613) 789-4720, 1-800-742-6016
fax: (613) 789-4724
CSTC@magi.com

● **Canadian Women in Communications**
372 Bay Street,
Toronto, Ontario M5H 2W9
tel: (416) 363-1880, 1-800-361-2978
fax: (416) 363-1882
75543.2556@compuserve.com
Beverley Dales, Executive Director

● **Carleton University**
1123 St. Patrick's Building,
1125 Colonel By Drive
Ottawa, Ontario K1S 5B6
tel: (613) 520 5606
fax: (613) 520 3975
liaison@admissions.carleton.ca

● **CFTPA National Training Programme**
175 Bloor St. East, Ste. 806, N. Tower,
Toronto, Ontario M4W 3R8
tel: 1-800-97-CFTPA
fax: (416) 922-4038
Cindy Lewis, Project Manager

● **CTV Television Network Ltd.**
250 Yonge St. 18th Floor,
Toronto, Ontario M5B 2N8
tel: (416) 595-4100
fax: (416) 595-7328

● **Department of Film & Video, York University**
Rom 224, Centre for Film and Theatre,
4700 Keele Street
North York, Ontario M3J 1P3
tel: (416) 736-5149
fax: (416) 736-5710

● **Directing, Acting & Writing for Camera Workshop**
50 Prince Arthur Ave., Ste. 1407,
Toronto, Ontario M5R 1B5
tel: (416) 922-5378
fax: (416) 922-5378
Maruska Stankova, Artistic Director

● **Global Television Network**
81 Barber Greene Road,
Don Mills, Ontario M3C 2A2
tel: (416) 446-5311
fax: (416) 446-5371
Laurel Kennedy

● **Humber College of Applied Arts and Technology**
205 Humber College Blvd.,
Etobicoke, Ontario M9W 5L7
tel: (416) 675-622 Ext. 4426
Rory Cummings, Program Coordinator

● **Ontario College of Art and Design**
100 McCaul St.,
Toronto, Ontario M5T 1W1
tel: (416) 977-5311

● **Praxis Film Development Workshop**
200-1140 Homer Street,
Vancouver, British Columbia V6B 2X6
tel: (604) 682-3100
fax: (604) 682-7909
praxis@sfu.ca

● **Queen's University**
Film Studies,
90 University Ave
Kingston, Ontario K7L 3N6
tel: (613) 545 2000
http://www.queensu.ca

● **Ryerson Polytechnic University -
Film Studies**
350 Victoria St.,
Toronto, Ontario M5B 2K3
tel: (416) 979-5167
fax: (416) 979-513-
Elvino Sauro, Program Director

● **Sheridan College**
1430 Trafalgar Road,
Oakville, Ontario L6H 2L1
tel: (905) 845-9430
fax: (905) 815-4067

● **Television and Film Institute for
Screenwriters**
10045-156 St. Rm. 441,
Edmonton, Alberta T5P 2P7
tel: (403) 497-4304
fax: (403) 497-4330
Ted Boniface

● **The National Screen Institute-
Canada**
3rd floor, 10022-103 Street,
Edmonton, Alberta T5J 0X2
tel: (403) 421-4084, 1-800-480-4084
fax: (403) 425-8098
Jan Miller, Executive Director

● **The Office of the Registrar**
The Banff Centre for the Arts,
Box 1020, Stn. 28
Banff, Alberta T0L 0C0
tel: (403) 762-6180
fax: (403) 762-6345
Sara Diamond, Artistic Director

● **University of Toronto- Innis
College**
Cinema Studies,2 Sussex Ave
Toronto, Ontario M5S 1J 5
tel: 978 5809 978 2011
http://www.utoronto.ca

● **University of Victoria**
Director of Film Studies,PO Box 1700
Victoria, B.C. V8W 2Y2
tel: (604) 721 6306
fax: (604) 721 7941
Imclarty@nero.uvic.ca
http://www.kafka.uvic.ca/film/

● **University of Waterloo**
200 University Ave. West,
Waterloo, Ontario   N2L 3G1
tel: (514) 885 1211
http://www.arts.uwaterloo.ca/FINE/
juhde/film.htm

● **University of Western Ontario**
Film Studies,
1151 Richmond St.
London, Ontario N6A 5B8
tel: (519) 679 2111
http://www.registar.uwo.ca/

● **University of Windsor**
401 Sunset Ave,
Windor, Ontario N9B 3P4
tel: (519) 253 4232

● **Vancouver Film School**
#400-1168 Hamilton St.,
Vancouver, B.C. V6B 2S2
tel: (604) 685 5808
http://www.multimedia.edu/

● **Women In Film & Television-Toronto**
20 Eglinton Ave. West,
Suite 902, Box 2009
Toronto, Ontario M4R 1K8
tel: (416) 322-3430, 322-3648
fax: (416) 322-3703
Deborah Day, Executive Director

● NOTES

● NOTES

International Producers and Distributors

● **Argentina**

● **Argentina Sono Film**
Lavalle 1973/75
1051 Buenos Aires
Argentina
tel: (54-1) 49 0216/17
fax: (54-1)814 4063

● **Distrifilms S.A.**
Lavalle 1860
1051 Buenos Aires
Argentina
tel: (54-1) 45 6347

● **Eurocine S.A.**
Tucuman 1968
1050 Buenos Aires
Argentina
tel: (54-1) 40 3631
fax: (54-1) 49 0547

● **Filmarte S.R.L.**
Ayacucho 595
1026 Buenos Aires
Argentina
tel: (54-1) 40 3662
fax: (54-1) 476 1739

● **Gea Cinematografica, S.A.**
Pacheo de Melo 2141
1126 Buenos Aires
Argentina
tel: (54-1) 803 7779

● **Jorge Estrada Mora Producciones**
Reconquista 609
1003 Buenos Aires
Argentina
fax: (54-1) 311 4498

● **Mandala Films**
Carlos Pellegrini
739 10 B Buenos Aires
Argentina
tel: (54-1) 322 8194
fax: (54-1) 322 8631

● **Oscar Kramer Producciones**
Libertad 12132
1012 Buenos Aires
Argentina
tel: (54-1) 41 6801
fax: (54-1) 804 1296

● **Transmundo Films S.A.**
Ayacucho 492
1026 Buenos Aires
Argentina
tel: (54-1) 953 3384
fax: (54-1) 11 2479

● **United International Pictures S.R.L.**
Ayacucho 520
1026 Buenos Aires
Argentina
tel: (54-1) 49 0261
fax: (54-1) 11 1303

● **Warner Bros.**
Tucuman 1938
1050 Buenos Aires
Argentina
tel: (54-1) 45 6094
fax: (54-1) 11 1191

● **Australia**

● **Annettework Pty Ltd**
A.C.N. 003 098 191, PO Box 394
Forestville, NSW 2087
Australia
tel: 61 2 452 6069
fax: 61 2 451 0719
Annette Shun Wah

● **Austria**

● Columbia Tri-Star
Wallgasse 21
1060 Vienna
Austria
tel: (43-1) 597 1515
fax: (43-1) 597 1516

● Extrafilm
Grobe Neugasse 44
1040 Vienna
Austria
tel: (43-1) 562 56 03
fax: (43-1) 587 27 43

● Filmladen
Mariahilferstrabe 58
1070 Vienna
Austria
tel: (43-1) 523 4362
fax: (43-1) 526 4749

● Lotus Film
Hietzinger Kai 169
1130 Vienna
Austria
tel: (43-1) 876 26 42
fax: (43-1) 876 26 45

● Odelga Film
Landhausgasse 2/37
1010 Vienna
Austria
tel: (43-1) 535 04 33
fax: (43-1) 532 84 96

● Satel Film
Computerstrabe 6
1101 Vienna
Austria
tel: (43-1) 66109
fax: (43-1) 667 56 50

● Stadtkino
Spittelberggasse 3
1070 Vienna
Austria
tel: (43-1) 522 4814
fax: (43-1) 522 4815

● Star Film
Konstanze Weber-Gasse 3
5020 Salzburg
Austria
tel: (43-662) 83 19 92
fax: (43-662) 82 26 88

● Terra Film
Lienfeldergasse 37
1160 Vienna
Austria
tel: (43-1) 45 80 96
fax: (43-1) 45 47 60

● Thalia Film
Schliessmanngasse 4
1130 Vienna
Austria
tel: (43-1) 877 6566
fax: (43-1) 876 5287

● Top Film
Lindengasse 56
1070 Vienna
Austria
tel: (43-1) 526 1919
fax: (43-1) 526 1918

● U.I.P.
Neubaugasse 1
1070 Vienna
Austria
tel: (43-1) 523 4631
fax: (43-1) 526 7548

● Warner Bros.
Zieglergasse 10
1070 Vienna
Austria
tel: (43-1) 93 86 26
fax: (43-1) 523 9462

● **Wega Film**
Hagelingasse 13
1140 Vienna
Austria
tel: (43-1) 982 5742
fax: (43-1) 982 5833

● **Belgium**

● **Corsan Productions**
J. De Hasquestraat 7
2000 Antwerpen
Belgium
tel: (32-3) 234 2518
fax: (32-3) 226 2158

● **Favourite Films**
Vandenbusschestraat 3
1030 Brussels
Belgium
tel: (32-2) 242 4510
fax: (32-2) 242 1408

● **Fugitive Cinema**
Prinsesstraat 35
2000 Antwerpen
Belgium
tel: (32-3) 234 3674
fax: (32-3) 232 8684

● **Kunst en Kino**
Avenue Louise 32/4
1050 Brussels
Belgium
tel: (32-2) 511 6341
fax: (32-2) 512 6874

● **La Nouvelle Imagerie**
Avenue Jacques Pastur 90
1080 Brussels
Belgium
tel: (32-2) 646 3946
fax: (32-2) 646 3946

● **Lamy Films**
Moensberg 57
1180 Brussels
Belgium
tel: (32-2) 375 3442
fax: (32-2) 375 3271

● **Man's Films**
Avenue Mostinck 65
1150 Brussels
Belgium
tel: (32-2) 771 7137
fax: (32-2) 771 9612

● **Brazil**

● **Belas Artes Cinematograficas**
Rua do Triunfo
34 Sao Paulo
Brazil
tel: (55-11) 221 3080
fax: (55-11) 220 6062

● **Columbia TriStar Films do Brasil Inc.**
Rua do Trinfo
134 Sao Paulo 01212 903
Brazil
tel: (55-11) 200 4022
fax: (55-11) 221 7423

● **Fox Filmes do Brasil**
Ave. Sao Joao, 802 Conj. 11
Sao Paulo 01036 000
Brazil
tel: (55-11) 222 1411
fax: (55-11) 220 7439

● **Look Films**
Rua Felix Sousa, 71 Campo Belo
04612 080 Sao Paulo
Brazil
tel: (55-11) 536 9366
fax: (55-11) 61 21 21
Denise Jancar

● **Pandora Films**
Rua do Estacao, Rua Augusta
1475 Sao Paulo
Brazil
tel: (55-11) 288 6780

● **Czech Republic**

● **Paris Filmes**
Av. Pacaembu
1702 Sao Paulo
Brazil
tel: (55-11) 864 3155
fax: (55-11) 872 4498

● **Bonton Films a.s.**
Severozapadhi 4/39
141 00 Prague 4
Czech Republic
tel: (42-2) 748 907
fax: (42-2) 765 750

● **Playarte Pictures/Playarte Home Video**
Ave. Republica do Libano, 2155
Sao Paulo 04502 300
Brazil
tel: (55-11) 575 6996
fax: (55-11) 570 0905

● **Czech Television**
Na Hrebenech 11
140 70 Prague 4
Czech Republic
tel: (42-2) 2423 0242
fax: (42-2) 2421 4254

● **United International Pictures**
Av. Sao Paulo
799 Sao Paulo 010 35 100
Brazil
tel: (55-11) 222 1411
fax: (55-11) 220 7439

● **Febio, Ltd.**
Ruzova ul. 13
110 00 Prague 1
Czech Republic
tel: (42-2) 2421 3933
fax: (42-2) 2421 4254

● **Filmexport Prague**
Na Morani 5
128 00 Prague 2
Czech Republic
tel: (42-2) 2491 5239
fax: (42-2) 293 312

● **Croatia**

● **Europa Video**
Kriznog puta 20
Zagreb
Croatia
tel: (385-1) 287 826
fax: (385-1) 255 748

● **Intersonic Taunus Production Ltd.**
Stare Grunty 34
842 24 Bratislava
Czech Republic
tel: (42-7) 711 005
fax: (42-7) 722 070

● **RZF Nausikaja**
Trg burze 2
Zagreb
Croatia
tel: (385-1) 430 373
fax: (385-1) 428 847

● **Mirofilm**
Na porici 14
110 00 Prague 1
Czech Republic
tel: (42-2) 2481 0966
fax: (42-2) 2481 0632

● **Denmark**

● **Penta Film**
Strandgade 4B
DK-1401 Kobenhavn K
Denmark
tel: (45) 3296 6230
fax: (45) 3296 0014

● **20th Century Fox**
Skelbaekgade 1
DK-1717 Kobenhavn V
Denmark
tel: (45) 3325 4000
fax: (45) 3325 4002

● **Scala Film**
Centrumpladsen
DK-5700 Svenborg
Denmark
tel: (45) 6221 8866
fax: (45) 6221 0821

● **Camera Film**
Mikkel Bryggers Gade 8
DK-1460 Kobenhavn K
Denmark
tel: (45) 3313 6112
fax: (45) 3315 0882

● **Superfilm Productions**
Forbindelssvej 5
DK-2100 Kobenhavn 0
Denmark
tel: (45) 3142 4611
fax: (45) 3142 4611

● **Crone Film Production A/S**
Blomstervaenget 52
DK-2800 Lyngby
Denmark
tel: (45) 4587 2700
fax: (45) 4587 2705

● **Egypt**

● **Danish Film Institute Workshop**
Vesterbrogade 24
Copenhagen 1264
Denmark
tel: (45) 31 24 16 24

● **Al-Ahram for Cinema and Video**
1 Abu El Karamat Square, Mohandessin
Cairo
Egypt
tel: (20-2) 346 5396
fax: (20-2) 347 0286

● **Domino Film and TV Production**
Kobenhavn N
DK-1411 Lanebrogade 6A
Denmark
tel: (45) 3296 6644
fax: (45) 3296 0644

● **Misr International**
35 Champollion St.
Cairo
Egypt
tel: (20-2) 578 8034
fax: (20-2) 578 8032

● **Gloria Film**
Vesterbrogade 149
DK-1620 Kobenhavn V
Denmark
tel: (45) 3327 0022
fax: (45) 3327 0099

● **Sobky for Film Production**
102 Tahrir St., Dokki
Cairo
Egypt
tel: (20-2) 349 9525
fax: (20-2) 713 384

● **Sphinx Film**
2 Behlar St.
Kasr El Nir St.
Cairo
Egypt
tel: (20-2) 392 0709
fax: (20-2) 392 0710

● **Finland**

● **Filminor**
Lemuntie 7C
SF-00510 Helsinki
Finland
tel: (358-0) 750 510
fax: (358-0) 750 900

● **Harlin/Selin Productions**
Mikonkatu 9
SF-00100 Hensinki
Finland
tel: (358-0) 174 191
fax: (358-0) 622 3403

● **Kinotar/Filmsolfo**
Meritullinkatu 33
00170 Helsinki
Finland
tel: (358-0) 135 1864
fax: (358-0) 135 7864

● **Kinotuotanto**
Katajanokankatu 6
SF-00160 Helsinki
Finland
tel: (358-0) 663 217
fax: (358-0) 622 048

● **Miofilm Oy/Urania Film Oy**
Hiidentie 1A 7
SF-90230 Oulu
Finland
tel: (358-81) 314 1732
fax: (358-81) 314 1730

● **Mondo Furioso Film Productions**
Nilsiankatu 15
00510 Helsinki
Finland
tel: (358-0) 701 2164
fax: (358-0) 7012 1681

● **United International Pictures Finland**
Kaisaniemenkatu 1C 98
SF-00100 Helsinki
Finland
tel: (358-0) 662 166
fax: (358-0) 665 005

● **Warner Bros. Finland**
Kaisaniemenkatu 1B a
SF-00100 Hensinki
Finland
tel: (358-0) 638 288
fax: (358-0) 638 161

● **France**

● **Argos Films**
4 rue Edouard Nortier
92200 Neuilly-sur-Seine
France
tel: (33-1) 4722 9126
fax: (33-1) 4640 0205

● **Celluloid Dreams**
24 rue Lamartine
Paris
France
tel: (33-1) 49 70 03 70
fax: (33-1) 49 70 03 71

● **Cine Classic**
6 rue de l'Ecole-de-Medecine
75006 Paris
France
tel: (33-1) 4634 7574
fax: (33-1) 4633 9760

● **Diaphana**
60 rue de Paradis
75010 Paris
France
tel: (33-1) 4479 9292
fax: (33-1) 4256 5448

● **Films du Losange**
22 avenue Pierre 1er de Serie
75116 Paris
France
tel: (33-1) 4443 8715
fax: (33-1) 4952 0640

● **Flach Film**
47 rue de la Colonie
75013 Paris
France
tel: (33-1) 4416 4000
fax: (33-1) 4580 4000

● **France 2 Cinema**
22 avenue Montaigne
75008 Paris
France
tel: (33-1) 4421 5613
fax: (33-1) 4421 5784

● **Gemini Films**
73 rue St. Denis
75001 Paris
France
tel: (33-1) 4039 0375
fax: (33-1) 4233 1213
Paulo Branco, Producer

● **Lazennec Productions**
36 rue Rene Boulanger
75011 Paris
France
tel: (33-1) 4240 5151
fax: (33-1) 4240 9210

● **Les Films Ariane**
15 rue du Colonel Pierre Avia
75015 Paris
France
tel: (33-1) 4662 1777
fax: (33-1) 4662 1797

● **Les Films des Trois Univers**
173 rue de Fg. St. Antoine
75011 Paris
France
tel: (33-1) 43 40 04 35
fax: (33-1) 44 74 93 44

● **Mercure**
47 rue de la Colonie
75013 Paris
France
tel: (33-1) 4589 8000
fax: (33-1) 4565 0747

● **Pan Europeenne**
107 boulevard Pereire
75017
France
tel: (33-1) 4415 6666
fax: (33-1) 4764 3638

● **Pyramide Film**
6 rue Callulle Mendes
75017 Paris
France
tel: (33-1) 4267 4411
fax: (33-1) 4267 8008

● **Renn Productions**
10 rue Lincoln
75008 Paris
France
tel: (33-1) 4076 9100
fax: (33-1) 4225 1289

● **Twentieth Century Fox**
8 rue Bellini
75782 Paris 16
France
tel: (33-1) 4434 6066
fax: (33-1) 4434 6101

● **U.I.P.**
1 rue Meyerbeer
75009 Paris
France
tel: (33-1) 4007 3838
fax: (33-1) 4742 5716

● **UGC Images**
24 avenue de Charles de Gaulle
92200 Neuilly
France
tel: (33-1) 4640 4400
fax: (33-1) 4624 3728

● **Germany**

● **Anthea Film**
Widenmayerstr. 4
80538 Munich
Germany
tel: (49-89) 226 194
fax: (49-89) 221 251

● **Atlas International**
Rumfordstrasse 29-31
D-80469 Munich
Germany
tel: (49-89) 227 525
fax: (49-89) 224 332
Dieter Menz, President and CEO

● **Bavaria Film**
Bavarafilmplatz 7
82031 Geiselgasteig
Germany
tel: (49-89) 6499 2681
fax: (49-89) 6499 2240
Ulrich Limmer, Producer

● **Cine International**
Leopoldstrasse 18
D-80802 Munich
Germany
tel: (49-89) 391 025
fax: (49-89) 331 089
Lilli Tyc-Holm, President

● **Delphi Film**
Kantsrasse 12a
10623 Berlin
Germany
tel: (49-30) 312 6070
fax: (49-30) 313 9996
Sonja Schmitt, Head of Distribution

● **Impuls Film**
Grazestr. 20
30519 Hannover
Germany
tel: (49-511) 835 001
fax: (49-511) 838 6253

● **Journal Film**
Potsdamer St. 18
12205 Berlin
Germany
tel: (49-30) 833 0151
fax: (49-30) 833 6349
Klaus Volkenborn, President

● **Lau Film International**
Uber Der Kaause 7a
81545 Munich
Germany
tel: (49-89) 6427 0007
fax: (49-89) 6427 0008
Ankie Lau, President

● **Mondada Film**
Klausenerstr. 19
8154 Munich
Germany
tel: (49-89) 692 5884
fax: (49-89) 691 6709

● **Veit Helmer Filmproduktion**
Wormestr. 4
10789 Berlin
Germany
tel: (49-30) 217 77 77
fax: (49-30) 217 77 77

● **Hong Kong**

● **The Film Library**
145 Waterloo Rd.
Kowloon
Hong Kong
tel: (852) 2337 9881
fax: (852) 2794 1345
Alexandra Sun, Managing Director

● **Association of Icelandic Film Producers**
Posthusstraeti 13, PO Box 476
121 Reykjavik
Iceland
tel: (354) 511 2525
fax: (354) 511 2550

● **Hungary**

● **Budapest Film**
Bathori u. 10
1054 Budapest
Hungary
tel: (36-1) 123 8198
fax: (36-1) 111 2494

● **Iran**

● **Focus Film**
Pasareti ut 122
1026 Budapest
Hungary
tel: (36-1) 176 7484
fax: (36-1) 176 7493

● **Children's Literature Mansion**
No. 135 Kashef (Noor) St., Hedayat Ave.
Tehran
Iran
tel: (98-21) 753 2181

● **Hungarian Film Institute**
Budakeszi u. 51B
1012 Budapest
Hungary
tel: (36-1) 176 1018
fax: (36-1) 176 7106

● **Jozan Film**
No. 5 Ghaffari Alley
Jam St. Motahari Ave.
Tehran
Iran
tel: (98-21) 882 2117

● **Hungarofilm Ltd./Cinemagyar**
Bathori u. 10
1054 Budapest
Hungary
tel: (36-1) 114 614
fax: (36-1) 531 317
Istvan Varadi, Managing Director

● **Mahab Film Organization**
No. 224 Sepahbod Qaraney Ave.
Tehran
Iran
tel: (98-21) 897 219

● **Majid Modarresi Film Production Company**
No. 39 Nilufar Alley
Apadana St. Shahid Beheshti Ave.
Tehran
Iran
tel: (98-21) 876 6110

● **Iceland**

● **Association of Icelandic Distributors**
Stjornubio
110 Laugavegi
Iceland
tel: (354) 551 6500
fax: (354) 562 4630

● **Ireland**

● **Temple Films**
4 Windmill Lane
Dublin 2
Ireland
tel: (353-1) 671 9313
fax: (353-1) 671 9323

● **Abbey Films**
35 Upper Abbey St.
Dublin 1
Ireland
tel: (353-1) 872 3422
fax: (353-1) 872 3687

● **The Good Film Company**
15 Vesey Place, Monkstown
Dublin
Ireland
tel: (353-1) 284 4881
fax: (353-1) 285 4882

● **Blue Light**
"The Barracks"; 76 Irishtown Road
Dublin 4
Ireland
tel: 353 1 668 7781
fax: 353 1 660 7654
Geraldine Creed

● **United International Pictures**
D'Olier Chambers, D'Olier St.
Dublin 2
Ireland
tel: (353-1) 679 2433
fax: (353-1) 679 8801

● **Clarence Pictures**
123 Lower Baggot St.
Dublin 2
Ireland
tel: (353-1) 661 4022
fax: (353-1) 661 4186

● **Isreal**

● **Ferndale Films**
4 Harcourt Terrance
Dublin 2
Ireland
tel: (353-1) 676 8890
fax: (353-1) 676 8874

● **Nachshon Films**
22 Harakevet St.
Tel Aviv
Israel
tel: (972-3) 566 0015
fax: (972-3) 615 112

● **Light House Cinema**
12 Anglesea St.
Dublin 2
Ireland
tel: (353-1) 679 9585
fax: (353-1) 679 9586

● **Shani Films**
Dizengoff Centre
Tel Aviv
Israel
tel: (972-3) 528 8282
fax: (972-3) 204 749

● **Little Bird Productions**
122 Lower Baggot St.
Dublin 2
Ireland
tel: (353-1) 661 4245
fax: (353-1) 660 0351

● **Shapira Films**
34 Allenby St.
Tel Aviv
Israel
tel: (972-3) 510 2530
fax: (972-3) 510 1370

● **Shoval Films**
32 Allenby St.
Tel Aviv
Israel
tel: (972-3) 659 288
fax: (972-3) 659 289

● **Italy**

● **Cecchi Gori Group**
Via Valadier 42
00100 Rome
Italy
tel: (39-6) 324 721
fax: (39-6) 3267 2300
Faruk Alatan, Int'l Acquisitions Manager

● **FilmExport Group**
Via Polonia 7/9
00198 Rome
Italy
tel: (39-6) 855 4266
fax: (39-6) 855 0248
Michel Freudenstein, President

● **Intra Films**
Viale Gorizia 25/0
00198 Rome
Italy
tel: (39-6) 884 1311
fax: (39-6) 8535 3790
Paolo Corvino, President

● **Medusa Film**
Via Aurelia Antica 422-424
00165 Rome
Italy
tel: (39-6) 663 901
fax: (39-6) 6639 0450
Mario Spedaletti, Managing Director

● **Penta Film**
Via Aurelia Antica 422
00165 Rome
Italy
tel: (39-6) 663 901
fax: (39-6) 6639 0405

● **Sacis**
Via Teulada 66
00195 Rome
Italy
tel: (39-6) 374 981
fax: (39-6) 370 1343
Sesto Cifola, Business Affairs

● **Surf Film**
Via Padre G.A.
Filippini 130
00144 Rome   Italy
tel: (39-6) 529 3811
fax: (39-6) 529 3816
Massimo Vigliar, President

● **Japan**

● **Daiei Co.**
1-1-16, Higashi-Shimbashi
Minato-ku, Tokyo 105
Japan
tel: (81-3) 3573 8716
fax: (81-3) 3573 8720
Ken Takeuchi, GM/Sales & Acquisitions

● **Latvia**

● **Baltic Cinema**
Kr. Barona St. 31
LV-1011 Riga
Latvia
tel: (371) 782 1485
fax: (371) 782 1486

● **National Film Centre**
Smerla St. 3
LV-1006 Riga
Latvia
tel: (371)252 0411
fax: (371) 782 8408

● **Malaysia**

● **Cineart Enterprises**
78 Jalan Combak
5300 Kuala Lumpur
Malaysia
tel: (60-3) 421 1282
fax: (60-3) 421 1848

● **Perkasa Film**
2786B Jalan Cangkat Permata
Taman Permata
53300 Kuala Lumpur
Malaysia
tel: (60-3) 408 9694
fax: (60-3) 408 4458

● **Mexico**

● **IMCINE**
Tepic 40
Roma Sur 06760
Mexico
tel: (525) 584 7283
fax: (525) 564 4187

● **The Netherlands**

● **Cine Ventura**
Hudsonstraat 52
1057 SN Amsterdam
The Netherlands
tel: (31-20) 683 7439
fax: (31-20) 616 0500

● **Cinemien**
Entrepotdok 66
1018 AD Amsterdam
The Netherlands
tel: (31-20) 627 9501
fax: (31-20) 620 9857

● **Concorde Film**
Lange Voorhout 35
2514 EC The Hague
The Netherlands
tel: (31-70) 360 5810
fax: (31-70) 360 4925

● **Fortissimo Film Sales**
Heremarkt 10-2
1013 ED Amsterdam
The Netherlands
tel: (31-20) 627 3215
fax: (31-20) 626 1155
Helen Loveridge, Co-chair

● **Holland Film**
Jan Luykenstraat 2
Amsterdam
The Netherlands
tel: (31-20) 664 4649
fax: (31-20) 664 9171
Claudia Landsberger, Int'l Relations

● **International Art Film**
Vondelpark 3
1071 AA Amsterdam
The Netherlands
tel: (31-20) 589 1418
fax: (31-20) 683 3401

● **Lowland Productions**
Duivendrechtsekade 82
1096 AJ Amsterdam
The Netherlands
tel: (31-20) 668 0492
fax: (31-20) 694 1018

● **Shooting Star Film Distributors**
Prinsengracht 546
1017 KK Amsterdam
The Netherlands
tel: (31-20) 624 7272
fax: (31-20) 626 8533

● New Zealand

● Essential Productions
PO Box 90056
Auckland Mailing Centre
Auckland
New Zealand
tel: (64-9) 378 0529
fax: (64-9) 378 1662

● Everard Films
PO Box 3664
Auckland
New Zealand
tel: (64-9) 302 1193
fax: (64-9) 302 1192

● Kiwi Film Productions
PO Box 6698
Wellington
New Zealand
tel: (64-4) 384 4060
fax: (64-4) 384 3774

● Roadshow Film Distributors
PO Box 68246
Auckland
New Zealand
tel: (64-9) 377 9669
fax: (64-9) 377 9449

● Norway

● Action Film A/S
Box 9343 Valerenga
N-0610 Oslo
Norway
tel: (47) 2267 3131
fax: (47) 2267 3005

● Europa film A/S
Stortingsgt. 30
N-0161 Oslo
Norway
tel: (47) 2283 4290
fax: (47) 2283 4151

● Montage Film & Video Produksjon A/S
Oscars gt. 59
N-0258 Oslo
Norway
tel: (47) 2244 0430
fax: (47) 2244 9750

● Norsk FilmDistribusjon A/S
Stortingsgt. 12
N-0161 Oslo
Norway
tel: (47) 2242 3600
fax: (47) 2242 2313

● Penelope Film A/S
Box 618
N-4601 Kristiansand
Norway
tel: (47) 3807 0040
fax: (47) 3802 6059

● Sherpa Film Norway A/S
Stensgt. 7
N-0358 Oslo
Norway
tel: (47) 2246 4640
fax: (47) 2246 6434.

● Tour de Force
Georgernes V.3
N-5011 Bergen
Norway
tel: (47) 5532 2590
fax: (47) 5532 3740

● Yellow Cottage A/S
Wedel Jarlsbergs vei 36
N-1342 Jar
Norway
tel: (47) 6752 5300
fax: (47) 6712 5108

Pakistan

MM Potocka Productions
Puzonistow 4
02876 Warsaw
Poland
tel: (48-2) 643 9556
fax: (48-2) 643 9553

Eveready Pictures
Mowlai Mansion
M.A. Jinnah Road
Karachi
Pakistan
tel: (92-21) 262 1775
fax: (92- 21) 262 7842

Syrena Entertainment Group
Marszal/kowska 138
00102 Warsaw
Poland
tel: (48-2) 273 503
fax: (48-22) 275 648

Mandviwalla Entertainment
Nishat Cinema Building
M.A. Jinnah Road
Karachi
Pakistan
tel: (92-21) 722 3535
fax: (92-21) 722 7259

Portugal

Animatografo/Companhia de Filmes do Principe Real
Rue de Rosa, 252, 2o
1200 Lisbon
Portugal
tel: (351-1) 347 5372
fax: (351-1) 347 3252

Poland

Apple Film Production Ltd.
Pl. Konstytucji 3/10
00647 Warsaw
Poland
tel: (48-22) 290 754
fax: (48-2) 290 754

Atalanta Filmes
Av. Joao Crisostomo, 38 C, 1o, Esc.3
1000 Lisbon
Portugal
tel: (351-1) 353 1585
fax: (351-1) 353 1636

Focus Producers Ltd.
Ryzowa 42
02495 Warsaw
Poland
tel: (48-2) 662 7586
fax: (48-2) 662 7083

Filmes Castelo Lopes
Rua de Sto Amaro a Estrela, 17A
1200 Lisbon
Portugal
tel: (351-1) 395 5951
fax: (351-1) 395 5924

Imperial Entertainment
Kolska 12
01045 Warsaw
Poland
tel: (48-22) 472 052
fax: (48-2)430 585

MGN Filmes
Rua de S. Bento, 644, 40 Esq.
1200 Lisbon
Portugal
tel: (351-1) 388 7276
fax: (351-1) 388 7281

● Russia

● Lenfilm Concern
10 Kamennoostrovsky Ave.
197101 St.Petersburg
Russia
tel: (812) 232 8374
fax: (812) 232 8881

● Mosfilm Concern
1 Misfilmovskaya St.
119858 Moscow
Russia
tel: (7-095) 143 9100
fax: (7-095) 938 2083

● Singapore

● Cathay Organisation
#5-00 Cathay Bldg.
11 Dhoby Ghaut
Singapore 0922
Singapore
tel: (65) 337 8181
fax: (65) 339 5609

● Golden Village Entertainment
#15-04 Cathay Bldg.
11 Dhoby Ghaut
Singapore 0922
Singapore
tel: (65) 334 3766
fax: (65) 334 8397

● Slovakia

● Mirofilm
Brectanova 1
833 14 Bratislava
Slovakia
tel: (42-7) 371 966
fax: (42-7) 371 126

● Saturn Entertainment
Viedenska cesta 20
851 01 Bratislava
Slovakia
tel: (42-7) 845 954
fax: (42-7) 845 969

● Slovenia

● Continental Film
61000 Ljubljana
Finzgarjeva 6
Slovenia
tel: (386) 61 219 364
fax: (386) 6121 4194

● Studio MI
61000 Ljubljana
Linhartova 8
Slovenia
tel: (386) 6130 2322
fax: (386) 6113 27085

● South Africa

● Nu Metro
6 Hood Avenue
Rosebank 2196
South Africa
tel: (27-11) 8807040
fax: (27-11) 442 7030

● **Philo Pieterse Productions**
PO Box 2299
Halfway House 1685
South Africa
tel: (27-11) 314 2080
fax: (27-11) 314 2265

● **Showdata**
P.O. Box 15756, Vlaeberg
Cape Town 8018
South Africa
tel: (27-21) 345 483

● **Sonneblom Films**
P.O. Box 3940
Honeydew 2040
South Africa
tel: (27-11) 794 2100
fax: (27-11) 791 2061
Katinka Heyns

● **Spain**

● **Alta Films**
Martin de los Heros 12
Madrid 28008
Spain
tel: (34-1) 542 2702
fax: (34-1) 542 8777

● **Atrium Films**
Fernan Gonzalez 28
Madrid 28009
Spain
tel: (34-1) 431 4790
fax: (34-1) 431 7555

● **Avanti Films**
Ronda de San Pedro 46
Barcelona 08010
Spain
tel: (34-3) 268 1233
fax: (34-3) 268 1617

● **Golem Distribution S.A.**
Avda. de Bayona 52
Pamplona 31008
Spain
tel: (34-1) 260 243
fax: (34-1) 171 058

● **Iberoamericana Films**
Velazquez 12
Madrid 28001
Spain
tel: (34-1) 431 4246
fax: (34-1) 435 5994

● **Lola Films**
Pintor Gimeno 12
Barcelona 08022
Spain
tel: (34-3) 418 4044
fax: (34-3) 418 4748

● **Musidora Films**
Princesa 17
Madrid 28008
Spain
tel: (34-1) 541 6869
fax: (34-1) 541 5482

● **Prime Films**
Clara del Rey 17
Madrid 28002
Spain
tel: (34-1) 519 0181
fax: (34-1) 413 0772

● **Sweden**

● **Atlantic Film**
Box 21112
S-100 31 Stockholm
Sweden
tel: (46-8) 305 230
fax: (46-8) 305 280

● **Capitol Film Distribution**
Sodra vagen 12
S-392 33 Kalmar
Sweden
tel: (46) 4801 2215
fax: (46) 4802 4085

● **Corona Film**
Brantingsgatan 35
S-115 35 Stockholm
Sweden
tel: (46-8) 661 0509
fax: (46-8) 702 9845

● **Egmont Film**
Box 507
183 25 Talby
Sweden
tel: (46) 7621 0050
fax: (46) 7621 2046

● **Fox Film**
Box 9501
S-102 74 Stockholm
Sweden
tel: (46-8) 658 1140
fax: (46-8) 841 204

● **Sandrew Film & Teater**
Box 5612
S-114 86 Stockholm
Sweden
tel: (46-8) 234 700
fax: (46-8) 103 850

● **Swedish Film**
Luntmakargatan 52
S-113 58 Stockholm
Sweden
tel: (46-8) 160 525
fax: (46-8) 345 900

● **Triangelfilm**
Box 17156
S-200 10 Malmo
Sweden
tel: (46-40) 125 547
fax: (46-40) 129 099

● **Switzerland**

● **Boa Filmproduktion AG**
Neugasse 6
CH-8005 Zurich
Switzerland
tel: (41-1) 271 0464
fax: (41-1) 271 0518

● **Carac Film AG**
Zinggstrasse 16
CH-3007 Berne
Switzerland
tel: (41-31) 372 0040
fax: (41-31) 372 0481

● **Condor Films AG**
Restelbergstrasse 107
CH-8044 Zurich
Switzerland
tel: (41-1) 361 9612
fax: (41-1) 361 9575

● **Elite Film AG**
Molkenstrasse 21
CH-8026 Zurich
Switzerland
tel: (41-1) 242 8822
fax: (41-1) 241 2123

● **Focus Film AG**
Zollikerstrasse 20
CH-8032 Zurich
Switzerland
tel: (41-1) 382 3388
fax: (41-1) 382 3389

● **Rialto Film AG**
Neugasse 6, P.O. Box 299
CH-8021 Zurich
Switzerland
tel: (41-1) 271 4200
fax: (41-1) 271 4203

● **Stamm Film AG**
Lowenstrasse 20, P.O. Box
CH-8023 Zurich
Switzerland
tel: (41-1) 216 615
fax: (41-1) 212 0369

● **TriLuna Film AG**
Neugasse 6, P.O. Box 299
CH-8021 Zurich
Switzerland
tel: (41-1) 273 0053
fax: (41-1) 271 2616

● **Turkey**

● **Alfa-Film**
Istiklal Caddesi No 140
Beyoglu, Istanbul

Turkey
tel: (90-212) 243 6340
fax: (90-212) 243 3108

● **Magnum Film**
P trak Sokak 7/4
34800 Yesilyurt
Istanbul
Turkey
tel: (90-212) 573 2879
fax: (90-212) 573 7343

● **United Kingdom**

● **Allied Entertainment**
3-4 Ashland Place
London W1M 3JH
United Kingdom
tel: ((44 171) 224 1992
fax: (44 171) 224 0111

● **Blue Dolphin Films**
40 Langham St.
London W1N 5RG
United Kingdom
tel: (44 171) 255 2494
fax: (44 171) 580 7670

● **British Lion**
Pinewoo Studios, Iver Heath
Bucks. SLO ONH
United Kingdom
tel: (44 1753) 651 700
fax: (44 1753) 656 391

● **Dakota Films**
6 Meard St.
London W1V 3HR
United Kingdom
tel: (44 171) 287 4329
fax: (44 171) 287 2303

● **Electric Pictures**
15 Percy St.
London W1P 9FD
United Kingdom
tel: (44 171) 636 1231
fax: (44 171) 696 1675

● **Enigma Productions**
13-15 Queens Gate Place Mews
London SW7 5BG
United Kingdom
tel: (44 171) 581 0238
fax: (44 171) 584 1799

● **Entertainment Film Distributors**
27 Soho Square
London W1V 5FL
United Kingdom
tel: (44 171) 439 1606
fax: (44 171) 734 2483

● **First Independent Films**
69 New Oxford St.
London WC1A 1DG
United Kingdom
tel: (44 171) 528 7767
fax: (44 171) 528 7771

Greenpoint Films
54 Noel St.
London W1V 3RB
United Kingdom
tel: (44 171) 437 6492
fax: (44 171) 437 0644

Guild Film Distribution
Kent House, 14-17 Market Place
Great Titchfield St.
London W1N 8AR
United Kingdom
tel: (44 171) 322 5151
fax: (44 171) 631 3568

Little Bird
91 Regent St.
London W1R 7TA
United Kingdom
tel: (44 171) 434 1131
fax: (44 171) 434 1803

Mainline Pictures
37 Museum St.
London WC1A 1LP
United Kingdom
tel: (44 171) 242 5523
fax: (44 171) 430 0170

Majestic Films International
Gloucester Mansions
Cambridge Circus
London WC2H 8HD
United Kingdom
tel: (44 171) 836 8630
fax: (44 171) 836 5819

Parallax Pictures
7 Denmark St.
London WC2H 8LS
United Kingdom
tel: (44 171) 836 1478
fax: (44 171) 497 8062

Prominent Features
68A Delancey St.
London NW1 7RY
United Kingdom
tel: (44 171) 284 0242
fax: (44 171) 284 1004

Rank Film Distributors
127-133 Wardour St.
London W1V 4AD
United Kingdom
tel: (44 171) 437 9020
fax: (44 171) 434 3689

Royal College of Art
88A Valetta Rd.
London W37TW
United Kingdom
tel: (44-171) 584 5020

Zoo Lane Productions
46 Stiven Crt.
Harrow, Middx. HA2 9AY
United Kingdom
tel: 44 181 423 0956
fax: 44 171 821 0231
An Vrombaut

● USA

40 Acres & A Mule Filmworks
124 Dekalb Ave.
Brooklyn, NY 11217
USA
tel: (718) 624 3703
fax: (718) 623 2008
Spike Lee

6th Man Films Inc. & Sauce Enterainment
100 Varick St.
New York, NY 10013
USA
tel: (212) 343 3000
fax: (212) 343 8503

Aban Entertainment
4000 West Alameda Ave. 5th Flr.
Burbank, CA 91505
USA
tel: (818) 972 4800
fax: (818) 972 4895

● **ABC Entertainment**
2020 Avenue of the Stars
Los Angeles, CA 90067
USA
tel: (310) 231 1650

● **Acme Filmworks**
6525 Sunset Blvd.; Garden Suite 10
Hollywood, CA 90028
USA
tel: 213 464 7805
fax: 213 464 6614
Ron Diamond

● **All Girl Productions**
500 South Buena Vista St.
Burbank, CA 91521
USA
tel: (818) 560 6547
fax: (818) 563 9648

● **American Zoetrope**
916 Kearny Street
San Francisco, CA 94133
USA
tel: (415) 78 7500
fax: (415) 989 7910

● **Beacon Pictures**
1041 North Formosa Ave. #200
Los Angeles, CA 90046
USA
tel: (213) 850 651
fax: (213) 850 2613

● **Blair/Levin Productions**
428 Cortland Ave
San Francisco, CA 94110
USA
tel: (415) 282 5240
fax: (415) 282 7202

● **Buena Vista Pictures Distribution, Inc.**
500 S Buena Vista
Burbank, CA 91521
USA
tel: (818) 567 5000

● **Caminer-Gallagher Productions**
305 Lexington Ave., Suite 7B
New York, NY 10016
USA
tel: 1 212 689 0104
fax: 1 212 689 5196
John Gallagher

● **Canyon Cinema**
2325 Third Street, Ste. 338
San Francisco, CA 94107
USA
tel: (415) 626 2255
fax: (415) 626 2255

● **Cappa Productions**
445 Park Ave.
New York, NY 10022
USA
tel: (44 212) 906 8800
fax: 44 212) 906 8891
Martin Scorsese

● **Carbo Films**
4086 Glencoe Ave.
Marina del Rey, CA 90292
USA
tel: (310) 578 5925
fax: (310) 306 0126

● **Carlson Films**
857 Fifteenth Street, Ste. B
Santa Monica, CA 90403
USA
tel: (310) 917 1988
fax: (310) 917 1988

● **Children's Media Project**
71 Robinson Lane
Wappingers Falls, NY 12590
USA
tel: 1 914 227 1838
fax: 1 914 227 1838
Maria Marewski, Director

● **Churchhill Media**
12210 Nebraska Ave., Dept. 200
Los Angeles, CA 90025
USA
tel: (800) 334 7830

Concorde/New Horizons Picture Corp.
11600 San Vincente Blvd.
Los Angeles, CA 90049
USA
tel: (310) 820 6733
fax: (310) 207 8825

Consentino Television Productions
118 West Mountain Rd.
Ridgefield, CT 06877
USA
tel: 203 438 4460
fax: 203 431 8533
Sandra & Joseph Consentino

Conspiracy Films, Inc.
6001 Skillman St., Ste. 243
Dallas, TX 75231
USA
tel: (214) 739 1432
fax: (214) 739 1432

Creative Thinking International, Ltd.
208 W 30th Street, Ste. 302
New York, NY 10001
USA
tel: (212) 629 5320
fax: (212) 629 5527

Dart Entertainment Group
345 Park Ave S., 2nd Floor
New York, NY 10010
USA
tel: 1 212 502 0810
fax: 1 212 685 0797
Michael Roban

Davis Entertainment
2121 Avenue of the Stars, Ste. 2900
Los Angeles, CA 90067
USA
tel: (310) 551 2266
fax: (310) 556 3760

Direct Cinema Limited
PO Box 10003
Santa Monica, CA 90410
USA
tel: (310) 396 4774

Documentary Arts Inc.
PO Box 140244
Dallas, TX 75214
USA
tel: (214) 824 3377
fax: (214) 824 3378

DreamWorks
100 Universal Plaza, Building 601
Universal City, CA 91608
USA
tel: 818 733 6001
fax: 818 733 7083

Electronic Arts Intermix
536 Broadway, 9th Floor
New York, NY 10012
USA
tel: (212) 966 4605
fax: (212) 941 6118

Elegant Films
1995 Broadway, Ste. 1801
New York, NY 10023
USA
tel: (212) 362 0409
fax: (212) 362 0079

Farmhouse Films
35 Boyce Road
Pine Bush, NY 12566
USA
tel: 1 914 744 3869
fax: 1 914 744 3869 (*3 to fax)
Meira Blaustein

Filmopolis Pictures
11300 W Olympic Blvd., Ste. 840
Los Angeles, CA 90064
USA
tel: (310) 914 1776
fax: (310) 914 1777

Films, Inc.
5547 Ravenswood
Chicago, IL 60640
USA
tel: (800) 323 4222

Fine Line Features
888 Seventh Ave., 20th Floor
New York, NY 10106
USA
tel: (212) 649 4800
fax: (212) 956 1942

Florida State University
School of Motion Picture, TV and
Recording Arts
Tallahassee, FL 32306
USA
tel: (213) 237 5000

Gotham Entertainment Group
99 Hudson Street, Suite 200
New York, NY 10013
USA
tel: 212 379 6063
fax: 212 376 6067
Joel Roodman   www.gothamcity.com

Gramercy Pictures
9247 Alden Dr.
Beverly Hills, CA 90210
USA
tel: (310) 777 1960
fax: (310) 777 1966

Guede Films, Inc.
P.O. Box 194140
San Juan, PR 00919-4140
USA
tel: (809) 783 5656
fax: (809) 782 8600

Hughes Entertainment
3450 W Touhy Ave.
Chicago, IL 60645
USA
tel: (708) 933 9014
fax: (708) 933 9013
John Hughes

Independent Film Channel
150 Crossway Park W
Woodbury, NJ 11797
USA
tel: (516) 364 2222
fax: (516) 364 7638

Inscrutable Films
PO Box 9053
Glendale, CA 91226
USA
tel: (818) 683 3283
fax: (818) 683 8797

Jim Henson Productions
117 East 69th Street
New York, NY 10021
USA
tel: 212 794 2400
fax: 212 988 3112
foundation@henson.com

Kit Parker Films
PO Box 16022
Monterey, CA 93942
USA
tel: (408) 393 0303
fax: (408) 393 0304

KJF Productions
1405 NE Madison St., Ste. 3
Minneapolis, MN 55413
USA
tel: (612) 782 3827
fax: (612) 782 3827

Lakeshore International
5555 Melrose Ave.
Hollywood, CA 90038
USA
tel: 213 956 4222
fax: 213 862 1456
Sharon Dietz, Manager, Mktng & Aq.

Lighter Than Air Film Marketing and Consulting
885 West End Ave., Suite 11-D
New York, NY 10025 USA
tel: 212-726-0443
fax: 212-749-7964
Scott Felixson LighterThanAir@Juno.com

Long Bow Group
55 Newton St.
Brookline, MA 02146
USA
tel: (617) 277 6400
fax: (617) 277 6843

● **Lucerne Films, Inc.**
37 Ground Pine Road
Morris Plains, NJ 07950
USA
tel: (800) 341 2293

● **Maverick Productions**
8000 Beverly Blvd.
Los Angeles, CA 90048
USA
tel: (213) 852 1177
fax: (213) 852 1505

● **McCann & Co. Films**
51 Kinney Street
Piermont , NY 10968
USA
tel: 914 365 3751
Tim McCann

● **Miramax Films**
375 Greenwich St.
New York, NY 10013
USA
tel: (212) 941 3800
fax: (212) 941 3949

● **Miramax Films**
7920 Sunselt Blvd. Suite 230
Los Angeles, CA 90046
USA
tel: (213) 969 2000
fax: (213) 969 9840

● **Morgan Creek Productions**
4000 Warner Blvd., Building 76
Burbank, CA 91522
USA
tel: (818) 954 4800
fax: (818) 954 4811

● **Moviebaby Productions**
109 West 85th Street
New York, NY 10024
USA
tel: 1 212 595 8593
fax: 1 212 769 0633
Fran Rizzo, President

● **National Film Board of Canada**
1251 Avenue of the Americas
New York, NY 10020
USA
tel: (212) 596 1770
fax: (212) 596 1779

● **New Line Cinema Corp.**
116 N Robertson Blvd., 2nd Floor
Los Angeles, CA 90048
USA
tel: (310) 854 5811
fax: (310) 854 1824

● **Oasis Film**
333 Fourth St., Ste. 31
Brooklyn, NY 11215
USA
tel: (718) 499 1650
fax: (718) 499 1650

● **October Films**
65 Bleecker St.
New York, NY 10012
USA
tel: (212) 539 4000
fax: (212) 539 4099

● **One Mind Productions, Inc.**
7906 Brookhollow Rd., Ste. C
Dallas, TX 75235
USA
tel: (214) 920 2464
fax: (214) 920 2460

● **Orion Pictures Corporation**
1888 Century Park East
Los Angeles, CA 90067
USA
tel: (310) 282 0550
fax: (310) 201 0798

● **Olivieri Films, Inc.**
171 East 88th Street, Suite 2C
New York, NY 10128
USA
tel: 212 996 4946
fax: 212 289 2058
Steven Olivieri, President

Overseas Filmgroup
8800 Sunset Blvd.
Los Angeles, CA 90069
USA
tel: (310) 855 1199
fax: (310) 855 0719

Pacific Data Images
3101 Park Blvd.
Palo Alto, CA 94306
USA
tel: 415 846 8100
fax: 415 846 8101
Judy Conner

Palomar Pictures
5657 Wilshire Blvd., 5th Floor
Los Angeles, CA 90036
USA
tel: (213) 525 2900
fax: (213) 525 2912

Pennant Productions
340 1/2 N Spaulding Ave.
Los Angeles, CA 90036
USA
tel: (213) 938 5108
fax: (213) 938 7138

Phoenix Films & Video
2349 Chaffee Drive
St. Louis, MO 63146
USA
tel: (314) 569 0211

Planet Pictures
PO Box 1151
Old Chelsea Station
New York, NY 10001
USA
tel: (212) 779 0660
fax: (212) 779 9129

Puerto Rico Film Commission
P.O. Box 362350
San Juan, PR 00936-2350
USA
tel: (809) 754 7110
fax: (809) 756 5706

Pyramid Film & Video
PO Box 1048
Santa Monica, CA 90406
USA
tel: (310) 828 7577

Rainbow Releasing
9165 Sunset Blvd., Penthouse
Los Angeles, CA 90069
USA
tel: (310) 271 0202
fax: (310) 271 2753

Red River Films
510 East 84th Street, Suite 4B
New York, NY 10028
USA
tel: 1 212 794 2313
fax: 1 212 794 3136
Walter Cohen

Red Wagon Productions
TriStar Building 212
10202 W. Washington Blvd.
Culver City, CA 90232
USA
tel: (310) 280 4466
fax: (310) 280 1480

Reitman Productions, Ivan
100 Universal City Plaza
Universal City, CA 91608
USA
tel: (818) 777 8080
fax: (818) 733 0689

Seven Rays Pictures
PO Box 1920
Santa Monica, CA 90406
USA
tel: (310) 450 3456
fax: (310) 395 4272

Seventh Art Releasing
7551 Sunset Blvd., Ste. 104
Los Angeles, CA 90046
USA
tel: (213) 845 1455
fax: (213) 845 4717

● **Shillelagh Pictures**
6041 Village Bend, Ste. 2109
Dallas, TX 75206
USA
tel: (214) 739 5011

● **The Disney Channel**
3800 W Alameda Ave.
Burbank, CA 91505
USA
tel: (818) 596 3279
fax: (818) 566 1358

● **The Shooting Gallery**
145 Avenue of the Americas, 7th Floor
New York, NY 10013 USA
tel: 1 212 243 3042
fax: 1 212 647 1392
http://www.shootinggallery.com
David Tuttle, Senior VP of Operations

● **The Goldwyn Company**
10203 Santa Monica Blvd.
Los Angeles, CA 90067
USA
tel: (310) 552 2255
fax: (310) 284 8493

● **Sony Picture Classics**
550 Madison Ave., 8th Floor
New York, NY 10022
USA
tel: (212) 833 8833
fax: (212) 833 8844

● **The Robert Evans Co.**
5555 Melrose Ave.
Lubitsch Building, #117
Hollywood, CA 90038
USA
tel: (213) 956 8800
fax: (213) 956 0070

● **Sony Pictures Repertory**
10202 W Washington Blvd.
Culver City, CA 90232
USA
tel: (310) 280 8000
fax: (310) 204 1300

● **Third World Newsreel**
335 West 38th Street, 5th Floor
New York, NY 10018
USA
tel: (212) 947 9277
fax: (212) 594 6417

● **SPB Films**
PO Box 684985
Austin, TX 78768
USA
tel: (512) 708 8740
fax: (512) 708 8740

● **Top Line Communications**
1123 Broadway, Ste. 817
New York, NY 10010
USA
tel: (212) 627 5522
fax: (212) 627 5802

● **Strand Releasing**
225 Santa Monica Blvd., Ste. 810
Santa Monica, CA 90401
USA
tel: (310) 395 5002
fax: (310) 395 2502

● **Tribeca Film Centre**
375 Greenwich St.
New York, NY 10013
USA
tel: (212) 941 2410
fax: (212) 941 2411

● **Swank Motion Pictures**
201 S Jefferson Ave.
St. Louis, MO 63013
USA
tel: (800) 876 5577
fax: (314) 289 2192

● **Universal**
100 Universal City Plaza, Bldg. 507-4H
Universal City, CA 91608
USA
tel: 818 777 1213
Ellen Cockrill

Contacts

Universal Pictures
100 Universal City Plaza
Universal City, CA 91608
USA
tel: (818) 777 1000
fax: (818) 777 6280

VCE, Inc.
13300 Ralston Ave.
Sylmar, CA 91342
USA
tel: (818) 367 9187
fax: (818) 362 3490

Video Data Bank
37 S Wabash
Chicago, IL 60603
USA
tel: (312) 345 3550
fax: (312) 541 8073

Walkow/Gruber Pictures
225 Santa Monica Blvd., Ste. 1106
Santa Monica, CA 90401
USA
tel: (310) 260 5570
fax: (310) 260 5572

Warner Bros.
500 N.Brand Blvd., Suite 1800
Glendale, CA 91203-1923   USA
tel: 818 977 7393
fax: 818 977 7596
dave_master@ccmailgw.wbfa.com
Dave Master

West City Films, Inc.
153A Mt. Auburn St.
Cambridge, MA 02138
USA
tel: (617) 497 9325
fax: (617) 497 1763

Weston Woods Studios
Weston, CT 06883
USA
tel: (203) 226 3355

Wildwood Productions
1101 Montana, Suite E
Santa Monica, CA 90403
USA
tel: (310) 395 5155
fax: (310) 395 3975

Xposure Productions
19th West 21st Street, Suite 201
New York, NY 10010
USA
tel: 1 212 352 1472
fax: 1 212 242 3983
Susan Bernstein

Zeitgeist
247 Centre Street, 2nd Floor
New York, NY 10013
USA
tel: (212) 274 1989
fax: (212) 274 1644

Leslie McCleave
734 Broadway, Ste. 5
New York, NY 10003
USA
tel: (212) 642 5275
fax: (212) 343 1850

Sherri M. Breyer
2135 Whitley Ave.
Los Angeles, CA 90068
USA
tel: (213) 464 5662
fax: (213) 464 5662

Bill Plympton
107 W 25th Street, Ste. 4B
New York, NY 10001
USA
tel: (212) 675 6021
fax: (212) 675 0233

Melissa Hacker
235 W 12th Street, Ste. 13
New York, NY 10014
USA
tel: (212) 255 5081
fax: (212) 255 5081

International Film Schools

● **Australia**

● **Australian Film Television & Radio School**
P.O. Box 126,
North Ryde NSW 2113
Australia
tel: (61-2) 9805 6611
fax: (61-2) 9887 1030

● **Denmark**

● **University of Copenhagen**
Department of Film & Media
Studies,Njalsgade 80
DK-2300 Kobenhavn S
Denmark
tel: (45) 3532 8100
fax: (45) 3532 8110

● **Finland**

● **University of Art and Design Helsinki**
Hameentie 135 C,
00560 Helsinki
Finland
tel: (358-0) 636 982
fax: (358-0) 634 303

● **Germany**

● **University of Mannheim**
Ew 292,
D-68131 Mannheim
Germany
tel: (49-621) 292 1449
fax: (49-621) 292 2850

● **Hong Kong**

● **The Hong Kong Academy of Performing Arts**
Academic Services Office,
1 Gloucester Road
Wanchai   Hong Kong
tel: (852) 2584 1554
fax: (852) 2802 4372

● **Ireland**

● **European School of Animation**
Senior College,Ballyfermot
Dublin 10
Ireland
tel: (353-1) 626 9421
fax: (353-1) 626 6754

● **Korea**

● **Kyungsung University**
110 Daeyon-Dong,
Nam-Ku, Pusan 608-736
Korea
tel: (82-51) 622 5331
fax: (82-51) 623 7803

● **Malaysia**

● **The Netherlands**

● **Ngee An Polytechnic- Department of Film & Media St**
535 Clementi Rd.,Block 23
599489 Singapore
Malaysia
tel: (65) 460 6784
fax: (65) 462 5617

● **Hogeschool van Utecht**
Faculty of Communication &
Journalism,
NL-3503 AB Utrecht
The Netherlands
tel: (31-30) 291 0273
fax: (31-30) 294 3093

● **Spain**

● **United Kingdom**

● **Film-Historia**
Centre for Cinematic Research,PO Box 12109
08080 Barcelona
Spain
tel: (34-3) 333 3466
fax: (34-3) 333 0614

● **Edinburgh College of Art**
Heriot-Watt University,
Lauriston Place
Edinburgh, Scotland
UK
tel: (44-131) 221 6000
fax: (44-131) 221 6001

● **The London International Film School**
Department IG11,
24 Shelton St.
London WC2H 9HP
UK
tel: (44-171) 836 0826

● **Sweden**

● **Halmstad University- Media and Communications**
Kristian IV :s vag 3,Box 823
S-301 18 Halmstad
Sweden
tel: (46-35) 167 100
fax: (46-35) 148 533

● **University of Bath**
Claverton Down,
Bath BA2 7BY
UK
tel: (44-1225) 826 826
fax: (44- 1225) 462 508

● **University of Karlstad Film Studies**
Admissions Office,
S-651 88 Karlstad
Sweden
tel: (46-54) 838 106
fax: (46-54) 838 496

● **University of Wales, Aberystwyth**
The Departme of Theatre, Film &
Television Studies,
1 Laura Place
Aberystwyth, Dyfed, Wales SY232AU
UK

● **Long Island University**
Southhampton Campus,
Montawk Highway
Southhampton, NY 11968
USA
tel: (516) 283 4000

● **USA**

● **California Institute**
24700 McBean Parkway,
Valencia, CA 91355
USA
tel: (805) 255 1050

● **New York Film Academy**
Tribeca Film Centre,
375 Greenwich St.
New York, NY 10013
USA
tel: (212) 941 4007

● **California State University -**
Fresno

Fresno, CA 93740-0046
USA
tel: (209) 278 4840

● **New York University**
Tisch School of the Arts,721 Broadway
New York, NY 10003
USA
tel: (212) 998 1820

● **City College of San Francisco**
50 Phelam Ave.,
San Francisco, CA 94112
USA
tel: (415) 239 3000

● **San Diego State University**
San Diego, CA 92182
USA
tel: (619) 594 5200

● **Columbia College - Hollywood**
925 N La Brea Ave.,
Hollywood, CA 90038
USA
tel: (213) 851 0550

● **Santa Monica College**
1900 Poco Blvd.,
Santa Monica, CA 90405
USA
tel: (310) 450 5150

● **Columbia University**

New York, NY 10027
USA
tel: (212) 854 1754

● **Sarah Lawrence College**
1 Meadway,
Bronxville, NY 10908
USA
tel: (914) 337 0700

● **Florida State University**
Undergraduate R-42,
Tallahassee, FL 32306-4021
USA
tel: (904) 644 2525

● **School of the Art Institute of**
Chicago
280 S Columbus,
Chicago, IL 60603
USA
tel: (312) 899 5100

● **School of Visual Arts**
209 E 23rd St.,
New York, NY 10010
USA
tel: (212) 592 2000

● **University of Southern California**
University Park,
Los Angeles, CA 90089-2111
USA
tel: (213) 740 2311

● **State University of New York**
Purchase,
35 Anderson Hill Rd.
Purchase, NY 10577
USA
tel: (914) 251 6000

● **Wesleyan University**
Middleton, CT 06457
USA
tel: (203) 347 9411

● **The American Film Insitute**
2021 N Western Ave.,
Los Angeles, CA 90027
USA
tel: (213) 856 7600

● **University of Alabama**

Tuscaloosa, AL 35487-0152
USA
tel: (205) 348 6000

● **University of California - Berkeley**
Berkeley, CA 94720
USA
tel: (510) 642 6000

● **University of California - Irvine**
Irvine, CA 92717-2435
USA

● **University of California - Los Angeles**
405 Hilgard Ave.,
Los Angeles, CA 90024
USA
tel: (310) 825 4321

Index

Festival Products

Festival Products

Index – By Country

Index

Festival Products

Index – By Genre

Index – By Submission Date

August

September

Festival Products

October

November

December

INTERNATIONAL FILM FESTIVAL GUIDE

If you are interested in having your festival included in our next edition, fill out the form below and send it to us.

We'll send you our profile form by return mail.

FESTIVAL PRODUCTS

713 Euclid Avenue
Toronto, Ontario
M6G 2V1
Phone: 416-410-0867
Fax: 416-633-1485
festival@interlog.com
www.festivalproducts.com

Festival Name: _____

Address: _____

_____

_____

_____

Telephone: _____

Fax: _____

E Mail: _____

Website: _____

Contact Name: _____

16.1

International film
festival guide.

1999 02 25